MW00774982

THE NIXON ADMINISTRATION AND THE DEATH OF ALLENDE'S CHILE

PREFACE

We have four thousand kilometres of frontier;
no one could defend it. We are to be found
here at the bottom of the continent, alone.
And we annoy many people.

Salvador Allende, November 1971[1]

Readers not strangers to this subject will doubtless remember the disturbing scenes in Costa Gavras's film *Missing*, which I watched at the time it was released, seated with Chilean exiles who relived a trauma they had never anticipated. The Chilean tragedy was an event imperfectly understood at the time; most certainly in the world beyond the *cordillera*. Since then archives have opened, though only one archive in Chile itself – that of the Foreign Ministry (no one will even say where the archives of the Allende régime are). Working through the story therefore entailed extensive use of all I could lay my hands on in several languages, including the files on Chile from a number of other archives, in Britain, the United States, Germany, Italy, France and Brazil; a range of memoirs; interviews published in the Chilean press; and off-the-record testimony from those in a position to know but who, for the time being, must remain anonymous.

The violent overthrow of any democratically elected régime was always bound to evoke mythology only loosely related to fact. Those who support the *coup d'état* necessarily need to legitimise it. Those who oppose the *coup* seek to deny justification. There are those who maintain that what was done was not only right but inevitable. There are those who argue that it was not only wrong but avoidable. And there is a minority third position which may be summed up as believing it wrong but inevitable.

---

[1] Interview, Rosanna Rossanda, "Successi, limiti e scogli di un anno di governo di 'Unità Popolare'", *Il Manifesto*, November 1971; reprinted in *Il Cile: saggi, documenti, interviste* (Milan 1973), p. 185.

Two strong myths have persisted since the death of Allende. One –
sustained not only on the right – is that the coup was entirely a domestic
matter;[2] the other – maintained only on the left – is that Allende was a
Chilean Willy Brandt overthrown by the CIA.[3] The story proves far more
complicated and far more fascinating, if equally tragic; yet it is sufficiently
clear on further examination and in the light of a mass of new evidence
to dispense with both stereotypes.

The *Unidad Popular* (Popular Unity) government of Salvador Allende in
Chile was overthrown on 11 September 1973. The questions as to how and
why stubbornly refuse to go away. William D. Rogers was once assistant
secretary of state for inter-American affairs (1974–76) under Henry Kissinger
as secretary of state. He is now vice-chairman of Kissinger Associates and
one of Kissinger's lawyers. He recently launched a fierce verbal barrage
in *Foreign Affairs* defending the Nixon administration against longstanding
allegations reiterated by Peter Kornbluh that the US government was
complicit in the overthrow of Allende. Rogers argues the innocence of the
United States largely in terms of the absence of evidence. In a measured
but firm riposte Latin Americanist Kenneth Maxwell insists, however:
"to claim that the United States was not actively involved in promoting
Allende's downfall in the face of overwhelming evidence to the contrary
verges on incredulity".[4] To say the least, therefore, the debate continues.

The aim of this work has been to research and elucidate all the elements
that resulted in the coup, both domestic and foreign; and to expand upon
factors hitherto relatively neglected, including the politics of the socialist
party prior to 1970, the mindset of the Chilean military and Patria y
Libertad, the role and significance of the Movimiento de Izquierda
Revolucionario, the Cuban dimension, the economic crisis, Russian
indifference, and the longstanding operations of US intelligence leading
to the decision for a coup. Against these are set the strengths and
weaknesses of Salvador Allende as the leader of the ruling coalition.

---

[2] Alan Angell, for instance, declared shortly after the coup that the "USA seems not to have been involved" (*Listener*, 20 September 1973) and sustains that view today (*Cambridge History of Latin America*, vol. VIII, ed. L. Bethell [Cambridge 1991], chapter 6).

[3] "He was basically a social democrat, very much of the European type." Noam Chomsky: *www.thethirdworldtraveler.com/Chomsky/SecretsLies_Chile_Chom.html.*

[4] "Fleeing the Chilean Coup: The Debate Over US Complicity", *Foreign Affairs*, January/February 2004, vol. 83, no. 1, pp. 160–5. Also, *http://drclas.pas.harvard.edu/uploads/images/104maxwellworking paper.pdf.*

THE NIXON ADMINISTRATION AND THE DEATH OF ALLENDE'S CHILE

A Case of Assisted Suicide

JONATHAN HASLAM

VERSO
London • New York

First published by Verso 2005
© Jonathan Haslam 2005
All rights reserved

1 3 5 7 9 10 8 6 4 2

Verso
UK: 6 Meard Street, London W1F 0EG
USA: 180 Varick Street, New York, NY 10014–4606
www.versobooks.com

Verso is the imprint of New Left Books

ISBN 1–84467–030–9

British Library Cataloguing in Publication Data
A catalogue record for this book is available from the British Library

Library of Congress Cataloging-in-Publication Data
A catalog record for this book is available from the Library of Congress

Typeset in Bembo
Printed in the USA by R.R. Donnelley & Sons

For Pasy and Gabriel,
who have the right to know

ultras de izquierda y ultras de derecha,
duros de la derecha y de la izquierda,
trabajan juntos en la misma brecha
para que la victoria conseguida
por un pueblo que lucha y que recuerda
(el cobre, el pueblo, la paz y la vida),
todo lo manden ellos a la mierda.

Pablo Neruda, "Incitement to Nixonicide
and praise for the Chilean revolution".[1]

We have our crazies and they have their crazies.

US ambassador Edward Korry, 1 July 1971[2]

---

[1] "Extremists and ultras of left and right, hardliners of right and left, are fighting on the same front so that the victory achieved by a people embattled and aware (of the copper, the countryside, peace and life) is shot completely to shit." Neruda, *Obras Completas III*, ed. Hernán Loyala (Barcelona 2000), p. 737.

[2] Testimony before the US House of Representatives: *United States and Chile During the Allende Years, 1970–1973: Hearings before the Subcommittee on Inter-American Affairs of the Committee on Foreign Affairs, House of Representatives* (Washington DC 1975), p. 13.

CONTENTS

GLOSSARY

AFL-CIO	American Federation of Labor-Committee on Industrial Organization
AID	Aid for International Development (US)
AIFLD	American Institute for Free Labor Development
API	Acción Popular Independiente
BOLSA	Bank of London and South America
CEPAL	Comisión Económica para América Latina
CIA	Central Intelligence Agency (US)
CODE	Confederación Democrática
CORA	Corporación de Reforma Agraria
CUT	Central Unificado de Trabajadores
DIA	Defense Intelligence Agency (US)
DGI	Dirección General de Inteligencia (Cuba)
DINA	Dirección Nacional de Inteligencia (Chile)
DIRINCO	Dirección de Industrias y Comercio
ENU	Escuela Nacional Unificada
FNPL	Frente Nacionalista Patria y Libertad
FRAP	Frente de Acción Popular
FRENDO	Frente de Dueñas de Casa
FTR	Frente de Trabajadores Revolucionarios
GAP	Grupo de Amigos Personales
GDP	Gross Domestic Product

GNP	Gross National Product
IBRD	International Bank for Reconstruction and Development
IC	Izquierda Cristiana
ICFTU	International Confederation of Free Trades Unions
INDAP	Instituto de Desarrollo Agropecuario
ITT	International Telephone and Telegraphs
JAPs	Juntas de Abastecimiento y Precios
MAPU	Movimiento de Acción Popular Unitaria
MCR	Movimiento Campesino Revolucionario
MININT	Ministerio de Interior
MIR	Movimiento de Izquierda Revolucionario
MLN	Movimiento de Liberación Nacional
NSDM	National Security Decision Memorandum (US)
OLAS	Organización Latinoamericana de Solidaridad
ORIT	Organización Regional Interamericana de Trabajadores
PCCh	Partido Comunista Chileno
PCI	Partito Comunista Italiano
PDC	Partido de Democracia Cristiana
PIR	Partido de Izquierda Radical
PN	Partido National
PR	Partido Radical
PS	Partido Socialista
PSD	Partido Social Democrata
PyL	Patria y Libertad
SED	Sozialistische Einheitspartei Deutschlands (East Germany)
SIM	Servicio de Inteligencia Militar (Chile)
UP	Unidad Popular
VOP	Vanguardia Organizada del Pueblo

The course of research was made easier by many who generously gave of their time while not necessarily sharing my views: Sir Reginald Secondé (British ambassador to Chile in 1973), who in turn led me to Senator Marco Cariola Barroilhet and his invaluable assistant Sebastián Donóso Rodríguez, who facilitated access to Chilean Foreign Ministry files and kindly introduced me to other people in Santiago – Roberto Kelly Vasquez, Hermógenes Pérez de Arce Ibieta and Ernesto Videla Cifuentes; Manuel Riesco Larraín, also in Santiago; in Rome, Maurizio Chierici, correspondent for *L'Unità*; Sir Nicholas Henderson and Richard Gott in London (where Luis Palma was of great assistance as Chile's chargé d'affaires). Professor Paul Sigmund of Princeton University and Professor Paul Drake of the University of California, San Diego, gave encouragement to this interloper on their preserve; unnamed insiders, and friends and colleagues Dr Stefan Halper here in Cambridge and Mr Jonathan Clarke at the Cato Institute, Washington DC, proved invaluable in fitting together the more obscure pieces of the jigsaw. Gabriel Ramírez kindly read and commented on the final draft. And lastly my thanks are due to Professor Robin Blackburn, Tariq Ali and colleagues for publishing a book that others rejected for both personal and political reasons.

The following archives were invaluable: the Chilean Foreign Ministry (Santiago), the US National Archives (College Park, Maryland), the Bundesarchiv in Berlin (both SAPMO and Ausamt), the Public Record Office (National Archives) in London, the archives of the Italian communist party at the Gramsci Foundation in Rome (courtesy of Silvio Pons and Giovanna Bosman), the Quai d'Orsay archive (Paris); the archives of the Brazilian Foreign Ministry (Brasilia); and the George Meany Memorial Archives (AFL-CIO) (College Park, Maryland). The Biblioteca Nacional de Chile, the Biblioteca Nazionale Centrale di Roma, the Widener Library at Harvard, Stanford University Library, the Library of Congress, the British Library, the British Newspaper Library and Cambridge University Library all provided the necessary periodicals, printed documents and secondary sources. Funding was secured from Cambridge University, including my own college, Corpus Christi, and the Centre of Latin American Studies, as well as from the British Academy (as part of an ongoing study of the Cold War).

Corpus Christi College, Cambridge, February 2005

Note: The reader from the northern hemisphere will have to bear in mind the inversion of the seasons – the "hot" summer of 1971 took place in January–February. And the non-Hispanic reader should note that the mother's maiden name follows the surname, but it is the latter that is commonly used. Where possible I present both when the character first appears; though the full name is on occasion never to be found in print, and a *Who's Who?* of Chile is sorely lacking.

I

DISINTEGRATION OF THE OLD RÉGIME

… the drama had begun long before September 4, 1970 …

General Augusto Pinochet[1]

The dramatic and bloody destruction of the Allende régime in Chile on 11 September 1973, just three years after his election to office, has naturally excited extensive interest and heightened emotion that has diminished little with the passage of time. For it occurred in a country best known in Latin America as a democracy long untroubled by the violence of dictatorship. The shock thus provoked a plethora of explanation in many languages, much of it plainly partisan, but one account of unquestionable quality: Paul Sigmund's *The Overthrow of Allende and the Politics of Chile, 1964–1976*, published only four years after events.[2] The doubting reader may therefore reasonably ask why yet another account is worth reading. The answer is that we now have an array of new sources hitherto unused that take us from the first cut of history to an interpretation rooted in formerly secret documents, not least those from the archives of the Soviet bloc and off-the-record disclosures from those in a position to know on this side of the Cold War divide.

Chile stretches for three thousand miles from north to south. It faces the Pacific and backs onto a massive mountain chain − the *cordillera* − isolating it from neighbouring Argentina and the distant Atlantic. As such it has extremes of climate: from burning desert in the far north to the

---

[1] A. Pinochet, *The Crucial Day: September 11, 1973* (Santiago 1982), p. 15.
[2] P. Sigmund, *The Overthrow of Allende and the Politics of Chile, 1964–1976* (Pittsburgh 1977).

frozen wastes of the deep south. This polarity could also be found in wealth. When senior British diplomat Nicholas (Nicko) Henderson arrived in the late fifties, his gardener asked for one of the large packing cases that had carried all Henderson's essentials, including Marmite, for a long stay. Several days later, typically unable any longer to contain his curiosity, Henderson asked what had become of the packing case only to learn with astonished consternation that the gardener was now living in it.[3] The people of the underclass, of whom the gardener was one, were known as *los rotos* (the broken); disenfranchised as illiterates, they lived on the margins of the vast estates and on the edges of the cities, wretched witnesses to conspicuous consumption by those who ran the country. It should also be borne in mind that, in contrast to its neighbour and rival across the *cordillera*, during the first half of the twentieth century only 80,000 people migrated to Chile, whereas Argentina benefited from 500,000 per year up to 1914. The bulk of Chile's working class and peasantry were unskilled Amerindians whose numbers were reinforced unintentionally by the annexation of territory to the north and a steady migration south from impoverished Bolivia. The members of Chile's dominant class were increasingly of Basque or German origin. Colour as well as class thus contributed to the distance between top and bottom in society. Just eight years before Allende's election as president the new archbishop of Santiago, Raúl, cardinal Silva Henríquez, commented that "considering the appalling conditions which the mass of the population had to put up with, it was not surprising that there were many Communists in Chile; what was, he said, surprising was that the poorer classes were not Communists to a man".[4] To make them so was of course the communist party's very intention. *El Siglo*, the party's daily newspaper, printed a series of reading lessons – "Armate aprendiendo a leer" (arm yourself by learning to read) – from April 1962. Gérard Raoul-Duval, the French ambassador, noted that when Eduardo Frei Montalva took the presidency a few years later, 50 percent of the people still lived in *callampas* – shanty towns – surrounding the larger conurbations, or in the countryside on marginal subsistence and in a "deplorable state". These Chileans were "on the fringes of national life, with no secure employment … no schools,

---

[3] Conversation with the author.

[4] Sir David Scott Fox (Santiago) to Lord Home (London), 4 August 1962: *Foreign Office* (hereafter FO) *371/162168.*

no doctors, no hospitals …"[5] And with the population growing at a rapid pace – it stood at 8,510,000 in 1965 and at 9,899,000 in 1973 – one does not have to look far to explain how such a country came to be convulsed by social and political turbulence, a turbulence that eventually brought Salvador ("Chicho") Allende Gossens to power.

Yet it is striking that Allende reached the presidential palace, La Moneda, democratically. This gave credence to the belief of creole hero Bernardo O'Higgins, who in 1818 liberated these lands from the Spanish, arguing that he could make of Chile "the England of South America". Whether from tradition or, more prosaically, the stark fact of geographical isolation, this sense of Chilean exceptionialism long permeated the political culture. "Chile is not like other countries" was a comment not untypical, even on the far left.[6] Whereas elsewhere in Latin America fleeting democracies were toppled by *caudillos* (leaders from the military or landed gentry) and military juntas, Chile unaccountably remained aloof.[7] This standing apart from the turmoil that beset other, less fortunate neighbouring societies inevitably prompted a sense of superiority, which was mitigated by a deep-seated scepticism that amused the celebrated Colombian novelist Gabriel García Marquez: "No Chilean believes that tomorrow is Tuesday, a Chilean once told me, and he did not believe it either."[8] It also created a political culture not unlike the *piccola politica* under Giovanni Giolitti in turn-of-the-20th-century Italy, a provincial setting with politicians all too "accustomed … to political manoeuvre and to bastardised solutions".[9]

Just as Chile seemed one of a kind, there was also much obviously unique about Salvador Allende and Unidad Popular. Allende emerged from a political family of good standing with roots in the Basque country: freethinkers to a man. His grandfather, Dr Ramón Allende Padín ("El Rojo"), had headed the army medical service in the Pacific war (1879–84). He was also a leading freemason – grandmaster of the Santiago lodge –

[5] Raoul-Duval (Santiago) to Paris, 8 March 1968: France. *MAE. Archives Diplomatiques.* Amérique 1964–1970. Chili. 69.

[6] Under secretary-general of the socialist party Adonis Sepúlveda, *Chile Hoy*, August 1973; reproduced in V. Farias, ed., *La izquierda chilena (1969–1973)* (Santiago 2000), p. 4854.

[7] A rather different angle is presented in H. Bichero, "Anti-Parliamentary Themes in Chilean History: 1920–1940", *Government and Opposition*, vol. 7, no. 3, summer 1972, pp. 351–88.

[8] "La última cueca feliz de Salvador Allende", in Alejandro Witker, ed., *Salvador Allende: una vida por la democracia y el socialismo* (Guadalajara 1988), p. 197.

[9] Raoul-Duval (Santiago) to Paris, 17 February 1967: *MAE*. Amérique 1964–1970. Chili. 68.

later a deputy and then a senator. He died early at forty. Salvador, born in Valparaíso on 26 June 1908 the son of a lawyer, grew up in a family linked by his aunt's marriage in the 1920s, to the soldier socialist Marmaduke Grove Vallejo. Salvador joined the army at sixteen to avoid breaking his education later. A slim, short-sighted young man of no great height, lively and generous to a fault, he was a medical student in Santiago from 1926 to 1932. He also followed in family footsteps by becoming a mason, in 1929. He worked part-time with the ambulance service, and here he came face to face with mass illiteracy as well as disease rooted in impoverishment. A strong social conscience drove him into student politics, resulting in two arrests, before election as socialist deputy for Quillota and Valparaíso in 1937. Just two years later, in 1939, he was appointed minister for health and social security in the Popular Front government. This appointment did not play to his strengths, however; administration was never his forte, as president Pedro Aguirre Cerda discovered. Allende resigned to take charge of the less onerous Caja de Seguro Obligatorio (national insurance for social security) in 1941. He rose, however, to become secretary-general of the *Partido Socialista* (PS), in 1943 and, at the end of 1944, senator for Valdivia, Osorno, Llanquihue, Chiloé, Aisén and Magellanes. He had every expectation of the presidency.

From his political youth Allende overtly championed revolution but, as foreign observers noted, "his good family, wealth and agreeable manner make him accepted (at least when electoral fever is dormant) in Chilean society".[10] He never demonstrated anything less than "a great confidence in his abilities",[11] yet he never struck others as steeped in culture or an outstanding thinker. He was most certainly no theoretician. In 1972 West German officials described him as "an adroit co-ordinator" but not as "a cool strategist of power" or "organisational tactician".[12] US ambassador Edward Korry reliably reported that he had "neither the temperament nor the intellectual experience to sustain systematic management …"[13]

[10] "Leading Personalities in Chile 1958": *FO 371/139131*. Also, R. Cruz-Coke M. "Síntesis biográfica del doctor Salvador Allende G.", *Revista médica de Chile*, vol. 131, no. 7, July 2003, pp. 809–14.

[11] Raúl Silva Henríquez, *Memorias*, vol. 2 (Santiago 1991), p. 249.

[12] Dr Wilhelm Hartlieb (Valparaíso) to secretary of state, 22 June 1972. Germany. *Bundesarchiv. Politisches Archiv der Auswärtiges Amt* (hereafter *AA*). Bestand 33. Band 639.

[13] United States. *NARA: Chile Declassification Project Collections*. Department of state. Amembassy (Santiago) to secretary of state (Washington), 28 April 1971.

Korry's successor Nathaniel Davis pointed out that he was "not always completely decisive in his handling of things".[14] Instead Allende's talent lay in his "shrewdness and quickness, a great capacity for taking the social pulse on particular occasions". Sociable though he was, he frequently had difficulty exercising self-control, "he often behaved impetuously, stubbornly, unreasonably".[15] "I am merely a man," he once disarmingly and publicly confessed, "with all the frailties and weaknesses of a man."[16] He made close friends across the political spectrum, notably among centre-left christian democrats – brother Bernardo Leighton Guzmán, Eduardo Frei and others – and it was all too easy for the unknowing observer to mistake this for only superficial attachment to beliefs professed. Here those on the right in Chile saw him more clearly than others. Senator Francisco Bulnes Sanfuentes – diehard of the Partido National (PN) – pointed out that "there were many people who did not believe that Allende was Marxist, but I knew it; we were colleagues for many years. I believe that he knew little of Marxist theory, but he had the faith of a true believer which is the most difficult to break."[17] Frei, after the breakdown of their friendship, openly "lamented Allende's personal habits, particularly his disdain for details and his penchant for indulgences … his drinking habits, his vanity, his liking for long lunches and daily siestas …" Yet Frei freely acknowledged "that Allende was a man of his word, that he liked to feel he was in command, that he was weak on ideology but strong on political tactics and loyal to his friends".[18]

The paradox of the bon viveur and the narcissistic *pije* (toff) as dedicated revolutionary was what astonished US military attaché colonel Paul Wimert.

> We were down at the beach and this beautiful yacht with sails that were not white, but they were cream and green colored, came gliding across the water to hook up to the wharf there and this gentleman in a white hat and a white

[14] George Washington University. *National Security Archive* (hereafter *GWU NSA*). *Cold War Oral History Project*. Interview 10844.

[15] Silva Henríquez, *Memorias*, p. 251.

[16] "Discurso de la Victoria", 4 September 1970: S. Allende, *Obras escogidas (1970–1973)*, ed. P. Quiroga (Barcelona 1989), p. 55.

[17] Quoted in Jorge Mario Eastman, *De Allende y Pinochet al 'milagro' chileno* (Bogotá 1997), p. 50.

[18] *NARA: Chile Declassification Project Collections*. Department of state. Conversation between Frei, assistant secretary of state Meyer, and ambassador Korry, 5 November 1970. Pol. 15–1 Chile. Amembassy (Santiago) to department of state, 20 November 1970.

cravat with a blue admiral's coat and white duck pants and white shoes, he looked as you say like one of the old wealthy people – the Vanderbilts of America – I couldn't believe he was Allende ... he was beautifully groomed, and of course his sailing ship was one of the nicest ones there ... and what was waiting for him was a Mercedes Benz.[19]

New York Times publisher Cyrus Sulzberger found Allende "a left-wing pro-Marxist liberal socialist" – a not untypical instance of the journalist as tourist seeing the expected and a gracious host doing his impeccable best to fulfil every flattering if inaccurate expectation.[20] Sulzberger would have done well to take ambassador Korry's advice that "in all conversations, Allende plays the tune his visitors wish to hear".[21] Sulzberger wrote:

I found him a likeable, garrulous man of sixty-two, small, stocky, quick moving, with a gray mustache, a ruddy face (he liked sailing), and wavy brown hair untouched by white. He wore thick, heavily rimmed spectacles and had a determined, obstinate face with small cleft chin ... He resembles a slightly overweight, agitated fox.[22]

Sulzberger's impression after Allende assumed power was "that of a clever but not profound man, energetic but undisciplined, intuitive but not intellectual; a man being rendered giddy with success".[23] What does ring particularly true in Sulzberger's account was, however, seriously underestimated by him: Allende's aside that "In thirty years' political life, I never failed to do what I said I would do."[24]

Allende was thus a very unusual figure; so was his coalition. Unidad Popular was an alliance of socialists, communists and other parties created not, as was the Front Populaire of the 1930s in France and elsewhere, to defend the country against the threat of fascism, but as a movement explicitly aimed at the implementation of Marxist socialism in Chile. The socialist tradition in Chile was also completely unlike that of its neighbours

---

[19] *GWU NSA. Cold War Oral History Project.* Interview 10837.

[20] C. Sulzberger, *The World and Richard Nixon* (New York 1987), p. 59.

[21] *NARA. Chilean Declassification Project Collections.* Department of state. Amembassy (Santiago) to secretary of state (Washington), 28 April 1971.

[22] Sulzberger, *The World and Richard Nixon*, p. 59.

[23] Ibid., p. 63.

[24] Ibid., p. 60.

or Western Europe. In the Mediterranean and in countries such as Argentina, communist parties emerged primarily out of the anarcho-syndicalist tradition. On 2 January 1922 in Chile the communist party (PCCh) rose from a less doctrinal socialist base, the northern deserts where the impoverished were exploited in the nitrate and copper mines that assured the country's wealth. It was from here that the PCCh's first leader, Luis Recabarren Serrano, emerged. The PCCh cultivated a combination of features unusual for a Latin American communist party, which no doubt reflected the relatively strong tradition of political democracy in Chile: a rigorous Leninist internal discipline and outward obedience to Moscow on the one hand, but an openness to collaboration with others and an avowed commitment to political democracy on the other. Although the rank and file were heavily working-class, the party was led from the middle and upper classes. Here it resembled more the postwar Partito Comunista Italiano (PCI) under Palmiro Togliatti than any other fraternal party. What was so unusual was that these remained its signal characteristics even when driven underground by the government in 1948. The PCCh also came to play a unique role *vis-à-vis* Moscow on the subcontinent. "They are the party that has coached the Soviets on how to deal with Latin America," US ambassador Korry testified, "and I think with great perception. They are the party that is advising the Soviets on how to deal with Castro today and which may have some longer term influences."[25] It was therefore on the face of it natural to expect that Russian interest in the fate of the Chilean experiment would not be negligible. Yet expectations were to be shattered.

The PCCh was matched by another unusual institution: that of the socialist party (PS), which was never sufficiently powerful to attain office without communist support, particularly given its identification with Marxism and its reluctance to ally with bourgeois parties. The sense of fraternity was symbolised in the use of the term 'comrade' – *compañero* rather than *camarada* – common to both parties. Otherwise, however, the two had little in common. They were as Siamese twins: indissolubly bound together at the head but forever separate at the heart. Whereas the PCCh was noted for its strict discipline, the PS was invariably riven by the chaos

---

[25] Testimony given 1 July 1971: *United States and Chile During the Allende Years, 1970–1973: Hearings before the Subcommittee on Inter-American Affairs of the Committee on Foreign Affairs, House of Representatives* (Washington DC 1975), p. 11.

of ideological fissures and personal rivalries. It had been formed on 19 April 1933 by self-declared Marxists opposed to the Moscow-controlled Communist International, insisting heretically on the accomplishment of the revolution by non-violent means. It thus had a potential appeal among middle-class professionals that the communists could not readily obtain. The party allied with the communists under the leadership of the radical party (PR), by far the oldest of the three, formed on 12 March 1862. And, with fortuitous backing from supporters of former dictator Carlos Ibañez del Campo, the presidential elections of 1938 were won by radical Aguirre Cerda. But the communists – obeying orders from Moscow – did not actually join the government. They turned out to be right. Disagreements multiplied within the administration and within the PS, with the result that the socialists split in 1940. Meanwhile PCCh freedom of action out of power combined with socialist dissension to make possible a greater gain for the communists in the congressional elections of 1941 than all the socialists – from both sides of the split – could muster. The following year both parties backed the radical presidential candidate Juan Antonio Ríos. Once again the PCCh stayed out of government and fortuitously reaped advantages from so doing. By the middle of 1944 Allende led the majority within the PS in a break with the administration; another split resulted. Those who had broken away in 1940 had by now joined the PCCh. The lesson for the socialists was by now fairly clear: participation in office without their communist rivals would merely give the latter an unfair advantage.

In 1946 the president's death prompted a further election. By now the socialists were but a shadow of their former selves. The communists again backed the radical party candidate, Gabriel González Videla. The lack of a clear majority in the country brought the final decision to congress, where the liberal party (a conservative force) played a crucial role. The resulting administration thus contained three radicals, three liberals and – Moscow now permitting – three communists. The temptation of government was reinforced for the PCCh by unprecedented gains at local elections in 1947 (16.5 percent), tripling the numbers attained in 1944 and double those for the PS. This made coalition partners nervous, as was the United States. And this mattered with the onset of the Cold War and the fact that 70 percent of inward direct investment came from the United States. The president dismissed communists from the cabinet. The PCCh then confronted those still in office with a coal strike. At this point the socialists jumped into government. But when the régime then imposed a ban on the PCCh – the law for the 'permanent defence of democracy' – in line with US policy, the socialists once again split.

Among those who broke ranks in solidarity with the communists were two who became prominent thereafter: the charismatic but unpredictable Titoist, Raúl Ampuero Díaz, and his polar opposite in temperament and image, Allende. Together with Aniceto Rodríguez Arenas, Clodomiro Almeyda Medina and others, they formed the popular socialist party (PPS). But when the 75-year-old erstwhile dictator, Carlos Ibañez, who seemed an honest alternative to *politiquería* of a weary and corrupt government, stood for the presidency in 1952, Ampuero, never averse to a gamble, supported him in what seemed to many a blatant act of opportunism. Allende, by nature more cautious and more committed to principle, left the popular socialists and instead took a more consistent if slower route to power and reconstituted the PS. To this he added the electoral ballast of the outlawed communist party in order to stand as presidential candidate for the Frente del Pueblo. At the high point of the Stalin era Allende told trusted private secretary Osvaldo Carlos Puccio Huidobro: "The communist party is the party of the working class. The communist party is the party of the Soviet Union, the first socialist state in the world. And whoever wishes to form a socialist government without the communists is not a Marxist. And I am a Marxist."[26] It was this presidential campaign in 1952 that created the initial precedent for Unidad Popular.

The results of Allende's first presidential campaign were depressing: less than 6 percent of the vote. None the less it soon became apparent that Ampuero and along with him younger followers such as lawyer Carlos Altamirano Orrego had badly misjudged the situation. The Ibañez régime turned out to be both repressive and inflationary. The latter was an inevitable consequence of the Korean War boom in raw materials – Chile now depended almost entirely on copper for foreign exchange earnings – which from the truce in 1953 led inexorably to bust. By the end of that year the PPS had left the administration, having failed to secure their demands. In the meantime Allende had become senator for Tarapacá and Antofagasta, representing the Frente del Pueblo, and in 1954, at the

---

[26] O. Puccio, *Un cuarto de siglo con Allende. Recuerdos de su secretario privado* (Santiago 1985), p. 25.

comparatively early age of forty-five, he capped this with the vice-presidency of the senate. Now able to encompass the popular socialists and others, in 1956 the Frente del Pueblo was transformed into the Frente de Acción Popular (FRAP), the formation of which became the immediate prelude to the reunification of the socialist party. In April FRAP won 25 percent of the vote at the local elections, but it lost congressional seats to the rising christian democrats in the following year.

FRAP's only hope lay in mounting popular unrest over the rising cost of living. In 1958 Allende once again stood for the presidency on behalf of the coalition. By now Ibañez had made matters easier by repealing the law banning communists from office and administration (in order to weaken the chances of the hated conservative Jorge Alessandri Rodríguez, who won anyway, not least because the liberals refused to back the clever and cultivated christian democrat Eduardo Frei). And the communists had more confidence in Allende than any other socialist. On this occasion he came very close to victory – with 29 percent of the vote – because the centre and right were split and some believed he lost only because a defrocked priest, formerly with FRAP, took 41,000 votes that Allende could conceivably have won. Yet, as British embassy officials noted – and this has relevance for later developments – Allende's near triumph was "largely thanks to party organisation rather than to his own qualities as a leader".[27]

In the parliamentary elections in 1961 a newly formed coalition combining liberals and conservatives (which formally became the National Party (PN) only on 16 May 1966) took 428,000 votes, christian democracy (PDC) 213,836 and FRAP an impressive 397,351. Allende took the senate seat of Valparaíso and Aconcagua. Clearly the country was shifting to the left, since christian democracy had been formed from the leftist Falange Nacional on 28 July 1957. Britain's ambassador reflected that "Chile was moving to the Left; the only question was how far Left she would go."[28] Friction between the communists and socialists, however, was never far away. The issues were both domestic and international. The PS had lost seats to the communists in the elections for the central council of trades unions (CUT) in December 1959. At the congressional elections

---

[27] Ivor Pink, ambassador, "Annual Report 1958": *FO 371/139130*.
[28] "Annual Report for 1964": Scott Fox (Santiago) to London, 7 January 1965: *FO 371/179282*.

in 1961 FRAP received 31 percent of the vote, and within this the communists were predominant. The election of Ampuero as secretary-general of the PS in December was bound to complicate relations with the communists still further.

Dissension between socialists and communists also arose over the PCCh's unwavering loyalty to the Soviet Union, now led by Nikita Khrushchev. This furthered a doctrinal dispute among the socialists. A militant element had existed since the 1940s that disliked the electoral route to power. After Moscow fixed this as the only route open to communists by a resolution of the Politburo on 10 November 1957,[29] the existing dividing line within the PS thus extended to create rifts with the PCCh. That was also the year in which Luis Nicolás Corvalán Lépez became general secretary of the PCCh. Known affectionately as *"Patas Cortas"* – Shorty – Corvalán had been born into poverty on 14 September 1916 in Pelluco (Puerto Montt) and abandoned by his father at the tender age of five. His upbringing and that of five siblings fell entirely into the hands of his mother, a seamstress and the illiterate daughter of peasants. He was taught to read by his mother's friend Audolita, who shared their quarters. He grew up shy and withdrawn but committed and determined.[30] Under his rule, the PCCh grew in strength and made for a remarkable combination of pluralism of opinion and ruthless discipline in practice.

As Moscow fell out with Beijing about the peaceful road to socialism – which China ostentatiously rejected – and as Fidel Castro also demonstrated dramatically in 1959 that revolution could be obtained at the barrel of a gun, the conflict within FRAP worsened. By March 1962 polemics between Orlando Millas Correa, a former socialist representing the PCCh leadership, and Ampuero for the socialists, reached the pages of the press. US ambassador Korry later told the US Congress that "The Socialists do not look on Soviet power as a bloc with any great favor. They fear it. They do not like what the Soviets have done to their man Castro. They don't intend that to be repeated in Chile."[31] In the crossfire Allende became an

---

[29] Protocol no. 124, 10 November 1957: *Prezidium TsK KPSS 1954–1964*, vol.1, ed. A. Fursenko (Moscow 2003), doc. 138

[30] L. Corvalán, *De lo vivido y lo peleado: memorias* (Santiago 1997), chapter 1. Unfortunately none of the foreign archives provides further details, which remain classified, presumably because the information comes from informants within the party destined to remain unidentified.

[31] *United States and Chile*, p.11.

indispensable element mediating between the two rival parties. Jaime Suárez Bastidas, still under Ampuero's spell, none the less marvelled at Allende's "true political mastery in the management of conflict".[32]

At this stage the socialists were still junior partners to the more formidable communists, despite growing electoral support. The PS was inevitably weakened by the continued insistence of some that elections were merely a means of mass mobilisation rather than the route to power. As early as March 1962 it seemed likely that "the FRAP ... has an excellent chance of getting its candidate in at the Presidential elections in 1964 and thus precipitating a probable Communist peaceful take-over".[33] The Americans therefore began serious preparations to forestall such an eventuality. President Kennedy passed on responsibility to his brother, the attorney-general.[34] Inside the Central Intelligence Agency (CIA) Latin America fell within the western hemisphere division, and Chile within branch 5 which covered Cono Sur – the Southern Cone.[35] The CIA presented papers to the special group on Chile with alternative options: support for the christian democrats or for the radical party. It was decided to go for both. Funding was authorised on 27 August 1962. Only when the radicals and their allies collapsed at a by-election in May 1964 did the Americans throw most of – but never all – their weight behind Frei.[36]

The by-election in Curicó, which resulted in victory for FRAP in what had hitherto been thought a conservative safe seat, electrified the political atmosphere in Chile, and in the United States as well. Chile was of considerable importance to the US government. It became the showcase for John Kennedy's Alliance for Progress – the US alternative to revolution – in Latin America. Chile held close to half the world's copper reserves, and as late as 1968 the United States possessed a massive $964 billion in direct investments in Chile, largely but not entirely in copper production. Between 1962 and 1969 Chile took more than $1 billion from the Americans in aid, loans and grants; between 1964 and 1970, $200–300

---

[32] Jaime Suárez Bastidas, *Allende: visión de un militante* (Santiago 1992), p. 64.

[33] Minute by Parsons, Latin American Department, on Scott Fox (Santiago) to London, 29 March 1962: *FO 371/162168*.

[34] Testimony of former ambassador Korry, quoted in Gregory Palast, "A Marxist threat to cola sales? Pepsi demands a US coup. Goodbye Allende. Hello Pinochet", *Observer*, 8 November 1998.

[35] P. Agee, *Inside the Company: CIA Diary* (London 1975), p. 101.

[36] *Covert Action in Chile 1963–1973. Staff Report of the Select Committee to Study Governmental Operations with Respect to Intelligence Activities. United States* (Washington DC 1975), pp. 14–15.

million in short-term credit was continuously open to Chile from US banks.[37] Jerome (Jerry) Levinson, counsel for the Church committee investigating US covert operations, has revealed that between 1963 and 1964 the United States spent "$12,000,000 – even more" to defeat Allende.[38] With some authority former ambassador Korry has described how this money found its way to Chile.

> When one examines the documentation of AID [Agency for International Development] with reference to aid to Chile, one sees that it was directed specifically in support of Christian Democracy and Frei in the 1964 elections. AID money had a specific objective according to instructions given by the White House. When people say that it was the CIA, well, the CIA was the organization that had the contacts and all these things, but the money came from different governmental sources. The CIA on its own account gave only $3 million. However, for example, an official of the State Department was handing over money in cash; the Church was handing over money in cash; AID handed over loans and grants; Cáritas obtained grants from AID … Thus from different accounts one concludes that the real figure amounted to tens of millions of dollars.[39]

This excluded assistance from the German christian democrats and other Catholic sources. In the circumstances, therefore, the vote gained by Allende – 975,210 – as against that obtained by Frei – 1,410,809 – was a considerable achievement. "Chile had had a lucky escape", commented the British ambassador with evident relief.[40]

But it should not be assumed that the Americans were alone in investing in Chilean political parties. Like other fraternal parties across the globe, the communists received regular subsidies from Moscow. In 1965, for example, the PCCh merited $275,000, which ranked it ninth in the list of recipients after Italy ($6.6 million, including both the communist party and the breakaway pro-Moscow socialists), France ($2 million), the USA

---

[37] Ibid., p. 4.

[38] This was stated one evening – within the hearing of former US ambassador to Chile Edward Korry – at a Conference on Multinational Corporations in Düsseldorf, West Germany, held between 5 and 7 January 1973: Korry to Church, 23 October 1975: *Covert Action*, exhibit 4.

[39] "Entrevista – El Embajador Edward M. Korry en el CEP", *Estudios Públicos*, no. 72, spring 1998, p. 77.

[40] Scott Fox, "Chile. Annual Report for 1964", 7 January 1965: *FO 371/179282*.

($1 million), Finland, Venezuela, South Africa, Israel and Greece. By 1969, however, the PCCh had risen to fourth place at $350,000, one below the USA in order of priority. In 1970 it received $400,000; in 1972, $550,000, and $645,000 in 1973.[41] Funds also found their way from the German Democratic Republic into socialist party coffers, as did aid from Cuba (see below).[42] Allende too was – in the blunt language of the robust US ambassador Korry – "the compromised recipient of large amounts of funds over many years from various Communist capitals and organi-zations".[43] Yet nothing equalled the scale of the US contribution to the centre and right in Chilean politics.

Having won the presidency in 1964, Frei was still without a majority in the legislature. Three days after the election this "expert magician"[44] had "made an indiscreet and premature approach to ask for co-operation" from FRAP.[45] But the response was cold: "Allende said that the election had been very dirtily fought …"[46] In these unforgiving circumstances the socialists were not prepared to make concessions. Allende was particularly hurt. He and Frei had been drinking companions for years; their wives continued to be friends (Hortensia Bussi Allende being more interested in family than in politics). Yet Frei had made no attempt to rein in the "campaign of terror" (funded and organised by the CIA) that had blackened Allende as a Soviet stooge, despite their close relations. It poisoned the atmosphere. And Frei soon decided he could advance without FRAP. The unprecedented size of the majority secured in September 1964 was matched by the results of the March 1965 elections for congress, where the PDC won 42 percent of the vote. Once again the United States bankrolled the campaign. "Covert support was provided to a number of candidates selected by the Ambassador and Station." A CIA election memorandum suggested that the project did have some impact, including the elimination of a number of FRAP candidates who might otherwise have won congressional

[41] These figures are from the Russian archives: Valerio Riva, *Oro da Mosca: i finanziamenti sovietici al PCI dalla rivoluzione d'ottobre al criollo dell'URSS con 240 documenti inediti dagli archivi moscoviti* (Milan 1999), pp. 702, 711, 715, 721, and 731. See, also, *Estudios Públicos*, no. 72, Spring 1998, pp. 397–400.

[42] Edward Korry to Senator Church, 23 October 1975: *Covert Action*, exhibit 4, pp. 116–17.

[43] Ibid., p. 109.

[44] P. Neruda, *Confieso que he vivido: memorias* (2nd edition, Buenos Aires 1974), p. 464.

[45] Told to Lord Shackleton by Allende and Altamirano on his visit to Chile (1–7 November 1964): *FO 371/179283*.

[46] Ibid. Also, (Maria) Isabel Allende's recollections, 7 September 2003: *www.pagina12.com.ar*

seats.[47] The agency chose twenty-five candidates for support, of whom nine succeeded. And it was calculated that eighteen FRAP candidates were blocked at the ballot as a result of the operation.[48]

Although still a minority in the senate, the christian democrats could effectively prevent the blocking of bills that required a two-thirds vote in the upper house. Frei could now rule without the aid of FRAP, and thereafter he sought to do so. Thus arose the arrogant assertion of christian democracy as the *partido unico*, a doctrine of self-sufficiency that was bound to end badly for the PDC. None the less the congressional elections, like the presidential ballot, demonstrated that the politically active were still shifting leftwards. PDC gains were drawn from voters on the right rather than FRAP; yet ironically many elected for the PDC stood far to the left of the party mainstream. The PCCh and the PS split in their response. In October 1965 the communist party congress agreed a policy of selective give-and-take with the new régime. But whereas the communists favoured supporting legislation deemed "progressive" – notably agrarian reform and the "chileanisation" of the copper industry – the socialists wished to block any and every proposal from the PDC.

The split widened as the PS drove further to the left in 1966 – and away from the PCCh and Moscow – aligning itself unconditionally with Cuba at the tricontinental conference in January and nominally rejecting the non-violent road to socialism at its congress later that year. Allende had been severely depressed at his third failure to win the presidency and all but gave up when at the Chillán congress in 1967 the newly elected party central committee (now under another rival: Aniceto Rodríguez Arenas) took an abrupt turn to the left. Allende was "virtually defeated in form and content at the Congress", recalls one of those present.[49] In one decisive act which showed its true colours this new leadership resolved that none could stand for parliament except the secretary-general on the grounds that parliament should not be overvalued in socialist politics.[50]

Although Allende had never ruled out an alliance with any bourgeois parties – he had, after all, served in the popular front government as a

---

[47] *Covert Action*, p. 9.

[48] Ibid., pp. 17–18.

[49] Suárez, *Allende*, p. 121.

[50] Ibid., p. 123. Suárez was elected a member of the Central Committee at this congress. The only exception allowed was for deputy secretary-general Sepúlveda in 1971.

minister under the leadership of the radical party – he did not dissociate himself entirely from the revolutionary posture adopted more openly by his colleagues. The contrast in attitude between the PS and the PCCh was highlighted at a Cuban occasion in July 1966. The Chilean delegation included both Allende and the communist Millas. At one point in his speech Castro not only lauded the "Association of Chilean Revolutionaries" living in Cuba (who were bent on the violent overthrow of capitalism in Chile) but also attacked "the pro-imperialist Christian Democratic regime of Señor Frei".[51] Millas stood up and left the platform and the country in protest. And although the congenitally more cautious Corvalán publicly disowned Millas's gesture and obliged him to renounce it, the damage had been done; it was evident in a subsequent meeting with Castro, at which the latter refused point blank to explain where exactly Che Guevara could be found, resulting in even more bitterness on the part of the PCCh when Guevara's death in the neighbouring country of Bolivia became public in October 1967.[52]

In vivid contrast Allende sat throughout the rest of the speech and later insisted he was "in agreement with the substance of Fidel Castro's criticism of the Frei government" and that the PS also viewed Frei as "pro-imperialist".[53] Allende was thus willing to accommodate to some bourgeois parties – notably the Partido Radical (PR) now in terminal decline and therefore in desperate search for allies – but not to the christian democrats: whether from tactical calculation or point of principle, or the happy coincidence of both. When in 1968 Jaime Suárez conducted a series of soundings on behalf of the PS with both the revolutionary Marxist Movimiento de Izquierda Revolucionario (MIR) and the PDC, Allende pronounced himself sceptical about the christian democrats as likely partners.[54] The PR was a different matter. Leaders Alberto Cortés Baltra and Luis Bossay Lieva were receiving financial aid from the East Germans.[55] Indeed, Baltra was "generally considered to be a dangerous fellow traveller. The present unholy alliance between the Radicals and Communists was largely his work," the British embassy reported, "and it

---

[51] *Granma* (weekly edition), 31 July 1966.
[52] Corvalán, *De lo vivido*, p. 127.
[53] *Granma*, 7 August 1966.
[54] Suárez, *Allende*, p. 139.
[55] "El Embajador Edward M. Korry en el CEP", *Estudios Públicos*, no. 72, spring 1998, p. 82.

was with strong Communist support that he was elected a Radical Senator less than two years ago in a by-election in Southern Chile."[56]

The US state department's bureau of intelligence and research did not take PS radicalism too seriously.

> It is important to note that the Socialists' position was entirely verbal: while praising revolution, they prepared for none; while deriding elections and parliamentary efforts, they continued to participate; while calling public attention to FRAP dissension, they made no move to dissolve the coalition.[57]

Verbal fireworks from the PS were assumed to be aimed at building a separate identity from the communists in Chile and at creating a popular appeal by providing a contrast on the left with traditional PCCh prudence. On returning from Cuba in 1967, firebrand Altamirano gave a baffling but none the less unintentionally revealing retort when asked the role of the PS in the armed guerrilla struggle: "Your question is organic and obvious, but actually that is what the Party is looking for. For now, we have no clear and organic answer to your question, comrade."[58] For those such as Altamirano this conviction was akin to spiritual identification with the revolution rather than a question of practical politics. The history of the Allende régime cannot be fully understood without grasping this unworldly reality. Yet it was not firebrand Altamirano but the practised parliamentarian Allende who, when three Cuban guerrillas[59] escaped across the Bolivian border in early 1968 and were brought safely into Iquique, rushed off to search for them in Arica in order to act as their protector, only to return to Santiago awkwardly empty-handed; when they were then flown over to Easter Island by the Frei government on a circuitous route back to Cuba via Tahiti and Czechoslovakia, Allende followed them two days later in a gratuitous gesture of solidarity, posed playing ping-pong with the guerrillas and, in a baffling gesture from a

[56] Chancery (Santiago) to London, 3 July 1969: *FCO 7/1125*.

[57] "Chile: The Socialist Party, Past and Present", 22 May 1970. *NARA*. US State Department Bureau of Intelligence and Research Research Study. RG 59, Box 2194, Pol 12 Chile, 12-1 Chile.

[58] Ibid.

[59] These were the fragments of Che Guevara's team: Harry Villegas Tamaño (Pombo); Daniel Alarcón Ramírez (Benigno); and Leonardo Tamaño Nuñez (Urbano). See Chancery to Department, 5 March 1968: *FCO 7/345*. Benigno defected to France in the 1990s. His memoirs are quoted below.

prewar world, presented them with a box of Havana cigars, risking wide-spread public ridicule in the process.[60]

This curious episode demonstrated Allende's stubbornness, the strength of his loyalties, his recently acquired mistrust of Frei and a deep-seated streak of romanticism that remained with him to the last. The episode also fitted the Soviet view of him: he was not a "down to earth person" but "idealistically minded, motivated by noble ideas and easily persuaded to do things which were not reasonable, economically or politically, and to take some gambles, which he lost. But no one ever actually doubted his honest intentions as a person and his integrity as a politician."[61] The doubts that did arise concerned his judgement and the likely impact on the choice for a presidential candidate by a united left, given that his political star within the socialist party already seemed in secular decline.[62]

By 1968 it was clear to everyone that Frei's "Revolution in Liberty" was going nowhere. It had diminished into a little more than a holding operation. Agrarian reform and the freeing of food prices had not increased productivity. Why should the vast estates threatened with appropriation invest further in the land? The result was twofold: "Whilst the poorer classes are impatient to see Frei redeem his promises, there is a good deal of alarm and despondency amongst the rich, who are resentful at the new taxes and at the threat that they will lose their properties through the agrarian reform."[63] Opinion thus began to polarise. The centre remained more or less where it was, but extremist activism of both left and right began to appear as a menacing feature on the political landscape. The only factor that kept Frei afloat economically was the rising price of copper on world markets – not least prompted by the war in Vietnam – as had happened as a result of the war in Korea. This made the growth of food imports possible: by 1967 Chile was spending £60 million abroad. There was, foreign observers noted, "very little sign that agriculture is being treated on a sound commercial basis or that efficiency

---

[60] Chancery (Santiago) to London, 5 March 1968: *FCO 7/345*. The press coverage was devastating.

[61] Yuri Pavlov, one-time head of the Latin American section of the Foreign Ministry in Moscow, and one-time ambassador to Chile: *GWU NSA. Cold War Oral History Project.* Interview 10841.

[62] Sentiment reflected in the French ambassador's despatch on the Tahiti episode: Raoul-Duval (Santiago) to Paris, 1 March 1968: *MAE.* Amérique 1964–1970. Chili. 69.

[63] Sir David Scott Fox, reflecting on Frei's first year: *FO 371/179284*.

and productivity are being taken as the true criteria for Government encouragement".[64] The year following, a major drought worsened conditions further, even though half the land remained unaffected. The bill for imports thus grew inexorably. And remorselessly every year congress voted a *reajuste* in wages to match rising inflation. The country was clearly living on borrowed time, pursuing social reform at the expense of investment and productivity, but doing so at a pace insufficiently rapid for the disadvantaged whose expectations had risen to Frei's bellicose rhetoric. And this was a young population: about half the country were under twenty years old, Chile had a higher percentage university population than anywhere else on the subcontinent, and the British embassy was certainly not alone in reckoning that over half the country's youth backed the left. The hopes of the young were bound to rise disproportionately in comparison with those of their elders.

The disenchantment with Frei that fed the undercurrent to the left was also pushing rank-and-file christian democrats in the same direction. At a meeting of the PDC in Cartagena, a resort near Santiago, on 1–3 April 1966, two members on a parliamentary trip to Cuba were condemned for openly sympathising with Castro. One, Patricio Hurtado, was excluded from the party entirely. Nevertheless, the slowness of agrarian and banking reform incited further attacks from the emerging left within the party: from such as Bosco Parra Alderete and Rafael Augustín Gumucio. Their first serious victory was when the young christian socialist Jacques Chonchol Chait, vice-president of the Instituto de Desarrollo Agropecuario (INDAP), had his radical proposals for "non-capitalist" development approved by the PDC congress in July 1967. A christian democrat since 1957, Chonchol had worked in Cuba for the FAO – the UN's food and agricultural organisation – during the initial phase of the Cuban revolution, where he had witnessed the transformation of the countryside at first hand. He was susequently one of those who helped frame Frei's electoral platform for change in 1964.[65] Chonchol went on to press for an acceleration of agrarian reform, backed by party rank and file but increasingly against opposition from PDC members in the cabinet and in congress. In August Chonchol confided

[64] Sir Frederick Mason's "First Impressions Despatch", 25 November 1967: *FCO 7/340*.

[65] "Jacques Chonchol. Ex ministro de Salvador Allende: La revolución en libertad y la socialista", Patricia Arancibia Clavel – *www.finisterrae.cl/cidoc/citahistoria/emol/emol_1*

that he expected the cleavage within the PDC to grow as presidential elections loomed in view.[66] In October, the president of the young christian democrats, Enrique Correa Ríos, warned that the choice lay between "socialist revolution or regression to the right".[67] This warning was echoed by Chonchol and Julio Silva Solar. After many failed attempts Frei's minister of the interior and vice-president, Edmundo Pérez Zujovic, long *bête noire* to the left, finally provoked Chonchol into resigning from INDAP on 11 November 1968. By then it had been assumed that christian socialist Radomiro Tomic Romero would be the next presidential candidate. But Tomic had been badly damaged in the eyes of the left by agreeing to become Frei's ambassador to the United States, representing his country at negotiations for the "chileanisation" of the copper industry – which was widely seen as a means of giving the illusion of nationalisation but not the substance.[68]

At a dinner for Chonchol on 29 November, Tomic was thus heckled incessantly by the leftist caucus under Silva Solar, who wanted Augustín Gumucio as president. Thereafter the party was riven by infighting. Party chairman Renán Fuentealba Moena reprimanded both wings and took disciplinary measures against Renato Valenzuela Labbé, a deputy, for claiming that infiltration of the PDC had been "cleverly engineered by the PCCh". The British embassy further noted that "The Communists, as so often, have achieved what they wanted, namely, a definite split in the Christian Democrat Party; but fortunately not to the extent they had hoped."[69] But the British had yet to understand the heterogeneity of the emerging left. When the idea of an alliance between the PCCh and the PDC emerged among left christian democrats, the first to attack it was none other than Corvalán, who was even more brutal in dismissing it than Frei.[70] In May 1969, two months after the congressional elections, Chonchol and Augustín Gumucio – both explicitly regarded by both

---

[66] Raoul-Dumas (Santiago) to Paris, 16 August 1968: *MAE*. Amérique 1964–1970. Chili. 69.

[67] Jean Ribo (Santiago) to Paris, 8 November 1968: ibid. He was removed in 1969.

[68] A point forcefully made by the communist poet Pablo Neruda: Neruda, *Confieso*, p. 464. They were friends.

[69] "The Split in the Christian Democrat Party" – Chancery (Santiago) to London, 9 December 1968: *FCO 7/1125*.

[70] Ribo (Santiago) to Paris, 8 November 1968: *MAE*. Amérique 1964–1970. Chili. 69. The politics of the splintered French left in 1968 undoubtedly gave France's diplomats more insight into the Chilean left than the British could achieve.

Washington and London as "submerged Communists"[71] – finally abandoned christian democracy to form their own party, MAPU, on 18 August. Not all leftists had deserted PDC ranks, however. Indeed, there remained "large elements" that "have developed an almost pathological hatred of the so-called *momios* ('mummies') of the Right ..."[72] By then Alessandri had thrown his hat back into the ring, attacking Frei for his "disastrous demagoguery"; "a brilliant journalist", he conceded, "but ... no depth and no true knowledge or grasp of public affairs". What Alessandri sought was to open the economy to free trade and greater domestic competition, to reverse the statisation of economic life accelerated by Frei.[73]

---

[71] Chancery (Santiago) to London, 19 August 1969: *FCO 7/1125*. US ambassador Korry claimed to Frei that Chonchol, Augustín Gumucio and Silva Solar had only very recently joined the PDC and that their views seemed to him "very similar in the last analysis to those that I had heard in the socialist countries" – "El Embajador Edward M. Korry en el CEP", *Estudios Públicos*, no. 72, Spring 1998, p. 83. This was certainly not true of Chonchol, however, a member of the PDC for some time.

[72] "Chile. Annual Report for 1969": *FCO 7/1519*.

[73] Mason (Santiago) to London, 11 September 1968: *FCO 7/346*.

2

THE ULTRA LEFT

Socialist Party militants must become aware of the
fact that ... the shortest path towards the qualitative
transformation of the current political system does not
necessarily have to occur by way of the collapse and
destruction of the prevailing constitutional order.

Salvador Allende[1]

Unity on the left was hard won and even harder to sustain. A vociferous minority favoured the use of force to secure a revolution. The Marxist alternative to socialist constitutionalism at its most extreme was represented by the Movimiento de Izquierda Revolucionario (MIR). The MIR shared much with the left wing of the socialist party. Indeed, US diplomats noted that "The more radical Altamirano wing has close ties with the MIR and has even helped establish several guerrilla training schools."[2] Its spiritual foundation took place at the university of Concepción in the mid-sixties, and involved – among others – two figures expelled from their various parties: Miguel Enríquez Espinoza (socialist party) and Luciano Cruz Aguayo (communist party). Both were *penquistas* (inhabitants of Concepción). Born 14 July 1944 the son of an army colonel, Cruz had moved from Santiago to Concepción in 1957 where he soon befriended Enríquez at school. A tall, good-looking extrovert, he is ironically remembered as having arrived with views to the right rather than the left, an activist in the Partido Liberal.[3] On 27 March 1944,

[1] "Discurso de la Habana", 13 December 1972: Allende, *Obras escogidas*, p. 166.

[2] "Chile: The Leftist Revolutionary Movement", 7 December 1970. *NARA*. Bureau of Intelligence and Research, State Department: United States. Department of State: RG 59, Pol 1.3–10 Chile to Pol 14 Chile, Box 2195.

[3] D. Avendaño and M. Palma, *El rebelde de la burguesía: la historia de Miguel Enríquez* (Santiago 2001), pp. 73–4.

Miguel was born the son of Edgardo Enríquez Froedden, an anatomist in the Talcahuano naval hospital, of which Edgardo later became director. In 1969 Edgardo left the navy at the rank of captain to become rector of the university of Concepción, and later, briefly, from 5 July 1973, Allende's short-lived education minister.[4] Miguel Enríquez and Luciano Cruz had started out in 1963 by joining the Vanguardia Revolucionaria Marxista formed in 1962 in rejection of socialist and communist attempts to form a broad front with christian democrats and other bourgeois parties against the reactionary régime of Alessandri. The *VRM* produced a mimeographed periodical *Revolución*, the first issue of which appeared in May 1963. Yet Enríquez also remained within the youth wing of the PS, hoping to capture it from within for the Leninist cause. Matters came to a head in February 1964 at the twentieth congress of the socialist party. Here Enríquez and his friends condemned the peaceful road to socialism the party followed as "electoral cretinism".[5] When in May he took the battle further, into the youth congress with a blatant attempt to split the party, secretary-general Ampuero promptly expelled him. Enríquez was anyway already looking much further afield. Around this time he made his first contacts with revolutionaries from other parts of Latin America inspired by Castro's success. At the end of that year Concepción hosted the Latin American congress of medical students, which included, as ever, a substantial quota from the extreme left.

The PS showed signs of radicalisation at its congress on 26–29 June 1965 in Linares. Here Ampuero was replaced by Aniceto Rodríguez. More importantly, a set of theses by the Trotskyist Adonis Sepúlveda Acuña was adopted after extensive debate. The theses reflected a natural disappointment with the election defeat of the previous year and argued that the fate of the revolution should not be allowed to hinge on the ballot, paving the way for more radical proposals in the years ahead.[6] But for Enríquez this was too little, too late. On 15 August 1965 the MIR formally emerged in Santiago out of a motley collection of Leninists, socialists, Trotskyists and anarchists, with as its secretary-general the paediatrician Dr Enrique Sepúlveda, formerly secretary-general of the Vanguardia Revolucionaria

---

[4] Pedro Naranjo Sandoval, *Biografía de Miguel Enríquez* (Havana 1999), p. 4. Pagination refers to the edition on the web: *http://home.bip.net/ceme/miguel_vida/biografia.htm*.

[5] Quoted in Julio Cesar Jobet, *El Partido Socialista de Chile*, vol. 2 (Santiago 1971), p. 100.

[6] Ibid., pp. 107–11.

Marxista Rebelde (VRMR).[7] Inevitably, with such heterogeneous beginnings – almost everyone was a dissentient from one or other Marxist–Leninist organization – it was anything but an organic union. Moreover, credentials were never scrutinised. As Enríquez later confessed, "no kind of selection for entry was put into effect, thus we had 'fans' of the revolution, the disengaged [*descomprometidos*], intellectualisers, etc".[8] It is claimed one of the key militants was in fact an infiltrator for the police, who were thereafter privy to the operations of the movement.[9] The armed forces also had some success in this direction – which became obvious after the coup of 1973 in respect of at least two figures, Patricio Maturana and Anatolio Hernández, who continued working with naval intelligence in Talcahuano.[10] Although the Americans had no "assets" of their own within the ranks of the MIR, they did have such assets within the socialist party "and at the Cabinet level of the Chilean government".[11]

In 1966 Enríquez visited China, then in the bloody turmoil of the Cultural Revolution, and travelled onwards to Peru to meet its leading revolutionaries. Something of a high point was reached in 1967 when Cruz succeeded in winning the student federation of Concepción for the extreme left. Latin America was in ferment. With Che Guevara still fighting in Bolivia, the Organización Latinoamericana de Solidaridad (OLAS) met in Havana. Prospects seemed limitless. Yet the MIR was patently inadequate to the task of revolution. Looking back on those years, Enríquez reflected that it was then "like herding cats" (*una bolsa de gatos*), little more than a scattering of groups and disputatious fractions. "It was not even minimally organic", he recalled. "The most immaculate 'ideologising' predominated. There was no strategy, even less tactics. Isolated from the masses. No serious attempt was made to resort to force, even if it was talked about and the movement defined itself in terms of armed struggle."[12]

For the first time, on 25–29 August 1965, communists and socialists together took effective control over the central council of trades unions,

---

[7] Naranjo, *Biografía, passim.*; Avendaño and Palma, *El Rebelde*, p. 60.

[8] "Contribuciones para una historia del MIR", *Estudios Públicos*, no. 85, Spring 2002, p. 335.

[9] Avendaño and Palma, *El Rebelde*, p. 62.

[10] Ibid.

[11] *Covert Action*, p. 9.

[12] Quoted in Naranjo, *Biografía*, p. 16.

THE ULTRA LEFT 25

the CUT. Some in the United States began to see the writing on the wall: rumours emerged from US southern command in Panama that special forces were turning their attention to studying options for Chile.[13] A turning point for the socialist party came at its twenty-second congress at Chillán on 24–26 November 1967. Here the attempt to include even leftist elements of the radical party within FRAP electoral lists was decisively rejected. Thus the candidacy of Baltra for the senate seat of Bío-Bío, Malleco and Cautín was denied PS support. Worse was to follow, from the viewpoint of Allende and the communist party, desperately trying to extend FRAP into the ranks of the bourgeois parties. The PS congress approved a resolution on national policy that had more in common with Enríquez and, indeed, Lenin than with party policy hitherto.

> Revolutionary violence is inevitable and legitimate. It constitutes the only way that leads to the seizure of political and economic power and to its ultimate defence and reinforcement. Only by destroying the bureaucratic and military apparatus of the bourgeois state can the socialist revolution be consolidated.

Peaceful means and the use of the ballot were of limited value only, "incorporated into a political process that brings us to the armed struggle".[14] It was at the Chillán congress that Altamirano joined the leadership. Adonis Sepúlveda was now rewarded with a position as one of the party's three under-secretaries.

Thus although purists such as Enríquez had departed, in a very real sense the party they had relinquished or which had relinquished them was rapidly moving closer to the revolution. A single-minded, intelligent, handsome and charismatic figure, Enríquez had by then, at the early age of twenty-three, come to Castro's attention. In November 1967 perhaps not accidentally, a month after Che Guevara's gruesome death at the hands of US agents hand in glove with the Bolivian military, Enríquez was invited to Cuba by the revolutionary government. Thus began the formalisation of contacts with Havana and military training at Punto Cero. Contrary

---

[13] French embassy in Panama to Paris, 14 October 1965: *MAE*. Amérique 1964–1970. Chili. 67.
[14] Quoted in full in Jobet, *El Partido Socialista*, pp. 130–3.

to popular misperception, Castro had not given up aid to revolutionary movements on the subcontinent, despite the friction it caused Havana's relations with Moscow, which saw this revolutionism as disruptive of a more realistic strategy of uniting existing Latin American régimes on the basis of anti-American sentiment. As late as February 1970 a hoarding could still be seen on the road from Havana to the airport saying "We will support any genuinely revolutionary movement."[15] Instead what followed was a less ostentatious and more secretive management of such operations: that is, a shift of style and tactics rather than a fundamental reconsideration of strategy, which was still focused on applying the model of "26 July" – Castro's early raid on the Moncada barracks in 1953 – to the rest of South America. Section 11-1 of the Dirección General de Inteligencia (DGI) provided "the money, the intelligence training, the false documents when necessary, the travel arrangements, the contact arrangements for all Cuban oriented and sponsored guerrilla activities in Latin America".[16] The DGI did not, however, provide guerrilla training; that was the job of the Cuban armed forces.[17] While Guevara was still alive and second only to Castro in the Cuban leadership, Ministry of the Interior (MININT) control over operations remained severely curtailed.[18] From 1967, however, the bureaucratic hierarchy was streamlined for greater efficiency.

The main link for Enríquez as for all foreign revolutionary leaders after the death of Guevara became Manuel Piñeiro Losada. Born on 14 March 1933 in the key port of Matanzas along the coast from Havana, and popularly known as "Barbaroja" (Redbeard), the ginger-haired Piñeiro had studied at Columbia University and had headed the rebel intelligence service during the fight for power. On 6 June 1961 he became vice-minister of MININT and head of the so-called "technical" vice-ministry that developed both foreign intelligence strategy and international

---

[15] "Secret. Memorandum. Cuban Subversive Activities Abroad", prepared by Chancery, British embassy, Havana, February 1970: *FCO 7/1602*.

[16] Testimony of Orlando Castro Hidalgo, who defected from the DGI Paris station on 31 March 1969: *Communist Threat to the United States Through the Caribbean (Testimony of Orlando Castro Hidalgo). Hearings Before the Subcommittee to Investigate the Administration of the Internal Security Act and Other Security Laws of the Committee on the Judiciary, United States Senate, Ninety-first Congress, First Session, Part 20, 16 October 1969* (Washington DC 1969), p. 1445.

[17] Ibid.

[18] This much is apparent from the memoirs of Jorge Risquet Valdés, *El segundo frente del Che en el Congo: Historia del Batallón Patricio Lumumba* (La Habana 2000).

revolutionary operations. From 1965 he was also a member of the ruling party's central committee. In line with the reorganisation of both intelligence and foreign revolutionary operations, he was appointed first vice-minister of MININT in 1970, head of its newly formed general national liberation department (DGLN) as well as head of the DGI.[19]

Chile tended to be seen in Havana as a "strategic reserve", as "a source of supply for guerrillas throughout South America". It was a country that "did not have the conditions for armed struggle".[20] The Cubans in support, none the less, Enríquez returned to Chile after the third congress of the MIR had already opened, on 8 December 1967. By then the Cubans were also discreetly publishing under cover a weekly in Santiago, *Punto Final*, which before long became the most widely circulated mouthpiece of the MIR; this was a cause of deep resentment on the part of the PCCh, because the Cubans refused to allow a communist to become editor.[21] Enríquez came back to head the movement as secretary-general after the majority of seats on the central committee fell to his supporters from Santiago and Concepción.

Clearly recognition by Castro had made a significant difference to his standing. His career also advanced. In March 1968, qualified as a doctor, he joined the hospital for neurosurgery in Santiago to train as a neurologist. But increasingly politics displaced medicine as his vocation. Despite his best efforts, however, the MIR remained heterogeneous and anarchic both organisationally and philosophically. A further step to self-definition arose with the Soviet invasion of Czechoslovakia in August 1968, which provoked explicit rejection of the bureaucratic model of Soviet-style socialism, which of course aroused intense hostility against the MIR from the communist party. "They are the spoiled darlings of the middle class", one leading communist commented bitterly.[22] Not that the socialist party took a stance different from the MIR. But in this

---

[19] Avendaño and Palma, *El Rebelde*, p. 64. Also, 'Barbaroja' Manuel Piñeiro, *Che Guevara and the Latin American Revolutionary Movements* (Melbourne 2001), pp. vii–viii. He died on 11 March 1998.
[20] 'Benigno' (Daniel Alarcón Ramírez), *Memorias de un soldado cubano: vida y muerte de la revolución* (Barcelona 2003), p. 119.
[21] Conversation in the Latin American Department of the GDR Foreign Ministry with Mario Zamorano of the PCCh central committee, 5 May 1967: Germany. *AA*. Beziehungen DDR/Chile 1967–1973, Az 4510 – Ministerium für Auswärtige Angelegenheiten der DDR: C 3319, 000202.
[22] José Yglesias, "1909–1973. Salvador Allende: A Personal Remembrance", *Ramparts*, vol. 12, no. 4, November 1973, p. 25.

instance the PCCh was still transfixed by the idea of FRAP-plus: a new movement that, encompassing the left of the bourgeois parties, would win power primarily through disillusionment with christian democracy.

It was during these turbulent months at home and abroad, the domestic political climate intensifying as the Frei government struggled to maintain its hold on power, that Enríquez finally threw aside his medical training to focus on the movement. He was determined to place the MIR centre stage as the national political temperature rose. At the end of 1968 he pressed the movement to adopt direct action and limited armed struggle. Facing the prospect of parliamentary elections the coming autumn, with the battle for the presidency expected eighteen months thereafter, Enríquez issued a statement in the name of the majority of the MIR leadership in January decisively rejecting the electoral route to power.

> We have to encourage and support all kinds of legal and illegal strikes, street battles, occupations of places of work, of estates and plots of land [*tierras y terrenos*], direct action, etc. In so far as the elections affect the political process itself, we cannot marginalise ourselves. On the contrary we will participate with all our strength. But it is not necessary, on the contrary it is harmful, to become electorally active; from this we will abstain absolutely and categorically.[23]

Effecting direct action and armed struggle was more easily said than done, however. By March, with the parliamentary election campaign under way, Enríquez later complained that "Enormous internal tension and conflicts had developed which made work impossible ... No way had been found to break the vicious circle: no use of force in the absence of clandestine organisation/clandestine organisation 'unnecessary' because there was no use of force; and no organic bonding of any significance with the mass movement."[24] During these months the leadership of Enríquez and Cruz was reinforced by Andrés Pascal, son of Laura Allende, Salvador Allende's favourite sister who had been deputy for Santiago Poniente. As leaders of the PS youth wing Pascal and Enríquez had worked together in the attempt to split the party at its youth congress in

---

[23] "No a las elecciones: lucha armada único camino", National Secretariat of the MIR, January 1969, quoted in Naranjo, *Biografía*, p. 19.
[24] Quoted in ibid., p. 19.

Concepción.[25] They failed and went their own ways. Pascal ended up heading an innocuous-sounding party: Grupos Universitarios Cristianos.[26] Connections with Allende did not stop there, however. Allende's favourite daughter, Beatriz – "Tati" – became the president's closest adviser. She had become involved with the revolutionary left in collaboration with Guevara's ill-fated expedition in Bolivia (being a member of the Chilean branch of the Ejército de Liberación Nacional). Tati had befriended Enríquez as a fellow medical student at Concepción.

Given the low profile the Cubans were now adopting, they were reluctant to provide arms. Instead local revolutionaries were encouraged to fund their own activities through crime: what Havana euphemistically called "economic coups". The formal admission of Pascal into the MIR leadership thus coincided with a shift to what he called "armed propaganda": bank robberies designed to raise funds and advertise the MIR's existence, in the tradition of anarchism rather than communism, Proudhon, Bakunin and the *Narodniki* rather than Marx and Lenin. Word reached the British in Santiago in April 1969 "that members of the M.I.R. (probably not more than 200) were planning to initiate activities here on the lines of the Tupamarus [sic] in Uruguay with whom they are believed to be in contact".[27] In June "a guerrilla training school was discovered some 40 Kms. from Santiago and four Germans who were expelled from Chile … were connected with this training centre".[28] One of the first operations was against the Banco Londrés–Sucursal Santa Elena in July 1969. In August the Bank of London and South America (BOLSA) was also hit. Enríquez made sure that these meticulously planned robberies had a "great impact on public opinion" by granting exclusive briefings to members of the press, emphasising that these raids were conducted by people from good families driven by high ideals. The publicity also gave the false impression that the movement was a good deal larger than it actually was. The French ambassador, René de Saint-Legier, caustically described the MIR as a "high command without troops".[29] It was reported

[25] Avendaño and Palma, *El Rebelde*, p. 57.

[26] "Chile: The Leftist Revolutionary Movement", 7 December 1970. *NARA*. State Department Bureau of Intelligence and Research. RG 59, Box 2195. Pol 13-10 Chile to Pol 14 Chile.

[27] Chancery (Santiago) to London, 11 September 1969: *FCO 7/1127*.

[28] Ibid.

[29] Saint-Légier (Santiago) to Paris, 20 March 1970: *MAE*. Amérique 1964–1970, Chili. 71.

that robbery also provided funds with which the movement acquired shares in various businesses: Industrial Minero de Schwager, Metalurgico de Lota, and fishery companies in Iquique and Talcahuano.[30] Meanwhile, regular contacts with Allende's inner circle were sustained from December 1969 even while the MIR was outlawed.[31]

Allende's attitude was one of benign tolerance verging on tacit complicity – even when it complicated his chances of election. This reflected his own schizophrenic attitude. He admired Castro's armed revolution and had taken pride in his own marksmanship from the time of military service in his late teens. Indeed, he "liked to train at home, in his garden, with all kinds of guns … "[32] On the other hand, for Chile he envisaged a revolution without the use of force. In 1961 Guevara had, after all, dedicated his book *Guerrilla War* "To Salvador Allende, who is trying to obtain the same result by other means."[33] "Other sectors of the left said that they disagreed politically with what we did, but that we were honest young people. For instance," recalls Pascal, "Salvador Allende, my uncle, had a shoebox delivered to me. On opening it, I found a Colt .45 revolver, completely new [*nuevecita*], and a note that said: 'You have chosen this route. Follow it through.'"[34]

These attitudes of Allende, which in retrospect seem foolhardy for one so publicly pledged to a peaceful road to socialism, have to be understood partly in terms of the heart ruling the head. His friend the celebrated Marxist journalist Régis Debray aptly observed that "This strange mix, this glorious incoherence, is the whole man" (*Ce décalage, cette glorieuse incohérence, c'est tout l'homme*).[35] Various elements of incoherence have been highlighted by different people but all point to the conflict between head and heart. Volodia Teitelboim, a leading figure in the PCCh, refers

[30] Note on the MIR by J. Norden, attaché at the East German embassy, 29 March 1972: *Bundesarchiv. SAPMO.* Zentralkomitee der SED. Abteilung Internationale Verbindungen. DY/30/IV. B 2/20. 355.

[31] "Contribuciones para una historia del MIR", p. 339.

[32] His friend Régis Debray, "Il est mort dans sa loi", *Nouvel Observateur*, no. 462, 17–23 September 1973, p. 36. Debray, like many leading leftists of this period, later turned away from his pro-revolutionary position. He became a leading adviser to President François Mitterand. But his comments here predate that switch.

[33] Proudly quoted by Allende: R. Debray, *Conversations with Allende: Socialism in Chile* (London 1971), p. 74.

[34] Andrés Pascal Allende, "El Mir, 35 anos", Part 2: website *La Haine*.

[35] Debray, "Il est mort", p. 36.

to Allende having "a personality both reasonable and proud at one and the same time".[36] Others, like Debray, emphasised that the calculating element – the ability to manoeuvre and manipulate (his renowned "wrist" *muñeca*) – was by no means predominant. Opponents such as Sergio Onofre Jarpa Reyes, leader of the PN, marvelled at Allende's "capacity to deceive anyone as to his intentions".[37] Pinochet, something of a dab hand himself, described the president as "a master of deceit".[38] Ambassador Korry also saw something of this. "As with all Allende dealings," he says, "and as he often boasted in private, appearance was much more important than reality … "[39] Allende himself liked to emphasise that "reality is stronger than theory".[40] Debray, however, saw the other face: "He was always identified as the shrewd politician but that was always his other side, his role, the image attributed to him [*son image fatidique*], which at times made him bitter." Allende's own self-image was very different. He could be like a child, "silent and stubborn about 'what is done' and 'what is not done' …"[41] Indeed Jaime Suárez talks admiringly of his "characteristic tenacity".[42] The emotions frequently took command.

Outsiders found these complex views of Allende too confusing, and instead substituted a simplistic and one-sided image that more closely matched their own temperament. British diplomats, for example, tended to see Allende as pragmatic, opportunist and rational. The British ambassador noted: "[He] gives the impression that his political ambitions are more important to him than are his Marxist principles; and he has

[36] "El Hombre de las Grandes Alamedas", in Witker, ed., *Salvador Allende* (Guadalajara 1988), p. 117.

[37] Patricia Arancibia Clavel et al., *Jarpa Confesiones Políticas* (Santiago 2002), p. 157. Arancibia is the sister of Enrique Arancibia Clavel who was tried and convicted in Argentina of complicity in the assassination of general Prats and his wife on 30 September 1974. According to testimony from ex-CIA and ex-DINA agent Michael Townley, found guilty of the assassination on 21 September 1976 of Orlando Letelier, one-time ambassador to the United States and one-time defence minister of Chile, in mid-1974 Pinochet declared that Prats was very dangerous to Chile. The order to eliminate him was given to the head of the DINA foreign service, Raúl Iturriaga, from whom Eduardo Arancibia took orders as head of the network in Buenos Aires: *Clarín* (Buenos Aires), 10 May 2000. "Now the DINA is worse than the Gestapo. I do not agree with this black legend that has been applied to the DINA", he told journalists (*Qué Pasa*, 15 February 1999).

[38] *El Mercurio*, 18 September 1973.

[39] Korry to Senator Church, 23 October 1975: *Covert Action*, p. 113.

[40] *Punto Final*, no. 132, 8 June 1971.

[41] *Nouvel Observateur*, p. 36.

[42] Suárez, *Allende*, p. 122.

assured me that if he comes to power he has no intention of allowing the Communists any key Ministries like the Interior, Defence or Foreign Affairs."[43] In such circumstances due allowance should have been made for Allende's habit of telling the listener what he wanted to hear. The puzzle for the British thus arose by 1972 as to why "In every crunch so far he [Allende] has moved to the Left ... "[44] In fact, it all came back to the emotional roots of his faith. Jarpa argues:

> ... if one analyses Allende's behaviour, at no time did he sacrifice revolutionary objectives nor enter into compromises of that nature. When it was felt that the government could founder and at any moment, the communists tried to slow down the process with this tactic of two steps forward and one step back. But the others demanded that they "carry on advancing without any concessions". Allende could have put the brakes on the process, including reaching an understanding with the christian democrats, but he did not do it.[45]

Debray noted, "A discouraging word from Fidel or a look of disapproval from 'Tati' ... held more importance for him than a motion in congress or a resolution from the central committee."[46] Commitment to the Marxist revolution was above all emotional. It ran deep: far deeper than rationalist onlookers could ever have anticipated. Alone among the leaders of UP, Allende killed himself rather than be taken alive on 11 September 1973. It is somehow hard to imagine the more bellicose of his own party doing likewise.

Personal and family attachments reinforced an instinctive solidarity with the revolutionary left. In 1969–70 Laura Allende "secretly rented various 'safe houses' [for MIR members fleeing the police] and encouraged young socialists in her district to join the MIR". Another daughter became emotionally involved with Enríquez. Allende's faithful secretary Puccio owned a building on Santo Domingo street, Santiago, where, in a small apartment on the third floor, the MIR leadership used to meet. On one

---

[43] "The Chilean Communist Party" – Sir David Scot-Fox (Santiago) to Lord Home (London), 4 August 1962: *FO 371/162168*.
[44] "Chile: Annual Review for 1971": *FCO 7/2210*.
[45] Arancibia et al., *Jarpa*, pp. 184–5.
[46] *Nouvel Observateur*, p. 36.

occasion Enríquez asked Pascal to stash the ill-gotten gains of a bank robbery. Pascal was sorting out the notes when in rushed a very agitated Puccio, telling him not to make a noise. In the room downstairs "the doctor" (Allende) was meeting Patricio Rojas (Frei's minister of the interior), who was in charge of prosecuting the MIR.[47] It was most unlikely that Allende was ignorant of Puccio's indulgence. He was just anxious to observe appearances.

On 25 September 1970, Luis Fernández Oña, hitherto head of the Chilean desk in the liberation department of the MININT, operating under the *nom de guerre* Demid, arrived in Santiago and shortly became counsellor at the Cuban embassy. He and Tati Allende had been lovers since 1968 and were now married. Moreover, in the autumn of 1971 one of Allende's other daughters, Isabel, married Romilio Tambutti, another DGI official doubling as a secretary at the embassy.[48] The links between the Allendes, the MIR and Cuba inevitably raised doubts in some minds about a presidential candidate vocally insistent on a peaceful route to revolution. And it was not just family that linked Allende to the MIR. Personal secretary Miria Orea Contreras Bell – "Payita" – was also his lover. They had much in common as well as physical attraction: politics, a love of irony, and a light-hearted sense of humour. With her, a friend and fellow militant noted with some surprise, "Allende had an unmistakably adolescent attitude."[49] Three of her children, Isabel, Max and Enrique, were members of the MIR. And Allende formalised the relationship once he took power, spending the weekends with her at El Cañaveral to the east of Santiago.[50] At Guardia Vieja 392, meanwhile, his wife, Hortensia Bussi – "*Tencha*" – cried in dignified silence.[51]

On Allende's death Debray insisted, "Even if his enemies profit by it, one must disclose … everything that this man has done to drag out from

[47] Pascal, "El Mir".

[48] Antônio Da Câmara Canto (Santiago) to Secretary of State (Brasilia), 26 November 1971: *Ministério das Relaçoes Exteriores (Brasilia). Arquivo Histórico* (hereafter *MRE*). *Ofícios Recibidos*. Chile. 1970–1973, vol. 8, 1971. Also, "Mio Zio Salvador Allende", *L'Unità*, 7 September 2003. P. Bravo, "Luis Fernández Oña, el yerno cubano de Salvador Allende", *Punto Final*, 2 March 2001.

[49] Suárez, *Allende*, p. 155. Born 28 April 1927, she was married to Andrés Enrique Robert Gallet, from whom she separated after going to work at La Moneda.

[50] "El itinerario de la Payita", *Qué Pasa*, 20 May 1995. See also a note from Stephen Clissold of the Foreign and Commonwealth Office Research Department, 14 August 1972: *FCO 7/2209*.

[51] Memories of Allende's niece, Maria Ines Bussi Missoni, who shared the house: Maurizio Chierici, "Undici Settembre", in Chierici, *L'altro 11 settembre/30 anni fa* (Rome 2003), p. 59.

the rut the armed continental revolution that bewitched his soul, even if his mind rejected it. As president of the senate he had risked his political future several times in order to help and on occasion save physically those underground in difficulty in their own countries." As "President of the Republic, he risked today for tomorrow: no Latin American guerrilla ... who turned to him failed to receive the armaments [*les moyens de lutte*] that he requested."[52] Indeed, Allende was "not fundamentally happy nor proud to be this conventional president, this 'circumspect politician', this expert in tactical accommodation".[53] According to Debray, "He made fun of those who have the strategy but not the resolution, but those who have them both at one and the same time bewitched him: Fidel, 'Che'."[54] With respect to Guevara, Debray maintained – no doubt on direct authority – that "'Che' knew, during his lifetime, that he could count on him, personally, for no matter what, including carrying his bags. And he carried them."[55] It is thus wrong to see Allende's relationship with the MIR anything other than as emotional. To Allende ideological consistency was unattainable. Debray testified: "He could attack the MIR and its policy on television in the afternoon, severely, and that same evening offer his house to a MIR leader under persecution."[56]

After the congressional elections in March 1969 and with a presidential ballot in prospect for the year ahead, the socialists convened a national plenum on 11–13 June 1969. It was here that the opposing camps – Allende for a broad-based coalition and Altamirano for a narrower revolutionary platform – fought out their positions. Overall the rhetoric was as radical as at Chillán, so Altamirano's prospects of gaining the upper hand seemed promising. But at a crucial meeting on 14 July, Altamirano stood down, at which point the leadership split between those backing Allende and those behind Rodríguez (now including Altamirano and Almeyda). Between this meeting and the meeting of the central committee at which the final decision would be made, the PCCh intervened. On 19 August Corvalán proposed a Unidad Popular coalition. Ten days later at the central committee of the PS, both candidates spoke.

---

[52] *Nouvel Observateur*, p. 36.
[53] Ibid.
[54] Ibid.
[55] Ibid.
[56] Ibid.

Jaime Suárez, now backing Allende, was appalled at his "repetitive, monotonous, extraordinarily insecure" speech which won him no new supporters.[57] Chile's greatest living poet, the communist Pablo Neruda, who always had a good word to say for Allende, had to admit that he "was never a great orator".[58] Rodríguez read a letter of withdrawal. But the votes were not good: 14 voted to abstain, and 13 voted for Allende.[59] The times were working to Allende's advantage, however. In May 1969 the Movimiento de Acción Popular Unitaria (MAPU) split from the PDC. The radical party shifted to the left. With these trends so evident, the argument for the broadest-based coalition sought by Allende and the PCCh suceeded. The new Undidad Popular coalition thus came into being, made up of the PS, the PCCh, the radicals (PR), MAPU, and the tiny Acción Popular Independiente (API) formed on 27 April 1968. They collectively approved the Basic Programme for change on 17 December 1969.

In the meantime, throughout the country the MIR had slowly built up *grupos politico-militares* (*GPMs*) as a preliminary to the use of force in local operations, which began systematically from September 1969.[60] The movement had begun by training in light arms with what they could "procure, borrow or buy", and in San Felipé and Los Andes they found retired miners who taught them to use dynamite. "We treked up the rugged heights of the Maipo Ravine to camp in protected and isolated watering places where we undertook instruction in combat."[61] In the countryside the MIR spearheaded forced expropriation of land by poor peasants and indians. In the cities it focused on small and medium-sized enterprises from 1969, when it embarked on what was termed "the revolutionary short-cut" − *el atajo revolucionario* − in the use of force. Through that year the party became involved in prolonged strikes, and factory occupations including a strike of six thousand peasants in Coquimbo, which led to land occupations and confrontation with the carabineros (national uniformed police). "In addition to strikes, in certain cases we used force as a means of pressure on owners", boasted Pascal.[62]

---

[57] Suárez, *Allende*, p. 150.

[58] Neruda, *Confieso*, p. 468.

[59] Suárez, *Allende*, p. 150.

[60] Naranjo, *Biografía*, p. 22.

[61] Pascal, "El Mir".

[62] Ibid.

Violent demonstrations took place in Santiago, Concepción and Talcahuano; there was a riot in Copiapo on 11 September. With the experience of the events of Paris 1968 in mind, French officials were only too aware of the damage all this could do:

> One takes a dim view … of the real danger that can be done to the state by the revolutionary romanticism of some extremists, few in number, politically isolated, recruited moreover from the bourgeois milieu, undoubtedly seduced by the example of "Che" but singularly ineffectual and disorganised, up to now at least in their first manifestations of violence even if, as certain papers affirm, they benefit from "technical assistance" from professional agitators trained in Cuba or in East Germany.[63]

By 1970 the MIR had also plunged into an inventive long-term subversive enterprise, penetrating the armed forces and emerging bands on the extreme right. The rationale was laid out in the pages of *Punto Final*:

> The army, the air force, the carabineros and the navy are being shaken by political processes; political ideas and opinions are erupting amidst the military. Generally, in respect of recruitment, forces are polarised into distinct factions: we see putschists financed by the CIA, those favouring a Frei coup from within [*autogolpe*] and confused nationalist forces of every stripe, mixing those from the right and those from the left. The more junior officers and above all the NCOs express opinions and are motivated by their own interests as they also discuss and "debate" political and national problems. The series of events that followed one another (military "pressure" in 1967; the Tacnazo and its consequences; the frustrated efforts of the CIA and the "nationalists" in 1969 and the Gamboa operetta in 1970) left an important political mark. On the one hand the shadow of a reactionary military coup became tangible as a possible political solution by the right; and on the other hand the political effervescence of junior officers, NCOs and ranks has turned into an irreversible process. Conscious of this the commander-in-chief of the armed forces has started internal repression; thus in the last days of April two officers and fourteen NCOs in the army have been demoted for their leftist ideas.[64]

---

[63] Saint-Legier (Santiago) to Paris, 27 June 1969: *MAE*. Amérique 1964–1970. Chili. 70.
[64] MIR (Secretariado Nacional), "El MIR y las elecciones presidenciales", *Punto Final*, 12 May 1970.

Pascal recalls:

> Clandestine political work began in the armed forces making use of family
> and social connections with members of these institutions (on occasion Cruz
> concealed himself within military units). We gave an important thrust to intel-
> ligence requirements not only with respect to the military and the police, but
> also the right and its armed groups supported by North American agencies.[65]

For constitutional reasons president Frei was unable to stand for yet
another term of office. Concern at the country's seemingly inexorable
drift to the left led to agreement that Tomic would step forward as
presidential candidate for the PDC. Foreign observers noted that, from
the beginning of 1969, the US government began taking a special interest
in Chile not seen in five years of relative stability. The country was still
the second highest recipient of aid in the hemisphere after Brazil. And
given the upsurge on the left so spectacularly evident in the socialist party,
this reawakening of keen interest should scarcely provoke surprise. At the
congressional elections on 2 March the Americans bankrolled various
candidates, including those standing for Ampuero's breakaway popular
socialist union, in order to split the socialist vote. They believed that this
effectively robbed the socialist party of seven seats, as well as ensuring
victory for ten out of twelve candidates favoured by the US government.[66]
None the less, the christian democrats lost their overall majority in the
chamber of deputies, where they were reduced to 55 out of 150, losing
to both the national party and the communists, though they still sustained
23 out of 50 seats in the senate. The extent of US involvement did not
pass unnoticed. The British ambassador reported that US ambassador
Korry, who had arrived in October 1967, "is taking a very interventionist
line in Chilean economic and political affairs" and had "made it clear
that he was not in any way kowtowing to the Chilean Government as his
predecessor [Ralph Dungan] did".[67] The background to this was that the
incoming Nixon administration in Washington refused further economic
aid to the Frei government, despite Korry's "explosive protests".[68]

---

[65] Pascal, "El Mir".
[66] *Covert Action*, p. 18.
[67] Sir Maurice Peterson to London, 20 March 1969: *FCO 7/1127*.
[68] *Covert Action*, p. 114.

The East Germans, deprived of global diplomatic recognition but possessed of a trade mission in Santiago that doubled as a listening post under Harry Spindler, remarked on the manner in which the rise of the left in Chile was prompting doubts in Washington as to whether the Frei government would be able to resist and the christian democrats to sustain themselves in power. East Berlin noted that the US priority in Chile would be to strengthen its influence at the top of the defence ministry, enhance its own economic and financial presence, and split the left in order to forestall its chances of election at the presidential ballot in 1970. The United States already had offices within the Chilean ministry of defence. Around 40 percent of the ninth floor accommodated the US army mission and 50 percent the navy mission; the seventh floor was made up by some 50 percent of the US military advisory group ("milgroup"); and on the second floor some 60 percent were from the US air force mission. These were all "officers of practical experience". They dressed as civilians. Under a co-operation agreement signed in 1959 NASA maintained an observation station 40 kilometres north of Santiago at latitude 33°09' south and longitude 70°40' west, some two and a half hours journey from the capital in the direction of Los Andes.[69] It had been reinforced by some eighty further personnel. "In political circles", the East Germans noted, "the opinion had been expressed that these were not just NASA specialists." The implication was that they were, instead, National Security Agency employees eavesdropping on communications – an assertion impossible to verify. The US quota for the training of Chilean army and air force officers in the United States or Central America (largely in Panama) in anti-guerrilla operations was significantly raised in recent months by around 300 percent. On 18–26 March 1969 the head of the US air force southern command, major-general Kenneth O. Sanborn, visited Chile. That same month a large number of US journalists came into the country and interviewed figures in various institutions, apparently to gauge opinion mainly on doubts about the fairness of the policies advocated by the left. Also noted in Berlin were the activities of the second secretary of the US embassy, Keith Wheelock (also of the CIA), who, since reaching Chile in 1966,

---

[69] See "Center for Space Studies, FCFM – Universidad de Chile": website *www.cee.uchile.cl/public/ instalaciones_en.html*.

had targeted the radical party (PR), getting to know the membership across the entire country. During the March congressional election campaign Wheelock without prior arrangement travelled south to see party members and convince them to maintain their independence *vis-à-vis* the left. Via the American Institute for Free Labor Development (AIFLD), the US government had also brought in an array of specialists to jobs on housing estates, in the organisation and promotion of men in the municipal transportation system, and the reorganisation and construction of electrical and telephonic systems. Signs of greater US activity were also evident in the University of Chile (the "California–Chile" programme), the introduction of military training in some universities, the Institute of Chile-North America, the Peace Corps, and increased investment in the copper industry despite Frei's "Chileanisation" of the same (which gave the government control over half of the assets).[70]

One area of intense East German interest was the activity of the Chilean military. Signs of anxiety and discontent continued to appear from within the officer corps that did not yet jeopardise the electoral process but which can now be seen as portents for the future. The *momios* of the right saw their last hope in Alessandri, and they were well represented among the military. It was a popular myth that in Chile, unlike the rest of the subcontinent, the armed forces had traditionally been a professional body above politics. But this was not exactly correct. "The Chilean army," wrote the French academic Alain Joxe before the end of the Allende government, "far from not having ever intervened in political affairs, has, on the contrary, been the main agent in the formation of the state that now exists … "[71] He added that "the intervention of the armed forces, after the War of the Pacific, has been in reality so important (the navy in 1891; the army in 1924) that they were able, in each instance, to remodel the State 'in form' with great efficiency, in such a way that numerous interventions were unnecessary … "[72] The intervention in 1924–25 was against both an inept but leftist government under Arturo Alessandri Palma and an obdurately conservative congress that blocked reformist legislation but voted itself a pay increase,

<hr>

[70] "Information: Verstärkung des Eindringens der USA in Chile", 27 March 1969: *AA. Ministerium für Auswärtige Angelegenheiten der DDR.* C3318. 000009.

[71] A. Joxe, *Las fuerzas armadas en el sistema politico chileno* (Santiago 1970) p. 40.

[72] Ibid., p. 43.

leaving everyone else in public service as badly off as before. The minister of war, Carlos Ibañez, was himself elected to the presidency but effectively became dictator before being ejected by army leftists in 1932. The socialist party had been founded by a utopian military officer, Marmaduke Grove, who had twice seized power (in 1925 and 1932).[73] Indeed, in 1932 the British embassy watched with morbid alarm and growing fascination as Santiago's main street, the Alameda, became "a tossing sea of red banners interspersed with the fluttering pennons of cavalry lances".[74]

Thirty years later Chile's apparently unremitting gravitation to the left made the military increasingly anxious. On 19 July 1964, with presidential elections in the offing, the Chilean defence council had proposed to president Alessandri that they conduct a *coup d'état* in the event of Allende's victory. And just in case the United States did not receive the message, on the following day an air force general approached the US deputy chief of mission threatening a coup if Allende succeeded.[75] Even after Frei's success at the polls, speculation about the risk of a "Communist-dominated régime" continued.[76] Military anxieties showed no sign of diminution. By November 1966 "the ugliest suggestion" that had reached the British embassy – "from a well-informed, sober-minded and eminently respectable person" – was "that there was real unrest in the Army and to a much lesser extent, in the other armed services. Officers at the Colonel level felt that the 'Revolution in Liberty' might get out of hand and that it might conceivably be advisable for the Services to step in to avert chaos."[77] Even the more moderate senior officers began not only thinking the unthinkable but also planning for that eventuality. Following the Chillán congress of the PS, general Carlos Prats González, then in charge of the military academy, is said to have formulated a plan for seizing power in the event of the PS acting upon its belief that only violence could bring about the revolution.[78] The idea that most of the

[73] J. Thomas, "The Evolution of a Chilean Socialist: Marmaduke Grove", *Hispanic American Historical Review*, vol. 47, 1967, no. 1, pp. 22–37. The most substantial, best documented and reliable account of socialism in Chile remains P. Drake, *Socialism and Populism in Chile*, 1932–52 (Urbana 1978).

[74] Sir Robert Mitchell, Annual Report for 1932: *FO 371/17508*.

[75] *Covert Action*, pp. 16–17.

[76] Valedictory despatch by Sir David Scott Fox, 12 September 1966: *FO 371/184703*.

[77] A. J. D. Stirling (Santiago) to London, 3 November 1966: ibid.

[78] Jarpa testimony: Arancibia et al., *Jarpa*, p. 188.

Chilean officer corps were ever apolitical with respect to the left coalition thus carries no conviction. At the very least they regarded themselves as the first line of defence of the constitutional order.

Politicisation of the armed forces was accelerated by officers' declining standards of living. Indeed in 1967 a US researcher described the army as "an organization in decline".[79] Based on extensive surveys of thirty-eight retired generals, questionnaires for those in active service and research into public opinion, Roy Hansen concluded: "For a professional group, officers' salaries were extremely low, and were perceived so, not only by officers."[80] This perception inevitably affected the prestige of the fighting services, though officers were loath to admit as much. The British ambassador noted:

> The situation in the Provinces is often aggravated by the proximity of relatively highly paid officials of new-found Government bodies such as the *Corporación de Reforma Agraria* [CORA], whose lowest paid officials, like the lowest paid workers in the copper mines, receive more than a Lieutenant General in the Army or his equivalent in other Services. The pay of an Army Major aged 35, probably with a family of three or four, is less than that of a newly qualified bilingual shorthand typist, and a qualified Engineer Officer of Lieutenant rank in any of the Services can obtain eight to ten times his salary in civilian life.[81]

Naval officers, such as captain Roberto Kelly Vasquez, with too many mouths to feed resigned from their posts; Kelly himself took his pension and bought land to farm chickens, only to find within a matter of months that the Frei government redefined the bases of land reform in such terms as to expropriate him of his property.[82] The government was well aware of the problem of officers' morale. Serving general Tulio Marambio was made minister of defence in May 1968 precisely in order to neutralise military discontent over pay.[83]

---

[79] R. Hansen, *Military Culture and Organisational Decline: A Study of the Chilean Army* (UCLA PhD thesis 1967) p. 193. Hansen made three trips of fifteen weeks in all between December 1964 and June 1965. He employed Jorge Contreras as a research assistant.

[80] Ibid., p. 200.

[81] Sir Frederick Mason to Mr Michael Stewart, 27 October 1969: *FCO 7/1127*.

[82] Interview. The right of extra-judicial appropriation of large estates – known as the Enmendia Aylwin (the Aylwin amendment) – was enunciated in the *Diario Oficial* on 17 January 1970.

[83] Raoul-Duval (Santiago) to Paris, 3 May 1968: *MAE*. Amérique 1964–1970. Chili. 69.

The military in Chile might not have seized power in recent years and they could not vote, but they were nevertheless politicised. The head of the Chilean air force at the time of the September 1973 coup, Gustavo Leigh Guzmán, commented with respect to anti-communism: "This sentiment was born long before Allende."[84] As early as September 1969 the papal nuncio, Monsignor Carlo Martini, spoke of the possibility "of an eventual coup [*golpe de fuerza*] in Chile, aimed at changing the constitutional order [*el orden institucional*]".[85] He had met leading officers in the army and navy. They had shown "great anxiety at the growing current of leftist subversion that is advancing in this country, and the possibility that this tendency will come to power in the next presidential changeover". Martini was convinced that "the armed forces will not permit the extreme left to assume power, even through elections".[86] The Argentinian chargé d'affaires, Calixto de la Torre, commented in the contorted language not unknown in diplomatic despatches that "officers and NCOs are becoming aware that they have been turned into a factor of power and that circumstances and contingent facts could lead them to attitudes alien to their professional role [*función específica*]".[87] Colonel Wimert, the US military attaché and veteran of the campaign against Guevara in Bolivia, knew these men best. When asked "Were they political at that time?" Wimert answered unhesitatingly: "Very much so."[88] Moreover malcontents in the military were matched by malcontents within christian democracy. The current to the left under Frei worried others at the top. "In May 1968," Prats later told the Valencian academic Joan Garcés Catalán, who was an adviser to Allende, "certain christian democrat ministers in the Frei government wanted to provoke a coup d'état."[89] This mattered to the United States once the March 1969 elections indicated that the left might soon achieve the power they had failed to gain in 1964. Hansen's work for the Rand Corporation on the Chilean military not accidentally held significance for US policy. "Under what circumstances would you probably support

[84] *Entrevistas de Sergio Marras: Confesiones* (Santiago 1988), p. 126.
[85] Quoted in Juan Bautista Yofre, *Misión Argentina (1970–1973): los registros secretos de una difícil gestión diplomática* (Santiago 2000), p. 31.
[86] Ibid., p. 32.
[87] Quoted in ibid., p. 37.
[88] *GWU NSA. Cold War Oral History Project*. Interview 10837.
[89] Prats statement, June 1974: article by Joan Garcés in *Le Monde*, 5 October 1974.

a military attempt to take control of the government?" was one of the questions Hansen put to officers, who were also canvassed as to their politics.[90]

Thus when increasing immiseration and the prospect of the left gaining power emboldened general Roberto Viaux Marambio to launch a coup attempt on 17–22 October 1969, only the deluded could really believe that this was merely a matter of money. Viaux, officer commanding the First Army Division in Antofagasta, had been scheduled for retirement but refused to go. Backed by the Tacna artillery regiment and the school of non-commissioned officers in Santiago, the *Tacnazo* – as it came to be called – failed lamentably, and a day later Viaux was under detention. Although some spoke of the affair disparagingly as a farce, it was undeniable that more lay behind the putsch than mere folly. And the fact that a nervous government immediately raised officers' salaries inadvertently but effectively legitimised the mutiny. Rumours were rife that the United States was involved. Indeed, military attaché Wimert recalls "a series of 'young' people doing 'dumb' things. I laid out in the grass until about 5 o'clock in the morning with the troops which were supposed to be attacking the city."[91] It could not have escaped the notice of most christian democrats – Frei in particular – that Nixon would have preferred an alternative government in Chile. US ambassador Korry had concluded within two months of arriving in Santiago in 1967 "that the political and economic situation in Chile was not healthy. The revolution in liberty of President Frei had begun to tire and inflation was accelerating. Furthermore, political games in the Chilean congress absorbed the energy of the country at a time when the military were deprived of the basic necessities."[92] This concern for the military matched that of Nixon, who himself had been deeply intolerant of the Latin American left ever since being stoned in Caracas on 13 May 1958. He took the firm view that governments run by the military were infinitely preferable. "I will never agree with the policy of downgrading the military in Latin America", he told the US

[90] Hansen, "Military Culture", pp. 103 and 333. Civilians were also asked, with respect to defence of the constitution: "under what circumstances do you believe that the military ought to act in this matter?" – ibid., p. 339. The public were overwhelmingly reported as being in favour of the army protecting the constitution – p. 100 – but did not favour military dictatorship.

[91] *GWU NSA*. Interview 10837. Unfortunately the transcription is bad, partly from Wimert's incoherence but partly also the typist's ignorance of Chilean history.

[92] Interview, *Qué Pasa*, no. 1444, 14–21 December 1998.

national security council. "They are the power centers subject to our influence. The others [intellectuals] are not subject to our influence."[93]

From Santiago, basing himself on intelligence sources, East Germany's envoy, Spindler, reported that both the Pentagon and CIA knew of the attempted coup before it took place. In the course of the year "a large number of advisers from the USA held intensive talks with young officers of the Chilean army". Spindler also reported that Keith Wheelock and Charles Yothers – both CIA under diplomatic cover at the US embassy – had been taken by surprise at the level of industrial unrest and "sought to drive sentiment in the direction of an eventual military coup".[94] It is hard to dismiss such evidence out of hand. In his memoirs, Prats, then officer commanding the Third Army Division, recalled:

> Civilians and military from the shadows prepared pieces for movement on the chessboard using Viaux as a pawn. The checkmate that would lead to the overthrow of Frei would have been obtained as a result of the dynamic of events if twenty-four hours earlier the principal moves of other key pieces had materialised; but the attitude of General [Emilio] Cheyre [commander-in-chief of the army], on the one hand – although it would be described as passive presumably for lack of some officers ready to obey his orders to react with force against his mutinous associates – the paralysis of the first division in Antofagasta on the other hand and, last, the open willingness of the third division to deploy in defence of the constitutional order, frustrated the attempted coup whose initial apparent leader was Viaux until the security of victory forced into daylight those who put him up to it.[95]

Whether the US officials were actively involved behind the scenes or merely complicit observers is still uncertain. But the British embassy reported a secret session of the Chilean senate – presumably a committee thereof – at which a leading christian democrat, Renán Fuentealba, denounced the CIA for interfering in Chile's internal affairs, notably by furthering sedition within the army.[96]

---

[93] 6 November 1970: Minutes in photocopy can be found in P. Kornbluh, *The Pinochet File: A Declassified Dossier on Atrocity and Accountability* (New York 2003), p. 119.

[94] Spindler, "Versuch eines Staatssreiches in Chile am 21.10.69", 3 November 1969. *AA Politisches Archiv.* Ministerium für Auswärtige Angelegenheiten der DDR: C 000146.

[95] C. Prats González, *Memorias: testimonio de un soldado* (4th edition, Santiago 1996), p. 127.

[96] Chancery (Santiago) to London, 18 December 1969: *FCO 7/1127.*

At the very least what occurred in 1969 was a forewarning that the armed forces were about to re-emerge in their historic role as the ultimate determinants of Chile's political and economic trajectory. Only a few read the omens. The French ambassador, René Saint-Legier, reported that the putsch had

… first of all confirmed by the reactions it provoked in [public] opinion as well as among [political] parties, the civil service and the trades unions … the strength of the attachment of Chileans to the democratic régime with which their country is blessed. But it has also revealed the dangerous weakness and the lack of sang-froid of a government that, largely responsible for the crisis by letting matters drift and its indecisiveness in the past, has exaggerated the dangers and found no other means of removing them than by calling on the people to come to their rescue with all the risks that such a resort implied. In sum it has cast a harsh light on the extreme seriousness of the malaise that inflicts the Chilean army and shows that the latter has to be considered from now on as a true political force, liable to exert its weight in the immediate future on governmental decisions, and to determine for the long term the orientation of the country.[97]

At the XIVth congress of the PCCh in November, general secretary Corvalán made the following comment:

Things must be recognised for what they are and reality must be recognised for what it is. It is, for example, a real fact that the armed forces constitute a new factor in national policy. It can be said that the period of abstention of the armed forces from political life – abstention that was never absolute, but which for several decades was reduced to one group of officers or another – has come to an end or is about to come to an end.

No one was now immune from the changes occurring around them: as Corvalán observed, "the winds that are blowing open all doors, reach into every corner". Corvalán recognised that in many ways the armed forces were "decrepid" and that the United States had, over the years, succeeded in instilling in the minds of the military the idea that internal

---

[97] Saint-Legier (Santiago) to Paris, 24 October 1969: *MAE*. Amérique 1964–1970. Chili. 70.

subversion was the great danger. Moreover, Corvalán did not see much prospect in "progressive" military régimes on the subcontinent (such as that in Peru), since the United States found in them a safer alternative to genuine revolution. At this stage all the PCCh could hope for was to keep the military politically neutral.[98]

Officers were not the only malcontents. In July 1969, anticipating a UP victory, small guerrilla bands began forming on the extreme right "composed of young men from politically rightist families". The US military received reliable information that these men were "trained in arms use and tactics by retired Chilean Army personnel. They are equipped with small arms up to and including sub-machine guns or machine pistols." The weapons came from foreign sources. At this point the informant nodded in the direction of Argentina.[99] It is worth noting that this was also the source of CIA supplies for covert paramilitary operations in Chile. On 18 December 1969 the British embassy in Santiago reported: "There is still some intrigue taking place mainly amongst officers of middle rank, who are showing signs of political ambitions."[100] And ten days later Prats warned minister of defence Sergio Ossa Pretot of the dangers that lay ahead: "continuity of democracy in power with the threat of eventual civil war, or the accession of a Marxist regime, with a foreseeable international war".[101]

Senior officers were alarmed to discover the penetration of their ranks by the extreme left. In April 1970 the army parachutist school was surprised to discover that two officers and fourteen non-commissioned officers were engaged in clandestine activity (unspecified).[102] Not much later further subversion of the ranks was uncovered at the air force base in Puerto Montt.[103] On a visit to the Argentinian embassy, ex-president Alessandri turned prophet. He warned that the *Tacnazo* "created consciousness of power in the bosom of the armed forces, and therefore [he] thought that Chilean democracy – here he put special emphasis on

[98] V. Farias, ed. *La izquierda chilena (1969–1973)* (Santiago 2000), pp. 156–8.
[99] *NARA: Chile Declassification Project Collections. DOD.* Department of Defense Intelligence Information Report, 10 September 1970.
[100] Chancery (Santiago) to London, 18 December 1969: *FCO 7/1127.*
[101] Prats, *Memorias*, p. 142.
[102] S. Huidobro Justiniano, *Decisión Naval* (Santiago 1999), p. 29.
[103] Ibid.

the confidential nature he gave his words – could disappear and be supplanted by a military government".[104] Indeed, there were many in Chile, commander-in-chief general René Schneider Chereau argued, who saw the armed forces as an "alternative power".[105]

Schneider himself by no means believed the armed forces forfeited any right to intervene under all circumstances, and in this sense he stood four-square with the tradition that the army was the ultimate guarantor of the constitutional order and that it had the right to decide when to protect that order by the means at its disposal. On this view the fighting services owed their ultimate loyalty to the nation rather than the state. In preparing the defence of Viaux, lawyer Pablo Rodríguez Grez obtained the records of three secret meetings of the Consejo de Generales del Ejército – the army high command. At the second of these meetings, held on 23 July 1970, Schneider stated the standard legal position that the armed forces were subordinate to the civil power. He then introduced a crucial caveat whose importance could not have been lost on fellow officers in that crucial election year.

> It is fitting, however, to have it clearly stated that this eminently legalist position and idea is limited only if the power of the state that is being sustained and supported abandons its own legal status. In such an instance, of course, the armed forces, that owe themselves to the nation, which is permanent, more than to the state, which is temporary, remain at liberty to resolve the problem when confronted with an absolutely abnormal situation which logically oversteps the mark set by the order that underlies the management of the country.[106]

The degree to which the fighting services were drawn in by forces external to Chile – largely, though not entirely, by the United States, as relations with Brazil were also close – or entered exclusively of their own volition is a matter for debate.

Frei could not stand for election as president again, and in his place the PDC proffered Tomic. Born in 1914 of Yugoslav origin and educated as

---

[104] Yofre, *Misión Argentina*, p. 62.
[105] Prats, *Memorias*, p. 157.
[106] Quoted at length in Manuel Fuentes, *Memorias secretas de Patria y Libertad y algunos confesiones sobre la guerra fría en Chile* (Santiago 1999), p. 140.

a lawyer, he also once edited *El Tarapacá* of Iquique. He served as deputy for Tarapacá from 1941 and senator from 1950 before translating to Valparaíso as senator in 1961. Tomic had been a staunch supporter of Frei in 1958 and 1964, before serving as Chile's ambassador to Washington, whence he returned in April 1968. He was described as clever, attractive and eccentric; and "apt to think in Marxist terms".[107] On assuming the presidency in 1969, Nixon not surprisingly refused to have anything to do with such christian democrats, who now dominated the party. Indeed, in private, foreign minister Gabriel Valdés Subercaseaux freely expressed his anxieties at the consequences of the Nixon election.[108] Tomic was thus denied financial support by the United States for good reason: the Russians were not alone in regarding his programme as "anti-imperialist".[109] The British saw him as less menacing, but their description of him as "a long-winded hothead" was no less damaging.[110] The Brazilian ambassador described him more coolly as a "recognised opportunist".[111] This was certainly how the communists saw him. Their overriding aim was to keep Alessandri from power and in this the PDC was not to be overlooked. As Antônio da Câmara Canto, the well-informed Brazilian ambassador, noted:

> … the PCCh has no absolute confidence in Tomic's sincerity … and is working still, if possible, to substitute him with another Christian Democrat who might be controllable or already controlled by themselves.

Foreign minister Gabriel Valdés Subercaseaux was seen as the most active, and his "behaviour in relation to the Cuban problem" was interpreted as "eloquent confirmation of his ambitions".[112]

Others, no less concerned at christian democracy's growing disavowal of conservative values, banked on the emergence of a more right-wing "independent" candidate for the September 1970 elections. The ageing,

[107] Chancery (Santiago) to London, 3 July 1969: *FCO 7/1125*.

[108] Saint-Legier (Santiago) to Paris, 13 May 1969: *MAE*. Amérique 1964–1970. Chili. 70.

[109] "The regrouping of political forces in Chile and negotiations between the PDC and the Left Bloc of Unidad Popular"; Soviet embassy (Santiago), 13 October 1970 – *Estudios Públicos* (Santiago), no. 72, spring 1998, p. 406.

[110] Sir Frederick Mason's Valedictory Despatch", 16 June 1970: *FCO 7/1521*.

[111] Câmara Canto (Santiago) to Secretary of State (Brasilia), 5 February 1970: *MRE. Oficios Recibidos*. Chile, vol. 1.

[112] Ibid.

infirm and "dyspeptic"[113] 73-year-old Alessandri – a business magnate, former president and the son of a president (Arturo) twice elected – was an ascetic bachelor, whose only hobby was antiques. His record in office (1958–64) was, on the view of more than one foreign observer, "undistinguished".[114] Having sat out the failure of the "Revolution in Liberty" almost entirely in sullen silence while discontent mounted and Tomic exhausted himself in a desperate effort to become the only candidate of the left, Alessandri finally announced his candidacy by radio on 2 November 1969. The French ambassador tartly noted that his singular advantage over opponents was that "no one listens to him and he has no need that anyone listens".[115] Alessandri had previously attempted and failed to resist the new wave of US policy under President Kennedy – the Alliance for Progress – which dictated land redistribution of Chile's *latifundia* (the roots of Alessandri's support) to transform the feudal nature of the agrarian economy. Although Alessandri was nominally independent, he was backed by the national party. The PN had been shattered by the electoral triumph of Eduardo Frei in 1964; it was the first victim of the leftward drift. Whatever Alessandri's weaknesses, he undoubtedly filled a political space left vacant by the leftward drift of both the PDC and the declining radical party.

In the United States on 25 March 1970, the 40 Committee, which oversaw covert operations for the US government, haplessly concluded that it would not back any one candidate for the presidential election in September. The PDC appeared to be falling apart. Of its fifty-five deputies, a maximum of twenty-five – and only twenty-two of them for sure – were aligned with Frei and would submit to party orders.[116] The 40 Committee therefore agreed that around $1 million was to be spent to block Allende's path instead. This decision was taken in the knowledge that Cuba was contributing around $350,000 to UP, matched by a Soviet contribution.[117] Looking ahead to one dread possibility, ambassador

---

[113] "Annual Report for 1969" – Sir Frederick Mason (Santiago) to London, 7 January 1970: *FCO 7/1519*.
[114] "Political Action Related to 1970 Chilean Presidential Election", Memorandum for the 40 Committee, March 1970: *NARA. NSC Declassification Review*. The British in turn described it as "mediocre" – Sir Frederick Mason's Valedictory Despatch, 16 June 1970: *FCO 7/1521*.
[115] Saint-Legier (Santiago) to Paris, 28 August 1970: *MAE*. Amérique 1964–1970. Chili. 71.
[116] Ibid.
[117] *Covert Action*, p. 20.

Korry recommended that the committee also look into what the United States should do if the Chilean congress had to choose between candidates in a situation when the margin of victory was narrow and Allende was the front runner.[118] At one of his weekly lunches with the Argentinian ambassador, however, Korry said that – on the best advice of his staff – he thought the votes would be 29 percent for Tomic, 33 percent for Allende, and 38 percent for Alessandri.[119]

Allende faced a battle for nomination as the leader of UP. In January 1970 the six parties of Unidad Popular, "after a bitter and prolonged struggle involving intense ideological and personality differences"[120] which had lasted five months, agreed to nominate Allende as their joint candidate. Chonchol gave up his bid. So did Baltra (PR), whose own party had been warned he stood no chance since he was no Marxist; moreover, his "austere mien and professoral rigidity" did "not seem of the kind to electrify the crowds".[121] Neruda (PCCh) also stepped down. And, after further sustained resistance, so did Rafael Tarud Sidawy (API), who had received backing from another minor grouping, the Partido Social Democrata, PSD. Hostile observers reported that Chonchol and Tarud were anyway "always, to a certain degree, creatures of the Central Committee of the Communist Party".[122] And a section of the radical party was effectively under PCCh control. Support for Allende from the communists was critical: without PCCh participation a coalition was impossible. Corvalán was blunt to Allende's face in recalling his defects. In recent years "we had observed ... that he repeated himself in his speeches, slipped into clichés and well-worn phrases. He showed signs of stagnation. The people's movement had developed further than he had."[123] Not surprisingly Allende did not react well to such criticism, being both a "strong personality and touchy".[124]

---

[118] Ibid., p. 21.

[119] No date given: Yofre, *Misión Argentina*, p. 55. Korry was not alone. McLellan at the AFL–CIO International Affairs Department commented on 2 September: "it appears that the Latin American observers in the State Department and at the White House assume that Alessandri will win." – *George Meany Memorial Archives*, International Affairs Department, RG 18–001, Series 4, Box 18//11.

[120] "Political Action related to 1970 Chilean Presidential Election", Memorandum for the 40 Committee, March 1970: *NARA. NSC Declassification Review*.

[121] Saint-Legier to Paris, 3 October 1969: *MAE*. Amérique 1964–1970. 70.

[122] Câmara Canto (Santiago) to Secretary of State (Brasilia), 5 February 1970: *MRE. Oficios Recibidas*, Chile: vol. 1, 1970.

[123] Corvalán, *De lo vivido*, p. 117.

[124] Ibid.

Corvalán had to reassure him that they would work together knowing all this but determined to overcome it. The communists in Chile were renowned for their sound common sense. The qualities Allende brought to the feast outweighed the defects. Not the least of these qualities was described thus by Neruda: "Salvador is indefatigable. We'd all be exhausted, unable to sleep, driving from town to town to speak at meetings. But if Salvador saw three people in a field, he would stop the car, give them a speech, and get back in and drop off to sleep without an effort."[125] If this were a long-distance race with the odds stacked against them, Allende was their man. He was finally proclaimed the presidential candidate for UP on 22 January 1970. But he came away having experienced "the most severe trauma". As a reliable witness relates: "There were casualties, there was scepticism and everything appeared to indicate a tiredness right across the left, a defeat foreshadowed with a UP so battered at its debut."[126]

It thus seemed very unlikely that UP could win. Not a man to contemplate defeat, however, Allende focused instead on practicalities. Among these was whether the MIR could be counted on to support him, for if the members could be prevailed upon to desist from their anarchistic antics they would rob the right of a propaganda advantage on the subject of law and order; moreover their support would also remove from his rivals the argument that Allende did not appeal to the revolutionary left. The first sign of progress came early in May when Enríquez said the MIR would not call for abstention in the elections, though neither would it come out in support of UP. The published statement from the MIR secretariat (which was essentially Enríquez, who at this stage ran the movement with an iron hand) said:

> There are those that seek to conquer power through electoral means. We believe that this is a mistaken path; at least it is not our own. But the fact of differing in methods does not convert them into our enemies. It merely makes it apparent that we walk distinctive paths. Only the right and those that wish to play their game seek to provoke confrontations between Unidad Popular and the MIR.[127]

[125] Yglesias, "1909–1973".
[126] Suárez, *Allende*, p. 157.
[127] *Punto Final*, 12 May 1970.

Furthermore, although the announcement did not say so, the MIR intended to continue bank raids and other acts of "armed propaganda". Allende appreciated the MIR's position on the elections but asked to meet Enríquez in order to persuade him to call a halt to operations that would inevitably damage the campaign by playing into the hands of the opposition. Allende was, according to a friend, "proud" that the police had been unable to track down his nephew and saw the young men of the MIR very much as prodigal sons. "If I am elected," he said, "I expect these young people to join in the building of socialism."[128] He and Enríquez met in a house in upper Colón. "The comrades met Allende in a distant quarter of Santiago, invited him into one of our cars, and after various manoeuvres to ensure no one was following them, arrived at the house where Miguel [Enríquez] and other comrades in the leadership were awaiting him."[129] The differences that divided them – over the wisdom of illegal expropriation and paramilitary activity – were thrashed out and a compromise was eventually reached in June 1970. As a result the MIR called a halt to its "armed propaganda" at the beginning of July. Enríquez recalls:

> Operations continued until the first days of July (the last was an attempt to blow up empty police stations in response to the death of two secondary school students as a result of police repression in Santiago while the CUT general strike was in full swing. It was a fiasco, three comrades were arrested with the first of the bombs and served as an event that showed the political risks entailed in carrying out operations at this time).[130]

It was the switch in tactics that may ultimately have caused Enríquez and Cruz to fall out, resulting in Cruz's boycott of the leadership to which he formally still belonged.[131] As the Unidad Popular campaign for election

[128] Yglesias, "1909–1973. Salvador Allende", *Ramparts*, vol. 12, no. 4, November 1973, p. 25.
[129] Pascal, "El Mir ".
[130] "Contribuciones para una historia del MIR", p. 340.
[131] "He and Cruz ruled the MIR with an iron hand until recently when a difference over opinion over tactics resulted in Cruz's expulsion from his position of leadership." – "Chile: The Leftist Revolutionary Movement", Bureau of Intelligence and Research, US State Department, *US National Archives*, Department of State: RG59, Pol 1.3-10 Chile to Pol 14 Chile, Box 2195. Cruz died in mysterious circumstances from carbon monoxide poisoning in his apartment on 14 August 1971.

got under way, Pascal recalls "We thought that it was very difficult for Allende to win, and if he succeeded we were sure that reaction would conspire to ensure that he could not assume the presidency."[132] In August 1970 Enríquez had permitted members of the MIR to vote for UP if they so chose.[133] The other part of the deal was that, if elected, Allende would amnesty MIR members in prison or under indictment.[134] At this stage the organisation numbered only 3,000 (excluding front organisations).[135] But because of the background, connexions and reputation of its leadership, its real weight on the political scene far exceeded numbers, as events were to show.

Since the socialists and the communists were natural competitors, relations between them were never easy, and given the MIR's criticism of the invasion of Czechoslovakia and of the bureaucratic model of Soviet-style socialism, relations between the PCCh and the MIR were invariably fraught with tension. However, an indirect compliment was paid by the MIR after Allende's election: Augusto Carmona acknowledged that the communists' longstanding "tactic" of a non-violent electoral route to office "had been shown to be right in so far as it resulted in a concrete and irrefutable electoral victory".[136] To Corvalán, however, the MIR and their like remained mere "soda-fountain guerrillas".

---

[132] Pascal, "El Mir".

[133] *NARA: Chile Declassification Project Collections*. DOD. Department of Defense Intelligence Information Report, 22 June 1971.

[134] The British embassy understood that this commitment was obtained from Carlos Altamirano, then only one of the Socialist Party leadership but with sympathies towards the MIR, in July 1970: P. Summerscale, "The Ultra-Left in Chile: How Serious a Force?" – *FCO 7/2209*. But this may just reflect chronic and persistent British underestimation of Allende's radicalism.

[135] Pascal, "El Mir", Part 4.

[136] "Elección de Allende: Cambio en el esquema": reprinted in *Estudios Públicos*, 83, winter 2001, p. 355.

3

PRESIDENT ELECT
BUT NOT IN POWER

I am not President of all Chileans.
Salvador Allende, 4 February 1971[1]

Allende's election as president of Chile on 4 September 1970 was wanting in two senses, the one short-term, the other for the duration of his office. The first problem was that his majority was insufficient to guarantee him the presidency without approval by congress; obtaining it would be a struggle. The second was alluded to by Allende at a later date: "Historical reality shows us that here in our country we have made use of a path that our reality has allowed us to avail ourselves of; and this path has been the battle within the electoral system. Many is the time, I can say, I was alone within my own party in defending such a possibility."[2] That battle, against both left and right, ran the entire stony road of Allende's fore-shortened presidential term. Not least of his problems was the United States.

A newly elected republican administration faced the prospect of defeat and humiliation in the war against communism in Vietnam. The president's special adviser for national security affairs, Henry Kissinger, strongly advised the reluctant president Richard Nixon that instead of immediate withdrawal, the United States should hold on and use force to safeguard a more dignified retreat after securing a compromise peace. As a result, early that year the United States attacked Cambodia to drive out communist supply routes; the Vietnam War thus grew inadvertently

[1] *La Nación*, 5 February 1971: M. González Pino and A. Fontaine Talavera ed., *Los mil días de Allende* (Santiago 1997), vol. 1, p. 64.
[2] *Punto Final*, no. 132, 8 June 1971.

instead of diminishing as expected. It was with US sensitivity to the expansion of communism at its height that Allende was hoping for power.

As the ultimate bulwark against revolutionary socialism, the US government had reason for concern. President Kennedy had committed himself to preventing Chile from becoming a second Soviet bridgehead in Latin America. Allende had been funded by the Soviet bloc. He was both pro-Soviet and pro-Cuban, and he was always more the preferred presidential candidate of the communists than of his own socialist party. Indeed in 1959, three years after the formation of FRAP and one year after he narrowly failed to win the presidential election, Allende seriously considered uniting his own party with the communist party.[3] And although he spoke out against the Warsaw Pact invasion of Czechoslovakia in 1968, he persisted in regarding the Soviet Union as "big sister" (no irony intended). Allende was bent on revolution for Chile and in solidarity with those governing Eastern Europe, China and Cuba. The indictment of him by US ambassador Korry was severe but not entirely inaccurate.

> Why hide the fact that the majority of this party's ruling Committee (by a vote of 12 for, 13 abstentions and six absent) had refused to endorse Allende as the party's candidate for President in 1970 because of his 18 years of close collaboration with the less violent, but stronger and totally subservient-to-Moscow Communist Party of Chile? Why shouldn't there be a sober study of the implications of Allende having been the compromised recipient of large amounts of funds over many years from various Communist capitals and organizations? Or that his first foreign political act on the very day of his inauguration was to promise covert support to the Puerto Rican independence movement?[4]

But, as the CIA acknowledged, to the irritation of Nixon as well as Castro, Allende was committed to so doing entirely through electoral means.

The assessment later presented by Kissinger to the US national security council argued that, given Allende's aims, his consolidation in power *"would pose some very serious threats to our interests and position in the hemisphere,*

---

[3] Puccio, *Un cuarto de siglo con Allende*, p. 98.
[4] Letter to Senator Church, 23 October 1975: *Covert Action*, Exhibit 4.

and would affect developments and our relations to them elsewhere in the world". Not only would he deprive the United States of its investments in Chile, Allende could also be expected to default on debts. "Chile would probably become a leader of opposition to us in the inter-American system, a source of disruption in the hemisphere, and a focal point of support for subversion in the rest of Latin America." Chile could be expected to "become part of the Soviet/Socialist world, not only philosophically but in terms of power dynamics; and it might constitute a support base and entry point for expansion of Soviet and Cuban presence and activity in the region". The example set of "a successfully elected Marxist government in Chile would surely have an impact on – and even precedent value for – other parts of the world, especially Italy; the imitative spread of similar phenomena elsewhere would in turn significantly affect the world balance and our own position in it". Tactically for the United States the problem was that "Allende was elected legally". Working to US advantage, however, were "tensions in his supporting coalition", "strong if diffuse resistance in Chilean society to moving to a Marxist or totalitarian state", "serious suspicion of Allende in the military" and "serious economic problems and constraints".[5]

The results of the presidential ballot once announced, it immediately became apparent that the votes of the centre and right had split two ways, while the left stood *en bloc*. Allende received 36.3 percent with 1,075,616 votes, Alessandri, 34.9 percent with 1,036,278 votes, and Tomic, 27.8 percent, with a mere 824,849 votes. The vote was thus divided almost evenly between left and right, leaving the centre a poor third. The strength of the left lay in the alliance between the socialist party and the communist party, with a supporting role for smaller parties such as the breakaway left christian democrats, MAPU, and the radical party (PR). Alessandri, though relatively popular in the country, stood at a severe disadvantage with respect to votes in congress without a party of his own. Allende was the one upon whom the parties could all agree, though reluctantly. Tomic's immediate response was to concede victory. The PDC youth wing under Pedro Felipe Ramírez, a deputy, astonished many by abruptly backing UP. It sent a delegation to counterparts in the socialist party to offer

---

[5] "Memorandum for the President", 5 November 1970: *NARA. Chile Declassification Project Collections.* NSC Chile.

congratulations. The Brazilian ambassador, representing a military dictatorship of the right, was contemptuous: "There is a deliberate attempt very typical of the Chilean psychology to conceal with a solemn democratic gesture a farce that strikes the eye of any attentive observer."[6]

According to one CIA official, the agency "had its nose rubbed in the dirt in Chile. We had staked our reputation on keeping Allende out. [The] loss hurt the CIA's standing [in the White House] and its pride." Nixon and Kissinger were both apoplectic.[7] The Soviet bloc took heart. "The victory of the forces of the left in the presidential elections of 1970 is of historic importance for Chile ..." the East German embassy concluded, "... Thereby Chile is, after Cuba, the second country on the Latin American continent to break out of the influence of imperialism and to orient itself towards a socialist order as government policy."[8] On the other side, as early as 10 September the French ambassador reported with some alarm that "The Communist Party is advancing its pawns much more rapidly than one had expected ... The Communist Party did not ask of Mr Allende more than two ministerial posts but demanded 800 senior administrative posts out of the 1,200 at the disposal of the newly elected president."[9] The prospect of such a régime establishing itself on the American continent thereafter became an *idée fixe* of both the US president and his national security adviser. The fact that such a régime originated in a popular vote made it all the more otiose and dangerous, since it could serve as a model elsewhere. For although Castro had presented a direct menace to the security of the hemisphere from communism, he had nowhere yet succeeded in exporting his own and more violent model to the subcontinent, despite his best efforts and those of Guevara. But direct US intervention on the model of the Dominican Republic in 1965 was not an option because of the continuing war in Vietnam and the damage it would do to relations with the hemisphere as a whole. Everything therefore turned on the willingness of the Chilean military to act.

---

[6] Câmara Canto (Santiago) to Secretary of State (Brasilia), 11 September 1970: *MRE. Oficios Recibidos*. Chile, 1970, vol. 4.

[7] D. Corn, *The Blond Ghost: Ted Shackley and the CIA's Crusades* (New York 1994), p. 248. Head of covert operations Thomas Karamessines told the US senate of the "heavy pressures" exerted by top Nixon officials – Obituary, *Washington Post*, 8 September 1978.

[8] GDR embassy in Santiago, "Ein Jahr Regierung der Unidad Popular", 10 December 1971: *AA. Ministerium für Auswärtige Angelegenheiten der DDR ... , AZ0214.*

[9] Saint-Legier (Santiago) to Paris, 10 September 1970: *MAE*. Amérique 1964–1970. Chili. 72.

When UP declared victory, the head of the marines, rear-admiral Sergio Huidobro Justiniano promptly dictated a letter of resignation to his secretary because he did not wish to serve a Marxist government.[10] He was successfully dissuaded, but not because his colleagues were complacent. On the contrary, the department of intelligence of the first naval zone, based at Valparaíso, two hours north-west of the capital, reported that when news of the election results came in, shouts of "Long Live Allende" could be heard within the fleet – and not just from the navy, within army barracks as well.[11] Instead of resigning, Huidobro was persuaded to see commander-in-chief admiral Fernando Porta Angulo on the following day. The director general of naval services, admiral José (Pepe) Toribio Merino Castro, had also submitted his resignation until this information came in.[12]

To forestall resignations, Porta agreed to arrange a meeting between leading flag officers and Allende in an effort to obtain reassurances about the government's intentions. The meeting took place in great secrecy on 12 September: commander of the fleet admiral Raúl Montero Cornejo and the next most senior officer, Merino, met Allende (with secretary Puccio), José Tohá González, Hugo Fazio, Luis Corvalán, Jorge Insunza, Manuel Mandujano, Jorge Molina, Volodia Teitelboim, Hugo Coloma and Luis Guastavino.[13] The president, at his consummate best in face-to-face encounters and unflinching in his ability to tell visitors what they wanted to hear, was all reassurance. When word of the meeting leaked to commanders-in-chief of the army and air force, however, they reacted with fury. Those present at the meeting had been encouraged to believe Allende was sincere in his stated intention not to interfere politically within the armed forces.[14] The credulous admiral Porta even came away from meeting Allende with the impression that the president would sooner or later break with the communist party.[15] The net result of the political initiative was to force Porta's resignation for allowing the meeting to take place. It is worthy of note, however, that there were others not unlike

[10] Huidobro, *Decisión Naval*, p. 23.

[11] Ibid., p. 24.

[12] José Toribio Merino Castro, *Bitácora de un almirante: memorias* (4th edition, Santiago 1999), p. 73.

[13] Ibid., p. 25. The complete list is given by Merino on p. 78.

[14] Yofre, *Misión Argentina*, p. 80.

[15] Ibid.

Porta of greater intelligence – such as Gustavo Leigh of the air force – who saw Allende as "a typical demagogic orator" and took it for granted, not unlike British diplomats, that although the president was heading for socialism, "after six months in government he would end up governing with the right or at least with the centre".[16] Similarly general Augusto Pinochet Ugarte later credibly recalled that "many of us believed that Allende would alter his course".[17]

No one, indeed, thought Allende's ascent to office would be untroubled. When news of his victory came in, commander-in-chief of the armed forces general Schneider looked at the bleak alternatives: a congressional vote for Alessandri that could provoke civil war; a deal between UP and the christian democrats that would lead to a slow but inevitable crisis; victory for Allende that would lead quickly either to dictatorship of the proletariat or a military dictatorship; or a coup provoked by the putschist Viaux before congress could pronounce – and promptly concluded that the destruction of the "professional army" was at stake.[18] The congressional vote on the presidency was due on 24 October. The battle lines were drawing up, and the political temperature began to rise inexorably.

On 21 September Schneider received a message from Viaux, expressing the wish to meet because he "wanted to participate in the activities of the officer corps" [*quería sumarse a la acción de los mandos*]. Schneider did not dignify this with a response. That evening he met with his generals to brief them and, responding to insistent pressures from within and without, insisted that they stand above politics.[19] The following evening a retired army officer came to see chief of staff Prats, and promptly announced that "The armed forces must save the country." He went on to say that "between Allende and Viaux, the latter was preferable, because one can throw him out later".[20] On 24 September a noted christian democrat then turned up and suggested that Prats take control of La Moneda, "send President Frei abroad, close congress, suspend the activities

---

[16] *Entrevistas de Sergio Marras*, p. 127.

[17] Pinochet, *The Crucial Day*, p. 16.

[18] Prats, *Memorias*, p. 166. It would therefore appear that the belief of Luciano Cruz that Schneider had originally been party to a coup plot was unfounded and was, likely as not, deliberate disinformation: Avendaño and Palma, *El Rebelde*, p. 126.

[19] Prats, *Memorias*, p. 171.

[20] Ibid., p. 172.

of political parties ... normalise the situation" and then "call new elections".[21] Further visits from retired officers suggesting a coup also resulted in a brusque, not to say bruising, response. Provoked by the presumptuousness of this trail of visitors, Prats asked one senior officer if it was indeed true that just before Viaux's putsch on 21 October 1969 he had told a journalist in confidence that "in the army there are two little leaders [*lidercitos*]: one in the north and the other in the south; but that in killing the bitches, you put an end to those sniffing them" [*que matando las perras, se acaban las levas*].[22] On 10 October another vain attempt was made to persuade Prats to meet Viaux.[23]

The Americans in the private sector were no less hostile to the prospect of UP in power. The involvement of the US corporation International Telephone and Telegraphs (ITT), interwoven with the CIA, in attempting to forestall Allende is well documented and burst onto the world in 1972. On 29 September 1970 the head of CIA clandestine operations in Latin America, William Broe, met Edward (Ned) Gerritty of ITT. Broe suggested the bases for the "invisible blockade" of Chile: withdrawal or denial of credits by banks; denial of goods by businesses; withdrawal of technical aid, etcetera.[24] The evident threat to the interests of private capital from the UP programme of nationalisation inevitably aroused extreme emotion. In 1965, Indonesian generals had massacred over 100,000 communist party members after an attempted coup, on the basis of lists handed over by the CIA. For some this was an exemplar. On 25 September 1970 Bob Eberhart from the parent company NIBCO in the USA wrote to Raúl Llorente at NIBCO Santiago. "We are anxious about the Chilean political situation", he wrote, "and strongly hope that a solution can be found to the present situation. Possibly Indonesia had the real solution to the threat of Communism."[25]

Still unsure of office, which had yet to be decided by congress, Allende had delivered a tough speech on 13 September, warning of unspecified but dire consequences were he denied office:

[21] Ibid., p. 173.

[22] Ibid., p. 174.

[23] Ibid., p. 181.

[24] The published version is coy about naming Broe: González and Talavera, *Los mil días*, vol. 2, pp. 1080–1. See also R. Sobel, *I.T.T. The Management of Opportunity* (London 1982), pp. 302–37.

[25] A copy found its way into the hands of the Allende government: *El Siglo*, 24 November 1970.

The people know how to defend its victory … If, in an act of insanity, [others] seek to provoke a situation that we reject, let them know that the country will come to a halt, that there would be no business, industry, workshops, schools, hospitals or farms [*campo*] that work, as the first demonstration of our power. Let them know that the workers will occupy the factories and let them know that the peasants will occupy the land. Let them know that employees will be in public offices expecting the voice and the mandate of Unidad Popular. Let them know very well that we have a sense of responsibility, but that we know well the power that a disciplined and organised people represent.[26]

The stakes thus raised and to the alarm of the United States and many within Chile, the christian democrats led by Frei caved in. Prior to the election Allende had refused to have anything to do with Tomic and the left-wing of the PDC – despite the urging of the communist party, always anxious to outflank the right and astutely banking on the chance of splitting the christian democrats. Yet in the immediate search for office after the election Allende took a friendlier view of collaboration where the programmes of the UP and PDC intersected. Moreover christian democrats such as senator Patricio Aylwin Azócar recalled the lack of surprise that Tomic had lost and that "the immense majority of the party thought that Allende had to be supported".[27] The Soviet embassy in Santiago was quick to commend the communists for their wisdom:

Without diminishing the importance of objective factors (the process of radicalisation of the masses and of the organisations at the base of the Christian Democratic Party as a result of the class struggle, the reinforcement of anti-imperialist tendencies on its left wing, the need to take into account the victory of Unidad Popular in the elections and its political power), it is also necessary to take note of an important subjective factor: the flexible tactical line of the Chilean communists in its attitude towards the Christian Democratic Party over the years.[28]

The compromise reached was that UP would accept constitutional guarantees which, it was hoped, could prevent a slide into dictatorship. This

[26] Reprinted in Merino, *Bitácora de un almirante*, p. 81.
[27] J. Eastman, *De Allende y Pinochet al 'milagro' chileno* (Bogotá 1997), p. 48.
[28] "The regrouping … ": *Estudios Públicos*, 72, spring 1998, p. 407.

directly contradicted the assurance given in Allende's victory speech that "We are neither in any way going to abandon nor negotiate away the UP program."[29] Yet one of its most significant articles – the creation of a single-chamber parliament (the assembly of the people) which would name the judges of the supreme court and stand in authority over the presidency – was a serious cause of anxiety among christian democrats.[30] Moreover, as even the relatively moderate leader of the PCCh, Corvalán, acknowledged, "Chilean legality" constituted an "obstacle". "This is undeniable. The need is to modify this legality, the nature of these institutions [*esta institucionalidad*], that is basically out of date. Obsolete."[31] The unanswered question was, how this was to be done when UP had only a minority of the popular vote. This was not, however, the first time a minority government was to take office in Chile by vote of congress. 1946, 1952 and 1958 were precedents. In 1958 Alessandri had won only 31.6 percent of the vote.

Attempting to play a "hidden" hand, Washington was left with few alternatives. When UP won as a minority coalition there were no illusions as to the threat, notably from Movimiento Cívico Patria y Libertad and from elements of the military inspired by Viaux. PyL had been set up by the CIA on 11 September 1970, after Allende's victory, via the leader of the PN, Jarpa. He suggested that the 32-year-old Alessandri activist and lawyer Pablo Rodríguez should take on the task of organising the movement. Rodríguez, the son of Manuel Rodríguez Valencia, minister of education in the 1940s, had defended Viaux in 1969. PyL was to act as a catalyst to the military seizure of power; and throughout its three years of existence, and against pressures from within for a more active paramilitary role, this remained the central aim – squarely within the policy of the White House.[32]

It was scarcely unnatural that the CIA should involve itself in association with extremists of the right. Chief of station in Chile was Henry Hecksher. Born in Hamburg and educated at the University of Berlin, in 1934 he fled to the United States. He reappeared with strong political backing in

[29] *Las Noticias de Ultima Hora*, 5 September 1970.

[30] See "Programa de Izquierda", *El Mercurio*, 28 December 1969.

[31] Interview with Luis Corvalán by Eduardo Labarca, December 1972: González and Talavera, *Los mil días*, vol. 2, p. 1192.

[32] For the recollections of a PyL notable, who is insistent on the CIA role, which was also highlighted by the Church committee on covert operations, see Fuentes, *Memorias Secretas*.

1950 as deputy head of the office of policy co-ordination in Berlin, which ran US covert operations against the communist regime in the East. There he achieved notoriety for recruiting and sending hundreds senselessly to their deaths in terrorist and subversive operations across the frontier despite growing awareness that the organisation had been penetrated by Soviet intelligence. One who knew him then and disliked him intensely caricatures Hecksher as "a cross between a joke and a loose cannon and a monumental jerk. He was a braggart with a direct line to Washington, a dangerous nut with clout in some high places, a damned fool who liked to throw his weight around."[33] Yet in the fevered atmosphere following Allende's election Hecksher was to appear moderate, as did more than a few agency officers, compared with opinion prevailing within the White House. Between 5 and 20 October some twenty-one contacts were made with officers of the armed forces and the carabineros in search of a coup.[34]

Finding the brakes had been cut during UP leadership campaigning on the road was only one of the frequent reminders of the extremes to which some elements in the opposition might resort. Waiting for the result, Allende lived in Payita's residence, at El Cañaveral, east of Santiago. On 6 September pro-Alessandri demonstrators appeared in a convoy of cars sounding their horns in protest at the election results. Fearing the worst, Allende's aide, the militant Marxist journalist Augusto ('*El Perro*' – 'The Dog') Olivares Becerra, called the police for protection; but none was forthcoming. A few days later Allende fired from his balcony to ward off audacious protestors. In one incident Tati was nearly run down by one of the cars. As the tension grew, Allende was under growing pressure to remove himself to greater safety.[35]

Something of a culminating point came when US ambassador Korry ignored channels to Washington and informed Allende he was a target for assassination. The assassin was to be retired major Arturo Marshall, a veteran of the Chilean Black Berets, implicated in the *Tacnazo*, and the right-hand man of Viaux.[36] At the time Korry had no idea that Marshall

[33] Quoted in J. Koehler, *STASI: The Untold Story of the East German Secret Police* (Boulder 1999), p. 133.

[34] Corn, *Blond Ghost*, p. 249.

[35] A. Olivares, "El pensamiento del comandante en jefe del ejército: General René Schneider", in *El Caso Schneider*, ed. Patricio García F. (Santiago 1972), p. 179.

[36] Korry's interview with *Qué Pasa*, no. 1444, 14–21 December 1998. Marshall is described as Viaux's right-hand man in a minute on Patria y Libertad written by Stephen Clissold: *FCO 7/2209.*

was linked to the CIA.[37] Under pressure from Allende the police were finally persuaded to arrest Marshall, who, after attempting to resist capture, was found with a rifle and telescopic sights. It was this episode that finally prompted Allende to ask the MIR to provide an armed bodyguard.[38] When subsequently asked by inquisitive journalists who exactly were these armed men, Allende quipped: "A group of personal friends." They thus became known as the *GAP* (*grupo de amigos personales*).[39] This group grew to around 300 members and was headed by a 23-year-old third-year architecture student, Ariel Fontana (an alias for Max Joel Marambio Rodríguez), the son of a prominent socialist deputy.[40] He had visited Cuba with his father in 1966, and the following year he began military training at Punto Cero which led directly to service in Cuban special forces under the command of Antonio (Tony) de la Guardia.[41] The move to draw in the assistance of the MIR was, however, far more significant than a symbolic act. It was also agreed that the MIR should "collaborate in intelligence activities and work in coordination with the socialist and communist parties".[42] For this purpose, Enríquez recalls, "we reinforced and reorganised what was 'an intelligence team'".[43]

Just as Allende had hitherto been reluctant to believe that anyone would arrange his assassination, there also existed a stunning naïveté as to the capacity (though not the will) of the US government to overthrow a government elected in a constitutional manner. Despite recent memory of the banishment of the communist party from 1948 to 1958 and bloody precedents in Latin America and elsewhere, Allende insisted:

> … we feel that the United States as a people and as a nation is today going through times which are very different from those of the past. They have deep-seated internal problems. Not just the race question, but problems with certain sectors of the working population, with the students and with the

---

[37] Testimony of Korry: Gregory Palast, "A Marxist …"

[38] "Contribuciones para una historia del MIR", p. 341. This dating is precise. Enríquez is usually meticulous about such things.

[39] Pascal, "El Mir".

[40] *NARA. Chile Declassification Project Collections. DOD.* Department of Defense Intelligence Information Report, 22 June 1971.

[41] Avendaño and Palma, *El Rebelde*, p. 128.

[42] Pascal, "El Mir".

[43] "Contribuciones para una historia del MIR", p. 342.

intellectuals who do not accept the policy of aggression. Also, they have provoked world-wide repulsion by their attitude in Vietnam, and it is therefore more difficult for them to operate in Latin America.

He added:

I believe that they will not do anything of this nature [economic measures, blockades even]: firstly, because as I say, we have acted within the laws of Chile, within the Constitution. It is for this reason … that I have maintained that victory through the polling booths was the way to pre-empt any such policy, because this way their hands are tied.[44]

The sense of exceptionalism in Chile was clearly as robust as ever: certainly at La Moneda.

In one sense Allende was justified. William Colby, head of the CIA in 1973, has told us of the "doubts within both the CIA and the State Department about large-scale CIA covert political action and subsidies".[45] But Allende also placed great confidence – some might say too much – in his own much-vaunted ability to master the tactics of the situation. From 1970 to 1973 in a country of less than 10 million people, at least $8 million was officially spent by the US government on destabilising the Allende government, an amount greatly enhanced by the collapse of the escudo and extensive use of the Chilean black market for foreign exchange.[46] The CIA moved through agents in place to reinforce the pluralism of the Chilean press by subsidies to *El Mercurio* via Hernán Cubillos; and through founding new publications: one was the periodical *Qué Pasa*, launched with characteristic discretion by, among others, Cristián Zegers Ariztía.[47] The other was the populist daily *Tribuna*. A third was *Sepa*, run by deputy Rafael Otero. Zegers, born in February 1940, came from a wealthy conservative and catholic family. A precocious child, active politically since the age of twelve, from early adulthood he combined the professions of journalism and the law with political activism. He had joined Alessandri's campaign in 1958, switched between the press and legal work through the 1960s,

[44] Debray, *Conversations*, p. 126.
[45] W. Colby, *Honourable Men: My Life in the CIA* (London 1978), p. 302.
[46] *Covert Action*, p. 148.
[47] Illustrative of this is Zegers's absence from the photograph of "founders" on the magazine's website.

and was among those who founded the school of journalism at the Universidad Católica. "From the first moment I was in the struggle against Allende," Zegers recalls, "we believed that the one thing we must not lose in Chile was freedom of information."[48]

Despite the extent of its operations, the CIA was never, however, the whole picture. Former director Richard Helms tells us:

> I think it is fairly clear that President Nixon was very distrustful of the CIA – largely because of the missile gap which was alleged to have existed at the time of his 1959 campaign against Mr Kennedy. He felt that he lost that election because of the so-called missile gap and held the CIA at fault. He had it in for the Agency in the sense that he was very distrustful of what was advocated and felt that our estimates had been wrong at times. There was not very much opportunity to talk to him personally. He liked to deal through Kissinger and [Alexander] Haig …[49]

This mistrust was part of a larger malaise that had hit the US government in 1969, a direct consequence of the combined personalities of Nixon and Kissinger, both of whom were, for different reasons, deeply contemptuous of those who worked in government. "It was fashionable in Washington throughout the Nixon Administration to scorn the staff officers in executive departments and agencies for their real or imagined sins", recalls Ray Cline, former deputy director of the CIA and latterly head of intelligence at the state department.[50]

Lack of trust in the agency was reinforced in the second half of 1970. Nixon "was very interested in preventing Allende's accession to the presidency", Helms recalls.

> There wasn't one of us [in the CIA] who thought we had any chance whatever of achieving that objective and I had tried to make that point but it was like talking into a gale … The possibilities of succeeding in the short time span were so remote that we had a most difficult time putting together anything that was even a semblance of an effort.

---

[48] "Cristián Zegers a Todo Dar", *Mundo Diners International*, IX, no. 107, October 1991, pp. 9–12.

[49] David Frost, "An Interview with Richard Helms", *Studies in Intelligence*, Fall 2000, p. 5.

[50] R. Cline, "Policy without Intelligence", *Foreign Policy*, no. 17, winter 1974–75, pp. 121–35.

For a successful covert operation assets – "real estate, individuals, money and sometimes automobiles, newspapers, printing plants and even loudspeakers" – had to be in place well in advance. "When President Kennedy launched the Agency into the 1964 Chilean election," Helms notes, "the work was started many months ahead of time so that there was some chance it would be effective. Against Allende it was started much too late to be effective. The thing went from bad to worse." "We had nothing in place in Chile. We really had to extemporize from the very beginning and it was an almost impossible situation."[51] This was an exaggeration, but keenly felt none the less.

The original aim was to bribe Chilean congressmen to deny Allende office, using funds from Anaconda and other interested US multinational companies. But when the CIA learned that Tomic would deliver the christian democratic vote to Allende, the plan fell through. The alternative, which became known as Track II, was born at an oval office meeting on 15 September, involving Nixon, Kissinger, Helms and attorney-general John Mitchell. This order was to be kept secret even from the 40 Committee: a precedent that was followed more than once more in Chilean matters. And, as usual, Kissinger cut secretary of state Bill Rogers out of the picture.[52] Colby reminds us that "this order was fully within the President's authority to order covert action".[53] Helms noted the following from the meeting:

> One in 10 chance perhaps, but save Chile!
> worth spending
> not concerned risks involved
> no involvement of embassy
> $10,000,000 available, more if necessary
> full-time job – best men we have
> game plan
> make the economy scream
> 48 hours for plan of action

---

[51] Frost, "An Interview", p. 9.

[52] See Sulzberger, *The World and Richard Nixon*, pp. 58 and 64.

[53] Colby, *Honourable Men*, p. 303.

The White House was not interested in hearing of Hecksher's scepticism. He "knew, and reported, that Viaux's circle had been infiltrated by the Chilean MIR".[54] This made no difference to the operation. The CIA in Santiago were to contact Viaux directly.[55]

Since ambassador Korry was not privy to these White House decisions and had forbidden the CIA station to contact the Chilean military for fear they would promote a coup, Nixon and Kissinger took a detour. In such operations the man they both trusted as a friend as well as a man counted on for his ruthless efficiency and complete discretion was the British-educated lieutenant-general Vernon (Bill) Walters, with whom military attaché Wimert of the US defense intelligence agency (DIA), a veteran of the Bolivian campaign, was closely associated[56]. Walters, who looms large later in the story, had been accompanying then vice-president Nixon on that fateful day in Caracas (13 May 1958) when their convoy was attacked by demonstrators who held the United States culpable for the Marcos Pérez Jiménez dictatorship that had finally collapsed under its own corrupt weight.[57] This shared trauma forged a special relationship, which Nixon and Walters allegedly celebrated each year on that very date. Walters was also posted as military attaché in Brazil preparatory to the overthrow of the João Goulart régime in 1964. Walters was no mere observer: he has himself pointed out that the US navy was waiting offshore.[58] His obituary in *The Times* made the point with customary tact: "Walters forecast the ensuing coup so accurately, down to the very date it would begin, that some suspected him of engineering it. This suspicion intensified when his old wartime friend, General Castel Branco, seized power."[59] Walters is also one of the very few that Kissinger privileges with praise in his memoirs.

Wimert says he duly received a communication from the chairman of the joint chiefs of staff, Admiral Thomas Moorer, instructing him to take

---

[54] Thomas Powers, "Inside the Department of Dirty Tricks", *Atlantic*, vol. 244, no. 2, August 1979, p. 48.

[55] This is confirmed by Viaux: Fuentes, *Memorias Secretas*, p. 333.

[56] "El embajador Edward M. Korry en el CEP", *Estudios Públicos*, no. 72, spring 1998, p. 90.

[57] Jiménez embezzled $200 million in less than six years and found refuge in Miami.

[58] Interview in *Istoé*, no. 1644, 20 December 2000.

[59] *The Times*, 13 February 2003. For more on this story: Elio Gaspari, *A Ditadura Envergonhada* (São Paolo 2002) pp. 59–62. As that account reveals, it was president Kennedy who first committed the United States to bringing the military to power in Brazil.

orders from the CIA.[60] Hecksher gave Wimert $250,000 to persuade the army to come around to the need to forestall Allende's entry into office. Wimert kept it in his riding boots. "It would sit in the closet and when the time came to give it out to various people, I did."[61] The carabineros and the navy were reportedly ready to move – but not without the senior service, the army. In retrospect Wimert believed the kidnapping of commander-in-chief Schneider to provoke a coup, by making it appear an action of the extreme left, "was stupid from the word go". But orders were orders.[62] According to Russian intelligence sources, Hecksher received instructions from the CIA at Langley to have Schneider "removed".[63]

On 15 October the project of working through Viaux was formally abandoned. Kissinger, however, told the CIA to maintain pressure on "every Allende weak spot in sight – now … and into the future until such time as new marching orders are given".[64] US officials in Santiago were then advised: "It is firm and continuing policy that Allende be overthrown by a coup … we are to continue to generate maximum pressure towards this end utilizing every appropriate resource. It is imperative that these actions be implemented clandestinely and securely so that the USG[overnment] and American hand be well hidden …"[65] On 17 October US intelligence veteran Thomas Karamessines, deputy director of plans at the CIA – who managed covert operations – was called in by the US president and told to find a military alternative to Viaux. Wimert therefore met a set of conspirators who were nominally general Camilo Valenzuela's people but were effectively no different from those of Viaux.[66]

Complicit were vice-admiral Hugo Tirado, the second most senior officer of the navy; Valenzuela, officer commanding the army in Santiago province; general Joaquín García, the second most senior officer in the air force; and the director-general of the carabineros, Vicente Huerta.[67]

---

[60] Russian sources claim it was a coded message from general Philpott, deputy head of the DIA, dated 28 September: Konstantin Tarasov and Vyacheslav Zubenko, *The CIA in Latin America* (Moscow 1984), p. 115.

[61] Interview: *GWU NSA. Cold War Oral History Project*. Interview 10837.

[62] Ibid., Interview 10838.

[63] Tarasov and Zubenko, *The CIA*, p. 116.

[64] Ibid., p. 50.

[65] Immediate Santiago (Eyes only [deleted]), 16 October 1970: a copy can be found on the web: *www.gwu.edu~nasarchiv/NSAEBB/NSAEBB8/ch05-01.htm*.

[66] Powers, "Inside … ", p. 50.

[67] Ibid., pp. 332–3.

The job was done under the direction of Juan Diego Dávila and Luis Gallardo Gallardo.[68]

The plan to kidnap Schneider was codenamed Alpha.[69] Viaux initially gave the conspirators their instructions on 17 October. But all kinds of things went wrong, in the hands of enthusiastic but nervous and desperate amateurs, some of whom had a criminal record, others of whom were barely out of school. A number of those accused, including British citizen Allan Leslie Cooper who held dual nationality, were members of the Grange School old boys' rugby club.[70] The conspirators tried again, just two days before congress was to declare Allende president, soon after 8.00am on 22 October under Viaux's further instruction. They were supposed to use tear gas if Schneider resisted; in fact Viaux handed Gallardo an aerosol for that purpose.[71] Yet Gallardo was not even present during the attempt. When Schneider ambushed, his own car cut off by the youths in four other vehicles, he predictably and instinctively drew his revolver and fired twice. He was shot at eight times. Three bullets hit and fatally wounded him.[72] The failed kidnap was by all acounts a complete fiasco, which those involved were very keen to blame on infiltration by the MIR, for which there is no known evidence.

The official position of the MIR remained, as stated in May and August, then restated soon after the election: "we will develop our nascent military apparatus and put it to the service of an eventual defence of an electoral victory of the left".[73] They were still attempting to develop a significant capability. "In terms of organisation," one internal document argued, "our job is to homogenise military training among all militants and in the immediate future attain the training of all militants, as specialists, not only in terms of the ability to act on their own initiative, but also to lead five

---

[68] Florencia Varas, *Conversaciones con Viaux* (Santiago 1972), p. 137.

[69] Testimony of Luis Gallardo: ibid., p. 157. Gallardo had worked with Alessandri's campaign, as had others on the extreme right.

[70] Cooper's father "practically admitted that his son had played some part in the incident", British diplomats noted. It was all very embarrassing since "The Coopers are a large and long established family in Chile, well known to the Embassy." – Lee (Santiago) to Robson (Latin American Department, London), 4 November 1970: *FCO 7/1522*.

[71] Varas, *Conversaciones con Viaux*, p. 163.

[72] Information obtained by the British embassy – Lee (Santiago) to Robson (London), 4 November 1970: *FCO 7/1522*.

[73] "El MIR frente a la situación política: A los obreros, campesinos, pobladores, estudiantes y soldados" – reprinted in *Estudios Públicos*, 83, winter 2001, p. 359.

or six comrades."[74] Expecting an amnesty from Allende, they had everything to lose from a premature confrontation. Indeed Pascal, who is invariably straightforward about MIR activities, tells us that they were not involved; in fact that they knew nothing of the plot. Neither was PyL party to the assassination – as one its former leaders Eduardo Díaz Herrera insists: "This was done by the most extreme members of the PN … During this period we did not have a strategy of threatening individuals. What I ran was sabotage, not terrorism."[75] And it was PyL, engaged in innumerable activities designed to provoke a coup by the military, that was the focus of MIR infiltration:

> The MIR intelligence team, headed by Luciano [Cruz], discovered the conspiracy by means of infiltrating Patria y Libertad, identifying some of those responsible for the 21 outrages [*atentados*] and cases of sabotage which that taken place, and finding out that they were planning to provoke a military intervention by 22 October. We denounced the conspiracy on the day of the 21st, relaying detailed information in an offprint from *Punto Final* that obliged the government to move against Patria y Libertad [that night Frei was obliged to raid the Patria y Libertad Santiago offices] … What we did not detect was the operation that was being prepared against Schneider.[76]

General (retired) Emilio Cheyre, backed by experienced detectives and military intelligence, uncovered the entire plot within days of Schneider's assassination.[77] As indicated above, the CIA and the extreme right were engaged in a range of disruptive activities designed to push the armed forces into action. From this viewpoint the assassination of Schneider was a disaster, and not merely for him and his family. The US connection was in danger of being exposed, and most probably the main cause of the murder of the US journalist Charles Horman in September 1973 was his proximity to finding out the truth. Wimert himself was "scared to death, because so many things led to me".[78] The Chilean sources of the plot on the right were known and, far from being eager to take action, the less

---

[74] September 1970: reprinted in ibid., p. 366.
[75] *Qué Pasa*, 5 September 2003.
[76] Pascal, "El Mir", Part 2.
[77] Prats, *Memorias*, p. 191.
[78] Interview: *GWU NSA. Cold War Oral History Project*. Interview 10838.

fanatical of the disgruntled senior officers were now risk-averse. Viaux was back in prison, along with those engaged in the assassination who had not managed to disappear over the border. "Any possibility of keeping the opposition organised and mobilised was shut down at that moment", recalls the leader of the PN, Jarpa.[79]

The coup option had been described to the 40 Committee in the US government. The role of that committee needs explanation. Proposals for covert action would come in to the committee from a branch of government. The deputy director for co-ordination at the state department's bureau of intelligence and research would liaise with the CIA. Proposals then went to the assistant secretary of state for the region in question or his deputy. When proposals such as these were approved they were forwarded to the 40 Committee, where the undersecretary for political affairs sat as the state department's principal. The committee was chaired by the national security adviser; in this case Kissinger. He is described as "the man who made the decision".[80] As we shall see, not all covert actions went before the committee, so its status, certainly under Nixon, was advisory rather than decisive. But in this case the coup option did go before the committee. It was described "as Chilean action with the US as catalyst".[81] Indeed, that remained the idea for the next three years. The problem now was how to assure the Chilean military that a low-risk option existed. The degree to which Nixon and Kissinger became obsessed with overthrowing Allende and distrustful of those who failed to follow through decisively is caught in later reports from informed sources that "Kissinger, in effect, became a Chilean desk officer".[82]

The operations initially approved included placement of disinformation in the media, black operations and attempts to stimulate an investigation by Chile's parliament "of Cuban activities in Chile to arouse a military reaction against certain factors of the coalition".[83] Differences that had

[79] Arancibia et al., *Jarpa*, p. 140.

[80] The structure as outlined by James Gardner, once deputy director for coordination – testimony, 7 October 1975: *US Intelligence Agencies and Activities: The Performance of the Intelligence Community. Hearings before the Select Committee on Intelligence. United States House of Representatives. 94th Congress. 1st Session* (Washington DC 1975), p. 820.

[81] *NARA. Chile Declassification Project Collections. NSC.* "Minutes of the Meeting of the 40 Committee, 29 September 1970", 30 September 1970.

[82] *New York Times*, 15 September 1974.

[83] *NARA. Chile Declassification Project Collections. NSC.* Arnold Nachmanoff, "40 Committee – Chile … December 22 1970", for Kissinger, dated 21 December 1970.

arisen within UP, in particular those between the communists and the socialists, and the communist party and the MIR, were consciously played upon by the Americans through covert action. In talking points for a 40 Committee meeting on 18 November 1970 which were accepted at the end of discussion as policy, additional step (c) ran as follows:

> To play devil's advocate for a moment, would it be in our interest to try to enhance the position of the most extreme groups within the coalition in order to disrupt Allende's game plan (i.e., maintain a moderate respectable image) and thereby force a polarization which might coalesce opposition against him?

Of further interest is a proposal which sustained the life of Track II through to more favourable times: "Maintaining contacts and influence in the military, not just for intelligence but for potential future action …"[84] The US government also adopted national security decision memorandum 93. This

> … established the following basic policy objectives in our relations with Chile: to prevent the consolidation of the Allende regime and to limit the ability of the Allende regime to carry out policies contrary to US and hemisphere interests. To achieve these objectives, NSDM 93 calls for maximizing pressure on the Allende government while maintaining a correct but cool public posture. Thus pressure is to be balanced by a restrained public posture so that measures intended to weaken the Allende regime do not contribute to its consolidation of power or its ability to rally external support.[85]

Alert to the hostility of the United States, Allende none the less behaved with complete lack of guile. On the day he took the oath of office he greeted the Soviet ambassador, Nikolai Alexeev, with customary formality. However, Allende then noticed Igor Rybalkin, the Chilean specialist in the Soviet party apparatus, who was on attachment to the embassy, *inter alia* interpreting for the ambassador. To the astonishment of all, Allende ostentatiously

---

[84] *NARA. Chile Declassification Project Collections. NSC.* "Talking Points for 40 Committee Meeting – Chile, Wednesday, November 18, 1970".
[85] Memorandum for Mr Henry A. Kissinger, The White House, 22 December 1971: *NARA. Chile Declassification Project. NSC.*

embraced his "friend".[86] The Russians were, however, extremely wary of the new régime. According to US state department intelligence:

> A Soviet diplomat in Santiago reportedly cautioned that Allende should delay recognizing Castro until he can do so in concert with other Latin American countries, perhaps Peru and Bolivia, thereby avoiding unnecessary early difficulties for the UP administration. There are indications that the USSR does not want Chile to become dependent on trade with communist countries. Six months prior to the Chilean election two Soviet diplomats in Santiago reportedly said the USSR could not logistically support an Allende government, and expressed the view that the policies of such a government would be completely different from those of Havana.

Overcommitted elsewhere, Moscow advised the PCCh to take the gradualist path.[87] Yet Allende incautiously ignored such advice. He took risks elsewhere too. On 18 December he followed through on a promise given to amnesty members of the MIR imprisoned or under indictment for their activities. This followed a gun battle in Concepción in which members of the PCCh Ramona Parra Brigade shot in the head and killed MIR militant Arnoldo Ríos after Ríos and his comrades surrounded and threatened brigade members putting up posters in the streets. During the nationwide election campaign for the student federation, where the communists predominated, to gain propaganda advantage the PCCh called on the MIR for support. But in Concepción, where the MIR held the local advantage, the communists refused to support the MIR. Both sent in paramilitary groups. The gun battle was therefore predictable. The fact that the MIR was still technically outlawed doubtless encouraged the use of force, though at the time of the incident its three main leaders – Cruz, Enríquez and Bautista van Schowen Vasey – were freely walking the streets of the city. After the incident Allende stepped in to heal the breach and had to use all his personal authority to dampen passions. No one was ever arrested and charged for the crime. But it was agreed that a single candidate would stand for the left in the city – MIR notable Nelson Gutiérrez.[88]

---

[86] *Don Américo: un chileno comunista. Homenaje postumo* (Santiago 1992), p. 50.

[87] *NARA.* Department of State: RG 59, Pol 15–1 Chile, Box 2197. "USSR-Chile: Soviets still play Allende in low key", Intelligence Note, Bureau of Intelligence and Research, 30 October 1970.

[88] Câmara Canto (Santiago) to Secretary of State (Brasilia), 11 December 1970: *MRE. Ofícios Recibidos.* Chile, 1970, vol. 5.

As a result of the subsequent amnesty forty-three militants were released and the prosecution of Luciano Cruz was closed. Those freed celebrated the new year at the house of Allende's private secretary, Osvaldo Puccio. Allende also hosted his own celebrations with the leaders of the MIR, at which he surprised one and all by the suggestion that they join Unidad Popular and that Miguel Enríquez become minister of health in the government. This was not just Allende's renowned *muñeca*. "In offering him the position that he himself had had as a young socialist leader in the government of Pedro Aguirre Cerda," Pascal points out, "it also constituted a gesture of affection."[89] But in adjusting to UP, the MIR was playing its own game as well: "We also took advantage of our participation in the business of presidential security to make silent progress in military training, logistics and intelligence", notes Pascal.[90] Cruz began building up small-arms stores in their various apartments.[91]

In the face of these contradictions, Cuba waited ominously and somewhat impatiently in the wings, the perennial ghost at the feast, a standing alternative to the Allende experiment, and possessed of a considerable reserve of sympathy within the ranks of the socialist party of Chile. At Allende's inauguration, Cuba's deputy prime minister, Carlos Rafael Rodríguez, who managed relations with fraternal parties, made public his government's acceptance of Chile's non-violent road to socialism. However, he simultaneously outlined the view that Chile was the only Latin American state where this project was conceivable. He warned, "It is essential not to be tolerant to enemies"[92] and announced, "We categorically refuse to consider the use of force ruled out", compounding the damage done highlighting the MIR's contribution to Allende's victory.[93] The extended visit to Chile by Castro a year later was to complicate matters further. In the meantime the Cuban embassy in Santiago became a hub of activity. Whereas the new Chilean mission in Havana under the pro-Cuban chargé d'affaires Jorge Edwards, a professional diplomat, was treated shabbily and with what appears to have

---

[89] Pascal, "El Mir", Part 3.

[90] Ibid.

[91] Naranjo, *Biografía*, p. 24.

[92] Press conference 11 November 1970: *Punto Final*, 24 November 1970.

[93] Quoted in Yofre, *Misión Argentina*, p. 105.

been calculated discourtesy,[94] the Cubans in Santiago acquired something close to *carte blanche*. The embassy comprised forty-eight people – the Chileans had a mere handful uncomfortably housed in Havana – of whom sixteen were diplomats, the rest administrative and support staff. The British concluded that this set-up was "not only very large but very sinister and … heavily weighted with officials engaged in subversive and intelligence operations".[95] The ambassador, Mario García Enchaustegui, had been ambassador to Uruguay, but was expelled for subversive activities. He later worked for Guevara, represented his country at the United Nations, directed the international organisations department at the foreign ministry and headed Cuba's UN office in Geneva. His minister-counsellor, Fernández Oña of the DGI, recalls that "we were enormously active" and, as Allende's son-in-law, "had a very close relationship with the president".[96] Others included the counsellor, Juan Carretero Ibáñez, the DGI station chief[97] (*nom de guerre* "Ariel"), who headed section 11-1 (the six branches of the Latin American department) and had been liaison officer in Havana for Che's guerrilla campaign in Bolivia. Carretero was reported to have been brought in to help set up a counter-intelligence unit for Allende. When the military eventually seized power they found Fernández Oña had a desk in Tati's office, next door to that of Allende. Two out of three first secretaries – Ramiro Rodríguez González and Manuel Martínez Galan – were also said to be DGI.[98] At the end of 1971 a DGI defector said that Santiago had replaced Paris as the centre for co-ordinating liberation movements in South America.[99]

Initially Allende had reason to be optimistic. He was now successfully in office, despite the odds that had been much against him. He had successfully neutralised christian democracy, apparently isolated the

---

[94] Jorge Edwards, *Persona Non Grata: An Envoy in Castro's Cuba* (London 1976). It was at that time expected that MAPU secretary-general Jaime Gazmuri would go to Havana as ambassador – Câmara Canto (Santiago) to Secretary of State (Brasilia), 4 December 1970: *MRE. Oficios Recibidos*. Chile, 1970, vol. 5. In the event Juan Henrique de la Vega (MAPU) was appointed.

[95] Stephen Clissold, "The Cuban Embassy in Santiago", Foreign and Commonwealth Office Research Department, 3 August 1971: *FCO 7/1991*.

[96] "Luis Fernández …", *Punto Final*, 2 March 2001.

[97] Identified as such by a DGI officer who defected to the US embassy in London at the end of 1971: *Daily Telegraph*, 18 December 1971; also *FCO 7/1991*.

[98] Ibid.

[99] *FCO 7/1991*. This has yet to be confirmed.

extreme right, and found a working compromise with the extreme left. And the US government had been forced to a longer-term strategy for his overthrow. Assistant undersecretary of state for Latin America Charles (Chuck) Meyer was a former Sears, Roebuck executive with direct experience of Latin America, who gained his post through the good offices of David Rockefeller, Kissinger's former patron. Despised by Kissinger for his "defeatist" approach to the problem, Meyer correctly pointed out in mid-November 1970 that "Any concept of a unified political opposition to Allende at the moment is virtually hopeless. The CDU [*sic*] is so badly split its factions cannot get together and there is no rock on which to build a solid political opposition."[100] Nevertheless, the issue remained for Allende as to whether he could effectively translate the ambitious Basic Programme into reality; whether he could do so and remain within the compromise secured with the christian democrats; or whether the hopes aroused by this unexpected victory would overwhelm every intention of proceeding at a steady and sober pace and thereby give Washington the opportunity it sought to bring down the government. The trouble was that the economy, upon which the success of UP so much depended, was already in serious straits. There had been a run on the banks and the stock market had plummeted. Much worse was to follow. Moreover the White House was no less committed to Allende's overthrow, despite continuing doubts at the CIA and state department. *Time* magazine later reported that "so many Marxist activists were pouring in from Cuba, Czechoslovakia and China that a special team of CIA clerks was dispatched to Chile to start indexing thousands of cards on their activities".[101] It was evidently this that explained the CIA presence at the Santiago consulate by the time of the coup in September 1973 and why the whereabouts of foreign militants and sympathisers were so easily obtained when it came to arrest and interrogation.

The core of the policy adopted by the White House, which required continued deception of the ambassador in Santiago, was that the downfall of Allende had at all costs to appear a consequence of Chilean events and come about at Chilean hands. The role of the United States had to be

---

[100] *NARA. Chile Declassification Project Collections. NSC.* "Minutes of the 40 Committee, 13 November 1970", 17 November 1970.
[101] *Time*, 30 September 1974.

entirely invisible. The five areas of action were: to create chaos in the economy; to encourage paramilitary activity which would foster a sense of chaos in society; to sustain a propaganda barrage against the régime by subsidising the opposition media; to reinforce the right through financial assistance; and to weaken and divide the left.[102] The official line that the CIA station in Santiago remained merely passive observers has long been sustained. Jack Devine, who arrived in Santiago in the autumn of 1971, gave an interview to the press nearly three decades later to reinforce the message that all they did was sit and watch. Unfortunately for him and the agency a "close colleague" of his "remembers no such line in the sand. I think our posture was a little more aggressive than that", Donald Winters recalls.[103] Indeed, it was.

[102] Decisions from the 40 Committee, gleaned from East German intelligence sources – a memorandum by Felipe Suárez of the PCCh, "Consideraciones sobre la situacion en Chile", November 1974: *AA*. Ministerium für Auswärtige Angelegenheiten der DDR. Abteilung Lateinamerika. C3352.000001.

[103] Vernon Loeb, "Spook Story", *Washington Post*, 17 September 2000. Winters was in Chile from late 1969 to mid-1973.

4

DESTROYING THE BASES OF CAPITALISM

... the Chilean process is irreversible ...

Augusto Olivares, adviser and
close friend to Allende, 1972[1]

The foremost political complaint levelled at the régime of Eduardo Frei
(1964–70) was that he ignored the size of the vote for the opposition
when he ruled Chile on a minority franchise, despite the readiness of
elements within the communist party to co-operate if Frei took on board
some of their concerns and policies. This omission and Frei's insistence
on government by one party only (*partido unico*) were to forge an
intransigent opposition of unusual unity. A bitter legacy thus remained
that made all talk of co-operation with christian democracy after
4 November 1970 on terms other than its unconditional surrender utterly
unthinkable to most socialists. Chile's seemingly irreversible drift to the
left made matters still worse. To the dispassionate observer – of whom
few were soon to be found – it was obvious that Allende should have
avoided making the same mistake as Frei by not rejecting the option of
aligning with the PDC, above all because of the ever-present possibility
of a military insurrection backed by the United States.

The extent of Chile's shift leftwards cannot be measured entirely by
the size of the vote for Allende. Judged in these terms, Chile had scarcely
moved at all. But the entire core of the political spectrum had shifted to
the left, taking the PS with it. The socialist party was no longer part of

---

[1] A. Olivares, *El diálogo de américa: F. Castro/S. Allende* (Santiago 1972), p. 2. Olivares headed TV
channel 7, was political editor of *La Ultima Hora*, a collaborator with *Clarín* and on the editorial
board of *Punto Final*.

the Second International, which it deemed too right-wing. Indeed, in 1973 the fortieth anniversary of the socialist party was celebrated with no invitations to fraternal socialist parties; only communist parties were present, including parties ruling within the Soviet bloc, and the PCCh were allowed in only for a brief salutation.[2] The christian democrats in Chile also stood markedly to the left of their counterparts in Europe or, indeed, in countries such as Venezuela. A back-handed tribute to the extent of PDC/UP convergence was rendered in retrospect by the then national leader of the Partido National (PN), Jarpa. "If you analyse the programmes of Tomic and Allende," he said, "that of Tomic was as socialist as that of Allende. They were two roads to arrive at the same objective."[3] Indeed, the PDC had declared as its essential task "the substitution of capitalism in Chile".[4] This was to be accomplished through co-operation with the socialist and communist parties as well as the trades unions. Before Tomic was named PDC candidate for the presidency, he had visited his friend Pablo Neruda, Chile's most distinguished living poet – who had initially been the PCCh candidate before withdrawing in favour of Allende – and suggested "a wider alliance of progressive forces as a substitute for our Unidad Popular movement, under the title of Unión de Pueblo [union of the people]".[5] Neruda was not encouraging, and Tomic had to go it alone, but the slogan of the right not surprisingly became: "A vote for Tomic is the same as a vote for Allende."[6] Even if Jarpa's characterisation of the PDC were merely the jaundiced view of a rival party in opposition, as such it has great significance because a united front against UP could be created only by PDC–PN co-operation, and the subsequent forging of that alliance spelled doom for Allende.

In hindsight it would have been reasonable for UP to seek to forestall a united front between the centre and the right. Yet, following constitutional amendments to safeguard democracy agreed by UP to

---

[2] Giancarlo Pajetta reporting to the Italian communist party (PCI) on his visit to Chile, 7 June 1973: *Archivio PCI* (Istituto Gramsci, Rome), Esteri. Cile. 046. 189–99.

[3] Onofre Jarpa, *Confesiones políticas* (Santiago 2000), p. 122.

[4] This was contained in the "Declaración política fundamental y bases programáticas para un segundo gobierno demócrata cristiano" approved in August 1969. See Radomiro Tomic, "Aclaraciones sobre ciertos hechos históricos", *Chile 1970–1973: Lecciónes de una Experiencia*, ed. F. Gil et al. (Madrid 1977), p. 196.

[5] Neruda, *Confieso*, p. 464–5.

[6] Ibid.

ensure Allende's accession to office, no sustained effort was made to win over the PDC until the majority were already alienated by government. Indeed, Allende's political adviser Joan Garcés cited only three attempts to reach out to the christian democrats; most significantly not one of these was made within the first year of reaching power, when it could have made all the difference. Indeed, we are told that "Garcés always considered as one of UP's most serious errors that it removed support from the most left-wing sections of christian democracy, thereby allowing the right within the party to take control of the leadership."[7] The reason why is simple. After a year in office Allende still harboured resentments against the PDC which had rekindled as opposition to the UP programme mounted. Italian journalist Rosanna Rossanda spent three hours with the president in November 1971 along with Paul Sweezy and Michel Gutelman. To her surprise Allende seemed more "decisive in both intention and expectation" than anticipated. And when questioned about the possibilities of co-operation with christian democracy, his response was completely negative: "All [christian democrats] are opposed; they are all in alliance." But what of Tomic? "Yes, but today they are all on the other side," he said, "with anger, bitterness, with a semi-smile ..."[8]

Those most actively reaching out to the PDC were, ironically, the communists, despite the fact that the PCCh was very much a working-class party. Its membership included 66.6 percent workers and 7.7 percent peasants. But communist memories of internal exile and the efforts made towards ending their isolation were too strong to be dismissed even when faced with the beguiling prospect of building the kind of socialism that had long been a waking dream. At the XIVth congress of the PCCh on 23 November 1969 Corvalán had asserted:

> We do not put all christian democrats in the same bag. We have borne in mind that the fact that an important part of those who had voted for Mr Frei and of government party militants took seriously the need for change and wished to advance it by attacking at the very least various centres of power on the right.

[7] Lía Levit, "Pinochet: la dictadura", *Cambio 16*, 12–19 September 1983.
[8] Rosanna Rossanda, "Successi, limiti e scogli", p. 185.

This line was followed despite the lack of understanding by "some circles on the left, which attempted to portray us as collaborators with ruling christian democracy".[9]

Indeed, the Soviet embassy attributed to the PCCh the "decisive role" in keeping the PDC in play; and in particular to its central committee plenum in September 1970, which invited the christian democrats to participate in a bloc of the left. "At the basis of this line one finds a realistic evaluation of fortifying progressive tendencies in the Christian Democratic Party and recognition of the importance of its role in the political life of the country." The manner in which Tomic and Benjamín Prado (chairman of the party's *consejo nacional*) supported Allende's election into office by congress showed the importance of this strategy, which was the outcome of several years' effort. The Russians also cited with evident approval such leading christian democrats as Valdés, Leighton, and others. The idea now, following Allende's election – in the Soviet embassy's view – was "attract to the side of Unidad Popular those vast sectors of the population that had supported the Tomic programme or had voted for Alessandri".[10] This made good sense. But the embassy had difficulty seeing a contradiction between draining the PDC of members and simultaneously sustaining or even developing good relations with its leadership. Although mainstream christian democrats had already seen members break away to form MAPU, they were not prepared to contemplate a repetition with even-handed tolerance, let alone resigned fatalism or beneficent good will.

When, after Allende's election, his daughter and special adviser Tati visited Havana, Castro dispensed various pieces of advice that echoed the message from Moscow. Among these was the conviction that the christian democrats were by no means homogeneous. Castro strongly recom-mended that UP should leave Valdés in post as foreign minister because he was "an anti-imperialist".[11] But it was not so easy for the PS to follow such advice even from Castro – let alone from the PCCh of whom, as a major element in the governing coalition, the PS were suspicious and

---

[9] Farias, *La izquierda chilena*, p. 143.

[10] Report dated 13 October 1970 by second secretary Yakovlev: reprinted in *Estudios Públicos*, no. 72, spring 1998, pp. 407–8.

[11] Volodia Teitelboim, member of the PCCh Politburo [*Comisión Política*], in conversation with ambassador Alexeev of the Soviet embassy, 14 October 1970: ibid., p. 413.

jealous. The PCCh always punched above its weight. Its membership was not that great: in 1971 it stood at 57,000, and rose to 153,470 in January 1972 and 165,000 that June.[12] But in stark contrast to the PS it was highly disciplined and well organised. "Its influence in the formation of Unidad Popular and in the government goes far beyond its electoral weight", noted the experienced Italian communist Giancarlo Pajetta.[13] The nervous PS leadership had insisted to Allende that the communists must not have any of the key political ministries: interior, defence or foreign affairs.[14] Moreover vested interests were at stake. The socialist Aniceto Rodríguez, for example, was determined to have the foreign ministry for himself; Allende, a long-time rival, was equally determined that he should not. But there were limits to his ability to restrict the influence of rivals within his own party. He had to operate as independently as he could from the PS, but at the same time he had to sustain unanimity within the co-ordinating committee that ran UP, which was reorganised into a political committee after the elections. Its initial members on 5 November 1970 were Corvalán (PCCh), Rodríguez (PS), Carlos Morales (PRh), Rodrigo Ambrosio (MAPU), Esteban Leyton (PSDh) and Alfonso David Lebon (*API*). Coalition unity obliged Allende to listen closely above all to the communists, socialists and MAPU. The point at which the radicals walked out of the government in the spring of 1971 should have indicated that he was listening insufficiently to others who were better aligned with mainstream opinion beyond La Moneda. The problem, which at the early stages was potential rather than actual, assumed major proportions when Altamirano replaced Rodríguez as secretary-general of the socialist party [see p. 91].

Whatever his sympathies for PCCh strategy, Allende held to his own beliefs and preferences. On 5 November, the minister of the interior, José Tohá, announced the dissolution of the "mobile group" of paramilitary policemen. Simultaneously proceedings against eight leaders of the MIR were called to a halt and all the accused were freed. At the end of the month many of those imprisoned, the bulk of whom belonged to the

[12] *AA. Ministerium für Auswärtige Angelegenheiten der DDR. DY/30/IV B 2/20.* 102. Information for the Politburo, 6 July 1972. "Zur gegenwärtigen Lage in Chile".
[13] Report in his visit to Chile: *Archivio PCI.* Estera. Cile. 046.189–99. Pajetta headed his party's section dealing with fraternal parties.
[14] *Estudios Públicos*, p. 411.

MIR, were set loose. On 12 November Allende announced the opening of diplomatic relations with Cuba – in spite of Castro's advice through Tati that he should take his time – and on 14 November ambassador Mario García Inchaustegi presented his credentials. Thereafter the number of Cubans appearing in Chile grew apace – it was reported in January 1972 that some 21,086 people had entered from the Soviet bloc, of whom the majority were Cubans.[15] And since Caribbean speech easily set Cubans apart from locals, and much of the same could also be heard from Venezuelans, rumours as to the number of Cubans in Chile soon far exceeded reality.

An ill omen for the economy appeared early. This was the call on 13 November 1970 by Luis Figueroa Mazuela, communist secretary-general of the CUT, for the working class to be prepared to make sacrifices. "Raising wages is vitally important", he said, "but not the main problem. The main point is the consolidation of the popular government … If sacrifices have to be made, we will make them and pull the country out of backwardness."[16] The unanswered question was whether he could deliver on that commitment. A further danger signal, more evidently fearful, was the unauthorised occupation of land within one and a half kilometres of Allende's house by eight hundred *sin casa* (homeless) on the following day. The movement of the *sin casa* was led by 28-year-old Victor Hugo Toro Ramírez of the MIR. But the government was at this point optimistic that all lay within its grasp, and on 26 November Allende announced the forthcoming nationalisation of US copper companies and of Chilean and foreign banks, insurance and industrial concerns. Furthermore he declared his intention to propose removal from the constitution of a guarantee for private property. The Basic Programme was now being implemented. The expectation among left christian democrats, in particular, was that all these measures – and not merely the nationalisation of copper, on which almost all agreed across the political spectrum – would be submitted for approval to congress.

At the PCCh's central committee plenum on 26–30 November, Corvalán underlined the importance of avoiding negative references to

[15] *El Mercurio*, 29 January 1972.

[16] Zorina et al., *Uroki Chili* (Moscow 1977), p. 271. This publication was drawn from classified files.

the christian democrats as the adversary.[17] This was not, however, the entire story. Although the communist party was committed to keeping the door open to christian democrats, it was equally – if not more – committed to pressing forward with state appropriation of the means of production, distribution and exchange as fast as possible in order to make the revolution, though piecemeal, irreversible. There was thus at the core of the PCCh strategy a fundamental contradiction never confronted and resolved. "It is too early to celebrate victory", Corvalán told *L'Humanité* on 7 December. "The course of events cannot be considered irreversible. It must be made irreversible … Now there is no task more revolutionary than completion of the government programme."[18] The question was, how this programme would be put into effect. What broke the spirit of the understanding with the opposition that made possible Allende's accession to office was that he did not turn to congress where the opposition could deny legislation or at least force a compromise. Instead, through the ingenious efforts of lawyer Eduardo Novoa Monreal the government resorted to laws effected some forty years before to expropriate businesses without the need for further legislation: decree 520 issued by the socialist republic in 1932, supplemented by economics ministry directive 338 from 1945 and law 1,262 of 1953. This and other ingenious but devious devices, which seriously undermined the régime's bona fides in the eyes of rival parties, were resorted to initially for the banal reason that factions within the UP coalition could not agree on the precise terms of legislation for the nationalisation of various sectors of the economy, and the balance to be struck between wholly state-owned, mixed enterprise and private possession. Given UP's hold on little more than a third of the popular vote, the government risked the accusation that it was carrying out a revolution with no popular mandate.

The under-secretary for the economy was Oscar Guillermo Garretón Purcell, a leading light in MAPU and, at a mere twenty-six years of age, the youngest and one of the most fanatical of Allende's team. The first use of executive authority began on 20 November when he announced that the government was taking over two businesses in Santiago for sabotaging production and breach of rules for the payment of agricultural

[17] Report on the meeting to ambassador Alexeev by Orlando Millas, member of the PCCh Politburo, 20 December 1970: *Estudios Públicos*, p. 416.
[18] Zorina et al., *Uroki Chili*, p. 277.

produce.[19] This set the pattern that circumvented the spirit of compromise with the PDC. On this the communists were as one with the socialists and MAPU; so much was evident at the plenum of the PCCh central committee, held between 26 and 30 November. Corvalán simultaneously reminded those assembled that, under previous constitutional changes initiated in February under Frei, the president had the right to call a plebiscite to dissolve parliament in the event of conflict between the executive and legislature. And he wanted the government to press ahead quickly to take maximum advantage of conditions favourable to change. Corvalán even declared the party's willingness to accept MIR co-operation with the government, provided the party dropped its ambivalent position towards UP and rejected hostility towards the PCCh.[20] Thus although the PCCh were ostensibly more willing to compromise with christian democracy, the substance of the revolution that it wished to press ahead with at great speed was unlikely to be acceptable to the PDC. This meant that serious pressure to neutralise mounting opposition was effectively nullified. The day after the plenum Allende signed another decree, this time expropriating a textile factory, whose owners too were accused of sabotaging production, as well as of withholding workers' pay and making workers redundant.[21]

Inevitably, with the failure of Tomic to win the elections, the PDC began to drift back towards the centre of Chilean politics, a compromise with the right that made further moves in this direction a real possibility. The circumvention of congress by Allende in his first measures nationalising industry also had its effect. At the *consejo nacional* of the PDC on 13–14 December it was agreed that the left and the right would be given equal representation in the party leadership.[22] The leader of the national party, Jarpa, recalls: "Gradually, a major separation opened up between UP and DC, though the latter had not sought it."[23] This was, as yet, merely a straw in the wind. It did not, however, prevent PDC collaboration in the nationalisation of the copper industry, which was brought to congress on 21 December. This measure was not out of line

[19] Ibid., p. 272.
[20] Ibid., pp. 273–4
[21] Ibid., p. 275.
[22] Ibid., pp. 277–8.
[23] Arancibia et al., *Jarpa*, p. 147.

with the actions of other less developed countries that were heavily reliant for foreign exchange earnings on one commodity. So it said less about sympathies for socialism within the PDC as a whole than nationalist sentiment readily found throughout the Third World: what Venezuelan christian democrat Rafael Caldera called "international social justice".

Another issue that tested PDC toleration was the handling of agrarian reform. Poverty in the countryside had long been a chronic problem. The interamerican committee for agricultural development in 1965 estimated that Chile had not only a greater number of families farming larger properties than elsewhere in Latin America but also the second largest number of agricultural labourers without land. Disguised unemployment and underemployment were said to account for some 30 percent of the labour force in the countryside. The Frei expropriations made no significant difference to this underclass, known as the *afuerinos*. When the great estates were seized and turned into co-operatives (*asentamientos*), the settled workers on the land – the *inquilinos* – were those who benefited most from tenure and a steadier income. The land reform implemented by the christian democrats thus left the countryside badly divided between a new class of "haves" and the longstanding class of "have-nots", whose financial position had worsened further with the higher inflation of Frei's last years.[24]

Ostensibly Allende's administration pursued land reform through legislation enacted by the christian democrats: law 16,640 of July 1967. This allowed for expropriation on grounds of size alone (not merely insufficient exploitation or breach of regulations): anything with the productivity equivalent to 80 hectares in the Maipo valley ("basic hectares"). The law had allowed exceptions, however, including viticulture, forestry, well-run enterprises and those sharing profits with the labourers; but these exceptions were for executive discretion, and the benevolent exercise of that discretion immediately disappeared under Allende. Frei had also reduced compensation to below market value, at a government-assessed rate, and the compensation awarded amounted to anything between 1 and 10 percent in cash; the rest was paid in bonds over the long term at a

---

[24] *NARA. Chilean Declassification Project Collections.* Department of State. "High Farm Unemployment One Factor in Rural Unrest". Amembassy (Santiago) to department of state, 26 April 1972. For more background, see R. Kaufman, *The Politics of Land Reform in Chile, 1950–1970: Public Policy, Political Institutions, and Social Change* (Cambridge, Mass. 1972).

mere 3 percent interest with only partial allowance for inflation. The odds were thus already stacked against landowners even before Allende took power, by which time some 3.6 million hectares had already been expropriated. A description of what followed is given by the World Bank:

> While Congressional opposition ruled out modifications of the Law, expropriations frequently spilled over the statutory boundaries. Parcels below the 80 BIH limit, legal reserves, and legally exempted forest lands were all taken. In some cases, the Government acted in response to land seizure by the workers on the grounds that expropriation was thereby made necessary to maintain public order. Almost 1,300 land seizures were reported in 1971, compared with 340 in 1969 and 1970 combined.[25]

Statements by government blatantly contradicted what was happening on the ground where MIR activists were furthering an intensive programme to "*concientizar*" (raise the consciousness) of the peasantry. On 18 December 1970, for instance, president Allende met sixty farmers' leaders and assured them that with respect to land reform "we will do it within the framework of the law".[26] Yet only three days later, events showed that this assurance bore little or no relationship with reality when the MIR's agrarian offshoot – the Movimiento Campesino Revolucionario (MCR) – organised the seizure of estates, provoking, *inter alia*, an armed confrontation in the province of Cautín. British journalist Alistair Horne tracked down the leader of these operations, "Comandante Pepe" – Gregorio José Liendo, the 26-year-old son of a dairy owner – who, with other MIR militants, launched a series of *tomas* (land seizures) that soon stretched from Cautín to Osorno, running the length of the Argentinian frontier to the south. Horne relates that the carabineros were "strictly ordered not to intervene when owners asked for protection against the MIR; on the other hand, one farmer defending his property with a shotgun was promptly arrested".[27] Once taken, the properties were given government funding to sustain them. Chonchol was all innocence, claiming he had never met Pepe, which scarcely rang true since Pepe boasted of their conversations. His comments – that "now it is the turn

---

[25] F. Levy et al. ed., *Chile: An Economy in Transition* (World Bank 1980), p. 68.
[26] Zorina et al., *Uroki Chili*, p. 278.
[27] A. Horne, "Comandante Pepe", *Encounter*, July 1971, vol. XXXVII, no. 1, p. 39.

of the majority to abuse the minority" and that "civil war in Chile is inevitable" – captured the spirit of the MIR.[28]

Allende arrived in Temuco and promptly called for order; yet the MIR's Miguel Enríquez, invariably an accurate witness, recalls a rather different outlook behind the scenes. At the end of December, he tells us, the MIR led "a wave of seizures of land … in order to push forward agrarian reform".[29] This we know; but he also remembers the government looked to "popular mobilisation as a source of strength".[30] At this time a "luke-warm" approach to dealing with land reform and the appropriation of big business was not appreciated. "As a consequence of this we began to take charge of the seizing of land in the provinces to the south of the country. In the beginning we succeeded in pressuring Allende and the PCCh into supporting us or at least keeping quiet and basically on the need to press ahead with agrarian reform in these zones (December)."[31]

The reaction of the farmers was predictable. "In the prevailing atmosphere of hopelessness," Horne recorded, "farmers are neglecting the land, not sowing or fertilising for next year. Large numbers of milch cows and breeding stock are being slaughtered for meat, or driven into Argentina, in return for ready cash at knock-down prices."[32] Given Enríquez's unforgiving candour in everything else, and given also his personal contact with the president at the time, it is hard to interpret all this as anything other than Allende's conscious complicity in the events that followed. But there was more to this. The mainspring of the acceleration in agrarian reform in government was Chonchol, now a leading figure in MAPU and a possible future contender for the presidency (he had put himself forward early in the previous round for UP): "the fact is", noted the Brazilian ambassador, "that in the interpretation of some sectors of UP Chonchol's activities are more unequivocal and revolutionary than those of president Allende himself". Chonchol seemed determined to ratchet up achievements for the government prior to the April elections. The ambassador noted that "of the personalities in government Chonchol was outdistancing his colleagues, be they [Pedro]

[28] Ibid., pp. 37 and 40.
[29] "Contribuciones para una historia del MIR", p. 342.
[30] Ibid.
[31] Ibid., p. 343.
[32] Horne, "Comandante", p. 39.

Vuskovic (timidity), [Orlando] Cantuarias (inefficiency), Almeyda (low popularity) and even [José] Tohá". In contrast Chonchol appeared to be "combative to the extreme". The price, of course, was paid in the alienation of the christian democrats. Senator Narciso Irrueta – president of the PDC – told Brazilian ambassador Câmara Canto that "Chonchol squandered on a spree all the loyalty, the support and the confidence that the PDC had always given him, by means of his various directives."[33]

In August 1971 Chonchol went one step further. He announced that all lands expropriated would be made agrarian reform centres (*centros de reforma agraria*), to which all workers aged over sixteen would belong. And he further made clear that the *asentamientos* formed under Frei were under attack:

> We believe that in the old asentamientos, fewer people remained on the land than when the latifundia existed. This has produced ill feeling among the outsiders and sharecroppers who believe the agrarian reform has been unsuccessful. In some asentamientos the members have become bosses of their fellow workers who work for a wage. This has given rise to first class and second class farm workers, which is something this Administration cannot tolerate.

A few months later Chonchol also declared that all farms above 80 irrigated acres would be expropriated by the winter of 1972.[34]

As already noted, Allende should not be seen entirely as a free agent. A major limitation on his freedom of manoeuvre where he chose to exercise it lay in the fact that all major policy decisions required unanimity within the leadership of Unidad Popular.[35] Communist party apart, those sharing power – with the exception of the radicals – generally stood further to the left, both in their greater tolerance of violence and in their urge to speed up the revolutionary process. A key figure was PS secretary-general, Altamirano, who (at least in his eyes) became something of the son Allende never had. Born on 18 December 1922, Altamirano came from an exceptionally wealthy home. His grandfather, the founder and

---

[33] Câmara Canto (Santiago) to Secretary of State (Brasilia), 23 February 1971: *MRE. Oficios Recibidos.* Chile, 1971, vol. 1.

[34] Davis (Santiago) to Washington, 26 April 1972: *NARA.* State Department, LAB 13. Chile.

[35] For an incisive summary by a Chilean historian: Gonzalo Vial Correa, "Salvador Allende (II)", *La Segunda*, 11 July 2000.

president of the Bank of Chile, had been one of the richest men in the country. Altamirano himself was a lawyer who had defended US companies against prosecution in Chile. A tall, skeletal figure, he was described by one Cuban journalist as "a man of anxious temperament" who was "constantly in movement".[36] The highly disciplined East Germans, who came to know him in exile, found him dangerously unpredictable. They might, of course, be seen as biased, since Altamirano had no love of Soviet-style socialism. But even the Whiggish British ambassador, David Hildyard, not altogether unsympathetic to UP, described Altamirano as "a strange unbalanced character".[37] And Hildyard's more conservative successor, World War Two veteran Reginald Secondé, regarded Altamirano as a truly destructive anarchist.[38] "The Chilean socialist party is an unusual party within the group of socialist parties of the Western capitalist world", Altamirano boasted. "Our party, as distinct from the European socialist or social democratic parties, has always defined itself as a Marxist-Leninist party."[39]

The socialists' congress at La Serena from 28 January to 2 February 1971 elected Altamirano secretary-general of the party over the head of Rodríguez. In this he had the quiet support of Allende.[40] The American ambassador commented: Allende "has designated de facto that his successor in 1976 will be the man that he got elected as the head of the Socialist Party even though he was his worst enemy within the SP in ideological terms, Senator Altamirano, the hardest liner of all".[41] Although Allende was undoubtedly relieved at the departure of Rodríguez – a rival of long standing who had tried to block his election as leader of UP – and had therefore supported Altamirano in his place, the rest of the party executive committee elected were also predominantly Altamirano supporters. And although Allende and Altamirano shared the same goals, they differed sharply on the way to achieve them. In contradistinction to Allende, Altamirano was wary of, if not hostile to, the Soviet bloc and

[36] *Bohemia* (Havana), 4 July 1971.
[37] Hildyard (Santiago) to Hankey (London), 8 March 1972: *FCO 7/2212.*
[38] Interview.
[39] *Bohemia,* 4 July 1971.
[40] *New York Times,* 2 February 1971.
[41] Testimony of Edward Korry, 1 July 1971: *United States and Chile,* p. 30. This is not the whole story. "Carlos never stopped considering him [Allende] a kind of spiritual father" – Maria Ines Bussi, "Mio Zio …", *L'Unitá,* 7 September 2003.

saw Cuba as a model with respect to means as well as ends. The perspicacious Argentinian ambassador correctly forecast that this "signalled the end of traditional Chilean socialism and is judged by many old leaders as the birth of a monster that will provoke with its behaviour the ruin and the annihilation of President Allende".[42] The latter had, not for the last time, overestimated his well-practised *muñeca*. The PS congress at La Serena also made very clear that it was having no truck with the PDC. Indeed, it resolved that "The so-called 'christian democratic left', by remaining in this party and by its indecision, is serving as a screen for the right and reactionary sectors that are taking part in the great plot against the government of comrade Salvador Allende and against the workers. Only a policy of profound transformation and accelerated growth of the revolutionary process will force a definition of groups of christian democratic workers." The resolution ended with an inflammatory and suicidal reference to preparing the party and the masses for "the decisive confrontation with the bourgeois and imperialism".[43]

Allende now moved to counter-balance the new influence. Soon after Altamirano's election he attempted to dampen rising expectations of greater radicalism by warning against any attempt to disrupt the more measured pace of change. The government did not carry all of the population with it, he said; a consensus had to be built and not assumed. He alluded, *inter alia*, to the constitutional compromise with the christian democrats that secured congressional support for his accession to power:

> I would be a hypocrite if I said that I am President of all Chileans. There are some people who would like to see me boiled in oil [*frito en aceite*], and they are Chileans. I am President of Unidad Popular, but I also have the duty to concern myself with Chile, which does not belong to Unidad Popular, and to concern myself with improving the life not of people from Unidad Popular but of all Chileans ... I am here to carry out the programme of Unidad Popular, which is not the programme of all Chileans. Senator Altamirano knows the compromises that the Socialist Party is making and that it is as a function of these compromises that I am in the presidency of the Republic.

---

[42] Despatch from Buenos Aires, 4 February 1971: Yofre, *Misión Argentina*, p. 112.

[43] *Resolución política del Congreso de La Serena* (Santiago 1970). Also reprinted in Farias, *La izquierda chilena*, pp. 619–21. The importance of this congress in cutting off the bridge to christian democracy was later noted by Jarpa: Arancibia et al., *Jarpa*, p. 162.

We have said that the transformations and changes are going to be made within bourgeois democracy. And if comrade Altamirano reckons that we ought to go faster, I say to him that we are not going to go faster. I am the president of Chile, and I have much respect for comrade Altamirano and I will always say so. I will listen to the political committee [of the Socialist Party], just as I listen to the opinion of the other parties. But I will not be told what to do by any party leader and of any party.[44]

At a press conference two days later, Altamirano outlined the forthcoming tasks of the PS, which he summed up as the creation of an "organised and ideologically united party" that would become "a genuinely revolutionary vanguard of the proletariat and peasantry". He insisted that UP would receive staunch support but he also heaped praise on the MIR: "the activity of MIR supporters has facilitated the development and strengthening of the revolutionary consciousness of our people".[45] Despite Allende's best efforts, however, the disruptive effects of Altamirano's elevation were not long in making themselves felt. On 4 March, for instance, the socialist party leadership demanded the resignation of the president of the supreme court on the grounds that the court remained in the hands of reactionaries and was "the only organ of power which has not undergone the changes taking place in the country".[46] Disarray set in as Allende was forced to assert himself to the point of exasperation in the face of internal opposition. At one particularly aggravating meeting of the UP leadership Allende demanded of his colleagues: "Will someone tell me who the hell is the President of the Republic in charge here?"[47] Altamirano later confessed that "relations between Salvador and the party were never a cup of tea [*una taza de leche*]".[48] This should scarcely occasion surprise: from the outset Allende's problem was that in some respects he was in office but not in power.

The MIR was ever more active in the countryside, encouraging seizure of land at will. This wave of expropriation began what was called the

---

[44] Statement delivered in Valparaíso, 4 February 1971: *La Nación*, 5 February 1971 – reprinted in González and Talavera, *Los mil días*, vol. 1, pp. 64–5.

[45] *La Nación*, 7 February 1971: quoted in Zorina et al., *Uroki Chili*, p. 283.

[46] Ibid., p. 284.

[47] Quoted from ex-minister Orlando Millas, in Yofre, *Misión Argentina*, p. 112.

[48] Patricia Politzer, *Altamirano* (Buenos Aires 1989), p. 54.

"hot summer". "The process of agrarian reform under the conditions of the People's Government cannot be achieved in anarchic form", Corvalán warned in an interview with the communist daily *El Siglo*. By acting this way the MIR was playing "reaction's game", giving the world "the impression that our agrarian policy is engulfed in chaos".[49] The MIR's reply was equally intransigent. The first congress of its peasant front, the MCR, held in Temuco at the beginning of March, condemned the law on agrarian reform as "a bourgeois law that does not contribute to the improvement of the standard of living of the peasantry" and called on agricultural labourers to overthrow the power of the agrarian oligarchy.[50] The MIR was unsatiated by the fact that in five months the government claimed to have expropriated 350 estates corresponding to 1,051,000 hectares. Chile was already importing basic foodstuffs to the value of $200 million per year. The situation now worsened. Those expecting to be expropriated were hardly likely to carry on investing in the land; and those now given land would need time and capital to develop it, if, that is, they expected to produce a surplus for the market beyond their own domestic needs. And that would require extensive assistance – both financial and technical. It was reasonable to ask how this would be paid for and where it would come from.

The government's failure to engage the PDC after Allende's attainment of office did not come without cost. The first omen appeared on 26 February when the government's newspaper, *La Nación*, exposed the existence of secret negotiations between the PDC and the PN about the backing of a joint candidate for a senate by-election in Valparaíso province due in July. The PDC was now in complete disarray, with one segment pushing in the direction of collaboration with the national party, the other in the direction of the government. As the UP programme rolled out across the country, the christian democrats soon began to splinter publicly: this began after the local elections on 4 April, where its vote dropped to 26 percent from 28 percent at the presidential ballot in September; whereas UP garnered a total of 49.73 percent socialists 22.38 percent, communists 16.97 percent, radicals 8.2 percent, social democrats 1.4 percent. UP's advance was partly a consequence of the extension of

---

[49] *El Siglo*, 14 February 1971; González and Talavera, *Los mil días*, pp. 66–7.
[50] *Punto Final*, 2 March 1971; ibid., p. 71.

the franchise not only to the illiterate, formerly denied the vote, but also to the 18–21 age group, more than 70 percent of whom voted for government parties. Most striking was the fact that the PS had doubled its vote; yet the communists had scarcely moved. The reaction of the christian democrat youth wing on 19 April was to declare itself in favour of socialism and co-operation with UP. This declaration was immediately welcomed by Millas on behalf of the communist party. Yet the boost to the confidence of the socialists made any substantive co-operation except on the basis of unilateral PDC concessions unthinkable. Instead, the wind fully in his sails, Allende told a press conference on 5 May that if the congressional majority spurned UP's key legislative proposals, he would go to the country with a plebiscite.[51]

The *consejo nacional* of the PDC met from 7 to 9 May in Cartagena. Leading from the left, Leighton declared the party's readiness to co-operate with the government at points where their programmes intersected. This was a position supported strongly by the party president, Irrureta; moreover, Tomic weighed in with the argument that the PDC had to lead the process of change, towards communitarian socialism as against the state socialism of UP. But the plenum rejected proposals for collaboration. The left's drive to dominance had stalled. The momentum now shifted to the right. Preliminary talks began between the PDC and UP as the process of copper nationalisation came before congress. But Frei, in Europe since 12 April, spoke out against negotiations with the government, threatening to resign from the party. Altamirano's declaration, in an interview with the Cuban journal *Bohemia* on 4 June, to the effect that congress should be dissolved and a new one-chamber assembly set up after a plebiscite, inevitably played into Frei's hands, setting a pattern for the next two and a half years. Meanwhile the PN issued a declaration calling for a broad front "against the establishment of a Marxist dictatorship in Chile".[52] The scene was thus set for some random incident to fix the pattern of opposition politics firmly in a new mould.

Among those on the far left to whom Allende gave amnesty were activists in the Vanguardia Organizada del Pueblo (VOP), a group that had broken with Miguel Enríquez in favour of terrorism. The amnesty

---

[51] Zorina et al., *Uroki Chili*, p. 287.
[52] Ibid., p. 292.

was in exchange for an agreement not to continue unlawful violence. But the VOP refused to conform. On 8 June a VOP cell, including the brothers Ronaldo and Arturo Rivera Calderón, assassinated former vice-president and former interior minister Edmundo Pérez Zujovic, a known hardliner in the PDC. The assassination sent shudders through christian democracy and appalled Allende, not least because these assassins were men who would not have been at liberty but for Allende's generous amnesty. There were rumours of fleeing Panamanians working for the CIA, but the unfortunate fact was that the agency did not have to do so much to stir up the atmosphere in Chile. Others were ready and willing to act entirely on their own account. The assassination should also have had a sobering effect on the PS. Allende certainly reacted with despatch. But, as ambassador Korry told a hearing in Washington: "an important segment of the Socialist Party regards this episode as ill-advised but heroic".[53]

Just a week later the consequences began to become evident. A majority in the chamber of deputies (78 to 44) voted out the chairman, who was from UP, and voted in a christian democrat. On 18 June the president of the PDC, Irrureta, who had formerly been in favour of collaboration with UP, condemned Allende for the amnesty granted to sections of the extreme left. And once the nationalisation of copper assets passed through congress on 11 July, all co-operation effectively came to an end. The success of the joint PDC–PN candidate at the Valparaíso election on 18 July then set an important precedent. At an extraordinary meeting of the christian democratic *consejo nacional* on 23–24 July a resolution against co-operation with the PN was decisively rejected. Frei's policy of opposing UP sectarianism and opening up relations with the national party won through, with the result that certain members, including the head of the youth wing, split away on 26 October 1971 to form a separate party – the Izquierda Cristiana (IC) – taking with them some 10,000 members of the PDC and joining UP. The radical party then split (18 July–1 August) when the leadership of Miranda installed an overtly Marxist platform. The party had long been unhappy that in the distribution of posts in government by Allende, the PR had lost out. Baltra and others then formed the left radical party (PIR) on 30 October but were prevailed upon to stay in the ruling coalition. MAPU also split, prompting Chonchol to move over to the IC.

---

[53] Testimony the following month, 1 July 1971 – *United States and Chile*, p. 12.

The underlying significance of these changes was by no means easily evaluated, as Allende himself admitted on 5 August; the only certainty was that they would further complicate the allocation of ministries which was done between parties rather than personalities. The Brazilian ambassador reported that both the PS and the PCCh, who held the real power within the governing coalition, "are beginning to tire of these schisms, which offer little of substance to the acceleration of the revolutionary process".[54] Only Altamirano, at the PS plenum on 15 August, appeared certain that the net result would strengthen the socialist party. The plenum reasserted the right to introduce a one-chamber assembly, expropriate monopolies, complete the agrarian reform and deny compensation to US companies for copper nationalisation.[55] The destruction of capitalism in Chile was thus well under way. The political consequences were, however, less obvious – except to the fundamentalists who now believed they had behind them a strong tail wind of indefinite duration. As to the economic consequences, they had barely been considered.

---

[54] Câmara Canto (Santiago) to Secretary of State (Brasilia), 28 September 1971: *MRE. Ofícios Recibidos*. Chile, 1971, vol. 6.
[55] Zorina et al., *Uroki Chili*, pp. 296–7.

5

THE ECONOMIC CONSEQUENCES OF PROFESSOR VUSKOVIC

Make the economy scream.

President Nixon, 15 September 1970[1]

Since the success or failure of UP rested upon improving the standard of living of the population of Chile, and since the most discreet and effective tools at the disposal of the United States with which to wreck the socialist experiment were financial, it might have been expected that the greatest care would be taken by UP to ensure the most prudent conduct of the economy within the framework of reform. "If we fail in the economic field," Allende recognised, "we will fail in the political field."[2] The government faced all the more difficulty because the economic situation it inherited was poor. Early in 1970 Tomic had visited Neruda in Isla Negra. There he outlined what the minister of finance, christian democrat Andrés Zaldívar, had told him: an economic storm was impending.[3] Inflation stood at 35 percent. Although net foreign exchange reserves were at an all-time high – $409 million – public external debt exceeded $2 billion.[4] Little did they know what lay ahead.

There was every reason for caution, particularly with regard to the earning of foreign exchange, which was Chile's achilles' heel. As to a

---

[1] Quoted in *Covert Action*, p. 14 and exhibit 2. Contrast this, and the events described in chapter 6, with the assertion "We did nothing to the economy", from deputy chief of the mission at the US embassy, Harry Shlaudeman: *El País*, 13 September 2003.

[2] "El futuro de la revolución Chilena está en manos de los trabajadores", 1 May 1971: Allende, *Obras*, p. 75.

[3] Neruda, *Confieso*, p. 465. A typographical error gives the year 1971 instead of 1970.

[4] Levy et al., *Chile: An Economy*, p. 63.

crucial potential source, US investment, however, Allende showed every sign of wishing to see it disappear. So much so that by the autumn of 1971 UP policy had created uproar in US business circles. The chairman of the US house committee on inter-American affairs, Dante Fascell, told US assistant secretary of state Meyer:

> I know what fantastic pressures you must be under because I have talked to an individual myself who is just absolutely frothing at the mouth – and I can't say that I blame him, don't misunderstand me. He is representing a company which, I know, has been to the White House beating on the walls. They want to send in the Marines … Any place they have the money they want to cut them [Chile] off.[5]

Taking over two US affiliates, Alimentos Purina and NIBSA, at the start of the presidency, Allende declared: "We don't want some Americans to stay too long in Chile."[6] The impression given was that he did not want any US businesses to remain in Chile.[7] He was well aware that if copper nationalisation were handled undiplomatically, a high price would be paid elsewhere, yet here – as with respect to all fundamentals – his heart ruled his head.

> We wish to avoid repression against Chile; we wish to avoid the closing of sources of credit; we wish to avoid reprisal measures; we wish to avoid the placing of obstacles on the technological development of our armed forces; we wish to avoid being denied technological collaboration and scientific progress; we wish to avoid these things, but not at the price of indignity.[8]

This meant alternative sources of capital would be required to sustain and raise investment in mining, manufacturing and services. But no thought had been given as to where these would readily be found. Indeed in 1970–71 capital expenditures in the public sector fell as an element of the

---

[5] 15 October 1971: *United States and Chile*, p. 60.

[6] *New York Times*, 7 January 1971.

[7] Chile expropriated the following US companies after nationalising copper in July: Allied Artists, Dow, Ford, General Cable, General Electric, International Basic Economy Corporation, International Chemical Filters, ITT, IRECO Chemical, MGM, Textron, 20th Century Fox, United Artists, Universal International Films, Warner Brothers.

[8] "Diálogo con los obreros del cobre", 7 February 1970: Allende, *Obras*, p. 237.

overall budget.[9] Moreover, the Basic Programme gave no clue about how to achieve what amounted to a political, economic and social revolution.[10]

Indeed, it was said that Allende characteristically was the only candidate at the elections who had no detailed platform. What the platform did support were key objectives familiar to students of the Bolshevik revolution, for although in many respects the more militant socialists looked not unlike the keep left group of the British labour party in the late 1940s, in other respects they more closely resembled the communist parties of Europe. Jorge Arrate MacNiven, once minister for mines, later commented that the great mistake of those years was not that Allende was no Leninist, but that he had "a party full of a tendency that wished to be Leninist".[11] Apart from the desirability of their objective, the core difficulty with the implementation of the UP programme was that, to succeed, it would require financial sacrifices from the very people who voted the government into power. Yet, wholly unlike the Attlee government of 1945 in Britain, which tumbled in on an unexpected landslide, in Chile the governing coalition squeezed in on a minority vote. It was therefore not only instinctively averse to calling for sacrifice, but was also under pressure to buy off the electorate in order to win a crucial second term. The socialist party was also concerned to gain votes at the expense of the communist party, which was particularly strong in the trades unions. It was thus all too tempting for the PS to support rather than discourage demands for higher wages, particularly once inflation accelerated. This created for UP a fatal dilemma which it failed to face up to and resolve.

Leading this coalition, Allende had no idea of economics and was content to leave such matters to others. Prior to winning the election he had barely spoken on such matters, and in his victory speech on 4 September 1970 he spoke emotionally of "overthrowing the arrogance of money".[12] US ambassador Korry, who was certainly well informed, told Washington that "Allende is a brilliant politician who understands Chile and Chileans but he has only a half-grasp of his true economic

---

[9] Levy et al., *Chile: An Economy*, p. 63.

[10] This much is acknowledged by a leading participant and defender of the original programme. Carlos Altamirano, *Dialéctica de una derrota* (Mexico 1979), p. 44.

[11] Jorge Arrate, "Ideólogo de la renovación socialista", *Época* (Buenos Aires), 4 October 1987.

[12] "Discurso de la Victoria", 4 September 1970: Allende, *Obras*, p. 57.

problems."[13] "He took no interest, certainly, in 'ways and means' of running the economy; nor did he make the effort to understand it", is the devastating lament of his chief economics minister.[14] Indeed, former foreign minister Valdés – sufficiently sympathetic initially to be rumoured likely to be a minister within the new government – recalled that "Allende had not expected to win the elections in 1970 and so, in keeping with his rather superficial approach to political and economic matters, had drawn up no clear plans for what he would do if he were elected."[15] This is consistent with what else we know of the president. Allende had always been regarded as "an extremely able politician but not a statesman of vision".[16] He was above all an accomplished parliamentary tactician rather than an adept administrator. As a result he delegated economic policy entirely to his ministers. Worse than that: "An increasing number of people believe … that he does not control or fully comprehend the chain reactions which have been set off by some of the Government's economic measures, or the forces which are at work in the country below the surface."[17] Moreover, having devolved responsibility, Allende was loath to wrench it back. As one former minister acknowledges, loyalty to his collaborators was "extreme". "At times it reached limits that were damaging to him, in the political sense."[18]

Certainly Allende made little preparation. The Marxist economist Professor Pedro Vuskovic Bravo,[19] born in Antofagasta on 25 November 1924 and recruited by Allende from CEPAL and the school of economics at the Universidad de Chile, was called in at late notice to create economic proposals on the lines of the Basic Programme within the space of a couple of months. He was not entirely new to these circles, having belonged to the team of specialist advisers working for Allende as far back as 1958 and

[13] *NARA*: Department of state. Amembassy (Santiago) to Secretary of State (Washington), 28 April 1971.

[14] "Recordando el Gobierno de Allende. 1986": Pedro Vuskovic, *Obras escogidas sobre Chile (1964–1992)* (Santiago 1993), p. 284.

[15] Told to Hankey at lunch, 6 April 1972, enclosed in Hankey to Sir Leslie Monson, 12 April 1972: *FCO 7/2212*.

[16] Hildyard, "Impressions of Chile under a Government of Popular Unity", 17 March 1972: *FCO 7/2212*.

[17] Ibid.

[18] *Don Américo*, p. 49. Américo Zorrilla was minister of finance, much against his own wishes.

[19] Christian democrat senator Renán Fuentealba described him as "the most Marxist of all the ministers" (March 1972): Yofre, *Misión Argentina*, p. 234.

worked closely with the communist party from that time on. Discussions opened at El Quisco on 4 September 1970. Veterans such as Almeyda, born in Santiago in 1923, a socialist member of the chamber of deputies for Valparaíso as early as 1937 and now something of a Maoist, were appalled that the specialists – social scientists from the universities – came up with little but generalisations divorced from economic and political realities.[20] He told the US ambassador, by way of explanation: "I am a Maoist, but you have to understand that Mao [*sic*] is a strategy and tactics is quite another thing."[21] Almeyda recalls:

> As was predictable in this atmosphere at the meeting in *El Quisco*, overwhelmingly favourable to structuralist schemes, my opinions were not only in the minority, but I was the only one to dissent completely from what was said … More than one said to me in private that I was the prisoner of conventional economic concepts – monetarist – and that now it was necessary to see things in another way, completely differently.[22]

In November the cabinet thus approved a "Basic Orientation of the Economic Programme for the Short-term" that had been improvised without probing analysis.

The head of planning, another "independent", who decades later was very critical of Vuskovic, does not appear to have been much different in outlook. At a revealing debate in the spring of 1971, Gonzalo Martner García was still more enthralled to the voluntaristic spirit with which power was taken than to the discipline in which he had been trained, underlining that "what interests us is to transform society and the economy and we are prepared to face the risks entailed in taking this road".[23] He insisted: "We do not think as a function of this traditional rationality. On the contrary, we know that certain incompatibilities are going to be produced, and we are ready to face them. Because our interest, I repeat, is in constructing a new economy. And we cannot attain one without producing certain imbalances."[24] Even the unrepentant

[20] Clodomiro Almeyda Medina, *Reencuentro con mi vida* (Santiago 1987/88), p. 174.

[21] *United States and Chile*, p. 30.

[22] Ibid., p. 176.

[23] *Panorama Económico*, April–May 1971, no. 261: Farias, *La izquierda chilena*, vol. 1, p. 757.

[24] Ibid., p. 761.

leader of the left within the socialist party, Altamirano, while sustaining the objectives,[25] freely acknowledged a fundamental error of omission of the Basic Programme.[26] But Altamirano was not complaining about inadequate attention to the contradictions inherent in socio-economic objectives. Instead his complaint was that: "The conquest of power thus stemmed not from the growth of popular power rising 'from the base' to displace the bourgeois State, as the program indicated, but from the progressive adapatation of the legal–institutional order to new realities introduced by socio-economic transformation."[27] In other words, Altamirano favoured more radical action to transform the political system from below, yet with no solution to the economic crisis that arose thereby.

One of the basic and flawed assumptions in Vuskovic's plan was that it constituted "a political compromise with economic need". It would more accurately be termed "economic need compromised to political purpose" in that there was no equality in the compromise between economics and politics. This had crucial implications. It meant that, where necessary, economic need would give way to political need: a triumph for voluntarism over an understanding of the market.

> A traditional scheme for running the economy, even under the pretext of overcoming immediate problems, would jeopardise this compromise and would not offer effective solutions to these problems. To put it bluntly, we cannot think at the first stage of purely conventional means, as a preliminary to economic 'revival' and a second stage in which we turn back to implementation of the Basic Programme; on the contrary, from the beginning we have to broach both simultaneously as both a political and economic requirement.[28]

The plan cited four major objectives: increasing growth, absorbing unemployment, changing the distribution of profit, and containing inflation. No thought was given to the likelihood that land reform would disrupt production, thereby also raising inflation; that nationalised

[25] Altamirano, *Dialéctica*, p. 39.

[26] Ibid., p. 44.

[27] Ibid., p. 63.

[28] The original economic programme, reprinted in Vuskovic, *Obras escogidas*, p. 198.

industries were bound to press for subsidies from government to keep them afloat; that increased demand was unlikely to increase investment in the private sector, which was more likely to expedite profits abroad for safety; and that price controls would distort the allocation of resources. The catastrophic fate of this policy is borne out in the complete absence of any further such documents in Vuskovic's selected works for the entire period of deterioration from August 1971 through to June 1972 when, with the country in economic crisis, he was eventually removed from office.

In effect Vuskovic cast aside his training in economics. He was not alone in this, but his role was crucial. Having claimed the policy he pursued was a great success, Vuskovic, in retrospect, went on to parcel out the blame to others above him for lack of co-ordination – "there was no unitary economic leadership", he claims[29] – and for continued political interference. Yet he had political ambitions of his own: a very good reason to place populist politics above the rigours of economics. He argued that the development of new forces of people's power would have aided the economy. It is hard to see how, though, for that would have required UP to demand economic sacrifices from its primary constituencies; and that it consistently failed to do. Instead rampant consumerism led inevitably to devaluation and a severe balance of payments crisis not unfamiliar to labour governments in Western Europe. The contradiction was funda- mental. Almeyda later pointed to "a notable inconsistency between short-term economic policy, which the Government promoted from the beginning with the aim of obtaining political support from the electorate, and the long-term objectives of socialist transformation of Chilean economy and society".[30]

An economic crisis was predicted. At the debate in April 1971 held by the journal *Panorama Económico*, christian democratic businessman and former vice-president of the central bank Jorge Cauas Lama warned that the programme adopted contained incompatible aims: low inflation, a rapid redistribution of incomes and significant increases in output and employment. "The traditional means of escape for situations of this kind", he advised, "has been increases in prices. If this mechanism is undesirable

[29] Ibid., p. 272.
[30] C. Almeyda, "The Reasons for Self-Criticism of the Unidad Popular Government", in S. Sideri ed., *Chile 1970–1973: Economic Development and its International Setting* (The Hague 1979), p. 8.

the road is open to a drastic augmentation of what is available through massive imports. The problems that this alternative brings in its wake are not insignificant: loss of reserves and competition for national enterprises at a time when they could do without it."[31] When faced with Martner's bland response that imbalances were merely to be expected, Cauas retorted:

> Well now, these imbalances must necessarily translate into inflation, loss of international reserves and/or shortage of certain goods. Which of these three means of escape does the government aim to adopt as a priority? To lay these things out and discuss them does not reflect "a difference of mentality"; it is simply to ask that will happen in the scheme designed by the government when serious imbalances arise between the separate goals laid out. And this has not been done thus far.
>
> The government's experts could, for instance, suggest that ultimately the goal most easily sacrificed would be price stability; but in that case it makes little sense to insist that inflation has been stemmed. If one chooses to go for imports, fine; other problems emerge that cannot be ignored. Or if one prefers rationing, the implications could also be serious.[32]

Others pointed out that, in the redistribution of income, some groups of workers had much greater leverage than others. A further complication subsequently outlined by Alberto Martínez, then director of the industry and trade department of the ministry of economics (DIRINCO), was that not only were there "vast differences in salary levels" but "there was a different wage system in each company, made worse by an extraordinary diversity in the companies' internal structures. Under these circumstances it was particularly difficult to establish any kind of link between increases in real wages and productivity."[33]

When Martner insisted that they could rely on the government's capacity to persuade and on the discipline of the workers, industrialist Sergio López tartly retorted: "Apparently the said capacity to persuade and for discipline is not so great, as President Allende himself in various public speeches has had to lay into exaggerated demands formulated by

---

[31] *Panorama Económico*, April–May 1971, no. 261: reprinted in Farias, *La izquierda chilena*, p. 759.

[32] Ibid., pp. 762–3.

[33] "The Industrial Sector", Sideri, *Chile 1970–73*, p. 250.

workers from various private enterprises."[34] In his defence Martner argued that the "system of imbalances is irrational in many aspects. But one has to take into account that government policy in this sphere is provisional, an emergency policy, that had to be put together shortly after assumption of power and at extremely short order."[35] When López commented on the "extraordinarily aggressive" behaviour of the workers in seeking wage rises, he met with a stout defence of their right to do so by Sergio Ramos Córdova (PCCh) who worked under Martner. Ramos in later years acknowledged the seriousness of the problem in a devastating analysis of UP economic policy.[36]

Others pointed out that resistance to excess wage demands led to "mediation" by the government which could lead to expropriation, and that therefore the impression was given that these demands were a part of government policy. Domingo Arteaga, another industrialist, agreed that some workers were, indeed, disciplined but that "other groups of workers, much more extensive, lack this conscience and, because Unidad Popular is in power, suppose that they have been freed from the internal discipline within the firm". Government confidence in the ability of the CUT to assure such discipline was, he claimed, "considerably less effective than it had been before, when it was dedicated to a struggle for the defence or conquest of wage demands". After all, if Allende himself was attacking absenteeism in companies under UP control, then discipline was not functioning well; that meant creating a new conscience, and enforcement "would be difficult".[37] On the human scale, we have the recollections of a PCCh trades union activist from the rank and file at SUMAR, a textile firm of some size, who rose to the very top. Juan Alarcón reminds us that "the workers had a poor understanding of the [revolutionary] process, in any meaning of the term". With much of the country in trouble, "people in effect wanted to ring-fence [*ponerle ruedas*] the company or divide it up among themselves, because people thought that the entire output was to be shared out among one another". The problem was that "some people were very self-centred. This is not a conservative country but the

[34] Farias, *La izquierda chilena*, p. 765.

[35] Ibid., p. 765.

[36] Ramos, "Inflation in Chile and the political economy of the Unidad Popular Government", in Sideri ed., *Chile 1970–73*, notably pp. 342–3.

[37] Farias, *La izquierda chilena*, p. 768.

phenomenon emerged of holding onto one's job, one's security, one's own well-being and not looking much beyond …"[38]

The régime's first six months in power were relatively trouble-free. Indeed, it achieved a great drop in inflation and an economic boom, because the immediate impact of policy was to reduce unemployment and raise consumer demand; growth therefore hid the underlying contradictions. But this was a false dawn and unfortunately encouraged the kind of practices that were soon to undermine UP economic policy entirely. Even at this stage some elements in the communist party leadership became concerned at the direction the economy was taking, and alarm was expressed at policy inspired by "methods of economic leadership copied from the practice prevailing in the Soviet Union, Cuba and, in general, the socialist countries".[39] Before long, consumer demand far outpaced supply – not least because of the dramatic cut in rates of interest. Moreover, government expenditure shot through the roof, the central bank printed money in profligate fashion, and very soon severe inflation began to take hold, hitting the working class and peasantry the hardest. The municipal elections on 4 April 1971 came too early to be affected, however; and it tended to encourage the régime in the rectitude of its programme. Moreover, the communist party, which was more cautious in economic matters, increased its vote only marginally from 15.9 percent to 16.9 percent, which did not enhance its steadying influence.

One of the reasons for spiralling inflation was excessive government expenditure. Revenues rose only 24 percent in 1971 but expenditures rose from 21 to 27 percent of GDP. The deficit thus stood at 8 percent of GDP as against 1 percent in 1970.[40] The gap between revenue and expenditure was made up in credit. To meet that need for credit, the money supply more than doubled in 1971.[41] Nominal interest rates dropped only from 24 percent to 18 percent, but that was not a true indicator of the availability of money because the régime operated

---

[38] F. Gaudichaud, ed., *Poder popular y cordones industriales: testimonios sobre el movimiento popular urbano 1970–1973* (Santiago 2004), p. 93.

[39] Orlando Millas Correa, *Memorias* (Santiago 1993), p. 69.

[40] Levy et al., *Chile: An Economy*, pp. 63–4.

[41] Ibid., p. 64. The World Bank calculations of Chilean inflation during this period were based on the growth of the money supply because the consumer price index was widely viewed as an inadequate true measure of the growth in prices. For a discussion of this issue, see the Appendix. I view the World Bank calculations as the better indicator.

selective credits – handing effectively negative rates of interest to the public sector, lower income groups, and expropriated estates etcetera.[42] Furthermore denial of credit is said to have been used to push private sector enterprises into bankruptcy in order to force through state expropriation of assets. Expenditure also rose because instead of consulting the chamber of deputies in nationalising various enterprises, such as the banks in March 1971, shares were bought using bills issued by the central bank. Yet even as inflation was rising that autumn as a direct result of government policy, Allende called on workers not to ask for privileges unavailable to other workers in the form of higher wages and to cease growing absenteeism. This was the subject of a lengthy speech he delivered at a poorly attended gathering in the Plaza de la Constitución on 30 March in anticipation of the local elections due on 3 April. In one instance employees were demanding wage rises of 190 percent; yet on one day alone as many as half of all employees were absent from work.[43] Even the nationalisation of the mines made no difference to workers' demands. At the El Salvador mine, which produced some $250,000 a day in exports, a ten-day strike for a 39 percent pay increase, augured ill for the future. At Chuquicamata, which was the most productive mine, where strikes were to erupt in the New Year, the opposition PDC and Ampuero's breakaway socialist party held the majority within the trades unions. The government had cause for anxiety. And just as public sector expenditure grew, so private sector expenditure declined. The private sector use of bank credit dropped from 77 percent of the total (1970) to a mere 40 percent (by December 1971).[44]

The entire picture was made damagingly blurred by two further non-economic factors at work: first, the rapid growth of new state agencies and enterprises incorporated into the public sector; and, second, "the breakdown of normal budgetary and accounting procedures".[45] The latter was just a part, but a crucial part, of the administrative chaos that engulfed Chile under Allende. At enterprises taken over, managers were not infrequently imposed who had no training to the task – engineers with degrees and little else. One militant recalls: "people were sent to take up

[42] Ibid., p. 65.
[43] *Puro Chile*, 31 March 1971: also González and Talavera, *Los mil días*, p. 79.
[44] Levy ed., *Chile: An Economy*, p. 65.
[45] Ibid., p. 64.

a position and it turned out that they were incapable". This was difficult to conceal over time and activists had to shoulder the burden in the short term until suitably qualified managers – from the right – could be found to substitute. "The fact is that no one was prepared for the revolution…"[46]

A worrying sign for those concerned at the danger of state control extending throughout the country – and this crucially affected the balance of power between left and right within the PDC – was the national assembly of journalists of the left which met on 11 April and called for the socialisation of the media, a proposal explicitly designed to reinforce support for UP in blatant contravention of the guarantees given to congress to secure Allende's accession to office. Contrary to the implausible claims of the CIA to the Church committee, attempting to explain away the vast sums it had expended in Chile, the media were not entirely in the hands of the left. Indeed, US ambassador Korry pointed out in July 1971: "You have a majority of the newspapers still in nonconformist hands."[47] Later, in January 1972, when visiting Santiago, the veteran Italian communist Pietro Secchia noted: "Another danger is presented by the great freedom of the press and especially of radio and television … In practice radio and television are largely channels in the hands of the enemy."[48] The assembly of journalists of the left did not succeed in their ambitious plans.

The political atmosphere steadily deteriorated as the régime increasingly ran into stronger opposition to its programme. Matters did not truly come to a head until July 1971, when a meeting was held at the presidential palace, Cerro Castillo, in the coastal resort of Viña del Mar, neighbouring Valparaíso, headquarters of the fleet. Here the differences that had been growing between the socialists and the communists came to a head. Américo Zorrilla, the communist minister of public finance (*Hacienda*), came to blows with Vuskovic. The latter seemed completely unable to see anything but the positive.[49] Altamirano backed Vuskovic; Orlando Millas, deputising for Corvalán (who was out of the country), stood behind Zorrilla, as did the head of the central bank, Inostroza, who bombarded the socialists with statistics to back the case for resisting

---

[46] Juan Alarcón, in Gaudichaud, *Poder popular*, p. 102.
[47] *United States and Chile*, p. 25.
[48] *Archivio PCI*. Esteri. Cile. 053. 1972. vol. IV. 1288.
[49] *Don Américo*, p. 63.

inflation, and Almeyda, the socialist foreign minister. Entirely in character, Allende told Millas he was right, but then did nothing to adjust policy to redress the problem.[50]

Corvalán himself was confident where the causes lay:

Anyone who knows something of Marxism knows that the laws of the economy are objective and that these laws cannot be dispensed with. More than that, there are economic laws that reign as much under capitalism as under socialism. One cannot, for example, ignore the fact that an increase in the income of the workers, in order that they be secure, must correspond to an increase in the goods available in the market or to the possibility of loading this change in income onto the profits of the firm. Similarly, if a particular factory increases wages without bothering too much [al lote] about the number of workers, without putting into production new machinery or machinery lying idle, the only thing that happens is a drop in productivity.

On his view this is what was happening under UP "in various companies that were nationalised or where the state moved in".

We communists are absolutely against these mistaken actions, as also against those who have underestimated completely the importance of raising production and productivity and have believed that what is important is to take and take industries, regardless of their size and profitability. In this sense the ultra-left have caused very great damage and have instilled fear into the small and medium-sized manufacturer, a fear that is one of the causes of the drop in investment in this sector.[51]

Nothing was resolved, however, after Cerro Castillo, and matters continued as before. Initially Vuskovic was protected by the apparent success of the policy overall. By the end of 1971, GNP was up an astonishing 8 percent; industrial output had risen by 12 percent. In addition to inflation, however, a worrying sign was that the share of income taken (as against profit) had also risen: from 51 to 59 percent, which promised ill for the balance between investment and consumer expenditure and the

---

[50] Ibid.
[51] Interview by Eduardo Labarca, December 1972: González and Talavera, Los mil días, vol. 2, p. 1164.

rising bill in imports of consumer goods. And for a régime aiming at liberating itself from imperialism, nothing could have been more damaging. When Secchia arrived for the PCCh anniversary celebrations in January 1972 he was briefed by Corvalán and Teitelboim on the situation. He reported serious difficulties, notwithstanding the high rate of economic growth and the fact that 60 percent of production now lay in the hands of the state. The working class did not realise that wages would have to drop because enterprises were in a perilous state of finance.[52] Levels of inefficiency in the bureaucracy were equally alarming. Secchia cited the instance of some twenty-four units in the ministry of agriculture performing the same functions.

On 9 November 1971 Chile had had to suspend payments on its external debt. By far its largest creditor was the United States, to whom it owed a colossal total, for a country of 10 million people, of $1.4 billion.[53] Negotiations with creditors – the so-called Paris Club – opened formally on 17 February 1972, the first of four meetings that lasted into mid-April. After the United States, which was owed 58 percent of the debt, came Britain – 9.3 percent, West Germany – 6.7 percent, and France – 6.1 percent. Britain pressed Chile to sign a letter of intent to the International Monetary Fund (IMF), which would have effectively constricted Allende's implementation of the Basic Programme. UP refused and restated its refusal the following month on the grounds that "The programme of reforms and social developments which the Government has set itself is a historical inevitability."[54] "Little progress was made at the first two meetings partly because the Chilean case was not adequately documented", noted the Foreign Office, "but also because Chile would make no concessions about the terms on which she was willing to negotiate."[55] Throughout, the United States took a low profile in order not to inflame further relations with Chile until the issue of compensation for US copper companies was satisfactorily settled. The British backed down on the letter of intent, and at the 17–18 April meeting it was agreed

[52] Report dated 13 January 1972: *Archivio PCI*. Esteri. Cile. 053. 1972. vol. IV.
[53] "Considerations Affecting Next Steps Options for Chile": Under-Secretary of State John Irwin II to Henry Kissinger, 22 December 1971. For the due date: Warren-Guest to H. de C. Taylor, 24 April 1972: *FCO 7/2221*.
[54] Embachile statement received by the Foreign Office 20 March 1972: *FCO 7/2219*.
[55] Warren-Gash, Latin American Department, to H. de C. Taylor, West African Department (FCO), 24 April 1972: *FCO 7/2221*.

to reschedule repayment over eight years, with two years' grace. For the next year, however, inflation rose inexorably and the balance of payments worsened relentlessly.

By mid-September 1971 the overheated exchanges between government and opposition had reached unprecedented heights. *La Tercera de la Hora* journalist María Eugenia Oyarzún called on the government to cease accusing those who opposed it of sedition. "Never before", she wrote, "has the country lived in an atmosphere of greater political hatred than that we breathe now."[56] Much of this hatred was prompted by the national party's attempt to block Vuskovic from appropriating companies without direct permission from congress. These moves were then backed by the PDC in the wake of the Castro visit. By this time there was no question but that the damaging backwash of UP economic policy had begun to alienate public opinion.

Castro's arrival was immediately preceded on 4 November by Chile's incorporation into the so-called Non-Aligned Movement: a movement overwhelmingly of those Third World countries informally aligned to the Soviet bloc against the United States and in receipt of substantial Soviet aid. On 9 November Allende sent his proposals for a single-chamber parliament to congress. The government was once again on the offensive. Castro arrived on board an Aeroflot Ilyushin-62 at Pudahuel airport late afternoon on the following day. Once in Chile he exerted strong pressure on Allende to drive the economy in the same direction as the Soviet bloc.[57] Indeed, as anticipated, Castro's very presence proved controversial. It afforded a welcome opportunity for the opposition, in particular the right-wing fundamentalists of the national party and PyL, to mobilise existing fears of Chile's Cubanisation. The mobilisation culminated on the evening of 1 December, while Castro was hosting a reception at the Cuban embassy to mark his departure. Thousands of women appeared beating pots and pans in a cacophonous display of hostility to the government; they were echoed by sympathisers shouting from their windows overlooking the streets slogans such as "the left united keeps us hungry" (*la izquierda unida nos tiene sin comida*). These housewives were far from ordinary. They were mobilised by the right into the Frente de Dueñas de

---

[56] *La Tercera de la Hora*, 13 September 1971.
[57] Millas, *Memorias*, pp. 393–4.

Casa (FRENDO), the housewives' front. The extreme left then confronted the demonstrators, who were themselves accompanied by violent shock groups from the extreme right, in the Plaza Vicuña Mackenna, throwing large stones and prompting confrontations with the police who released tear gas to prevent this agitated mass from reaching La Moneda. The incidents stemmed as much from police inflexibility as from the determination of the shock brigades of the various parties to win the street. A day later Santiago was declared a zone in a state of emergency. For a time Allende had effectively been trapped at a reception in the foreign ministry to celebrate the anniversary of its foundation.

With the Chilean president preoccupied with keeping public order on the streets, Castro told a sympathetic but disappointingly small crowd in the national stadium: "We have visited Chile not as tourists. We have made a visit to Chile as revolutionaries, as friends." Friends, of course, expect to be able to offer advice, though Castro had agreed not to air differences with Allende in public. The president had said that the Cubans had come to Chile neither to learn nor to teach. But Castro could barely contain his contempt: "I do not know what kind of fear grips those … saying that there is nothing to teach them, which perhaps reflects a kind of complex, a subconscious fear."[58] It was, to say the least, a visit of dubious value to Allende. It further damaged his image abroad as well as with the centre at home. "To go to such lengths to strengthen his position within the UP while accepting with equanimity so high a price in boredom and antagonisation of the opposition and floating voters hardly suggests he is concerned with democratic means of retaining power", commented a British official somewhat sourly.[59]

It was not hard to understand what the upsurge in violence augured. Up to now, as foreign observers noted, "a great advantage that Mr Allende was able to count on in his first year in office was not having an opposition conscious of its own power". The PDC went along with much of what UP did on the grounds that this was the compromise entered into by the Tomic platform. The government was thus kept afloat on support gratuitously given by "the more powerful grouping".[60] Indeed, christian

---

[58] *Punto Final*, 7 December 1971.

[59] J. Hunter (London) to Hildyard (Santiago), 3 January 1972: *FCO 7/1991*.

[60] Joaquim de Almeida Serra (Santiago) to Secretary of State (Brasilia), 7 December 1971: *MRE. Oficios Recibidos*. Chile, 1971, vol. 8.

democratic attempts to reach out to the new government on a reciprocal basis were decisively rebuffed. Four such attempts were made between October 1970 and July 1971, as Tomic has testified. First, in October 1970 a proposal was made for assistance in securing for Allende's vacated seat in the senate a christian democratic candidate of the left: Bosco Parra or Gabriel Valdés, for instance. This was deemed "impossible". Second, in December the new PDC leadership chaired by senator Narciso Irrueta visited Allende authorised to offer assistance. No response was forthcoming. Third, in April 1971 the senator tried again with the specific suggestion that the two sides co-operate in the election of all the mayors of Chile. At the end of the week the minister of the interior, José Tohá González, told Irrueta that it had been decided that it would be better not to continue the conversation. And, fourth, in June 1971 UP rejected the proposal that it should co-operate in the election of Luis Badilla as deputy for Valparaíso to replace another christian democrat who had died. Instead UP undertook a fierce election campaign which it lost disastrously anyway.[61] Such high-handed rejection of offers from the PDC came as an unpleasant surprise to its left-wing, which was to become fatally weakened under the strain. But it came as a tremendously welcome windfall to the White House, which had long expected that the artful Allende would "keep his opponents within Chile fragmented so that he can neutralize them one by one as he is able".[62]

It also opened up a key opportunity for the minority national party. The PN, in search of intransigent opposition, had hitherto found it hard to form common ground with the christian democrats. But the defections from the PDC youth wing and the formation of the Izquierda Cristiana paved the way for closer co-operation on the right. A significant symptom of this was the appearance of PDC youth brigades in the fighting on the streets. There the rival groups from the right formed "a blood bond". "If the authorities do not act with greater tact," the Brazilian chargé d'affaires predicted, "a much closer fusion could occur."[63] And opposition prospects had suddenly otherwise brightened. In a by-election for the chamber of

[61] Tomic, "Respuesta a Julio Silva Solar: acotaciones sobre los origines y la actitud de la corriente democratica cristiana de izquierda", F. Gil et al., *Chile 1970–1973* (Madrid 1977), pp. 330–1.
[62] Memorandum for the President, 5 November 1970: *NARA. Chile Declassification Project. NSC.*
[63] Almeida Serra (Santiago) to Brasilia, 7 December 1971: *MRE. Oficios Recibidos.* Chile 1971, vol. 8.

deputies in Valparaíso held at the beginning of November Dr Oscar Marín won a victory for the opposition PDC against hardline socialist Hernán del Canto, secretary-general of the CUT and an ally of Altamirano.

The president did take note. On 3 December Allende questioned the commander-in-chief, general Prats, particularly closely about senior officer appointments for 1972, which lay entirely beyond the presidential prerogative. "The fact is", Prats noted, "that the President is anxious because his fine political nose indicates that the 'march of the pots and pans' was not a fleeting and spontaneous women's protest. His attention is drawn to other intentions of a more far-reaching extent in the sustained protest of the opposition."[64] It could not have escaped Allende's notice that the downfall of the Goulart régime in Brazil seven years before at the hands of the CIA and the local military was preceded by similarly well-organised demonstrations by ordinary housewives. He now had serious concerns about what might lie ahead. In Chile the commander-in-chief had sole rights to make appointments within the service. It was thus with some surprise that on 7 December an astonished Prats was summoned by the normally sympathetic minister of defence Alejandro Ríos Valdivia, who, affecting an air of indifference, read out a list of officers for key units in the Santiago garrison at the express wish of the president. Prats said he would look into the matter.[65] Later, in Allende's presence, he gently proffered his own list.[66]

Minister of the interior Tohá ("*el flaco*" – "skinny"), had been born in 1927 in Chillán; formerly a socialist journalist of some note – he was for a decade editor of *Las Noticias de Última Hora* – intelligent, cultivated, and a personal friend of Allende, Tohá had fought at his side for the presidency since 1952. He vigorously condemned the manner in which the pots and pans demonstration turned violent. This was only natural. But Tohá overreached himself in using the occasion to gag the media. Declaring that "some radio stations have given out false, alarmist and seditious accounts of these events", he went on to announce that "Because of this … the government has arranged their immediate closure."[67] The closed station was Radio Balmaceda, owned by the PDC. The final straw for

[64] Prats, *Memorias*, p. 229.
[65] Ibid., pp. 229–30.
[66] Ibid., p. 232.
[67] The statement was published in *Clarín*, 3 December 1971.

La Moneda was when PyL journalist and propagandist Manuel Fuentes Wendling broadcast details of PCCh infiltration of the army that had been given to him by the MI6 station in Santiago.[68]

The opinions Tohá expressed were scarcely exceptional. Corvalán announced that "The working class and the people are ready to prevent fascist bands returning out into the streets. We will not permit another mob such as that on Wednesday."[69] Not surprisingly this emboldened the opposition still further. On 24 December the christian democrats presented congress with proposals to censure Tohá on a number of counts: infringement of the constitution and compromising of the security of the nation, toleration of illegal possession of arms, arbitrary detention and infringement of the rights of the media.[70] The PDC simultaneously pressed on with legislation (the Hamilton–Fuentealba Bill) to define the limits of the private, mixed and state sectors of the economy. It also backed the moves made by the national party to censure Vuskovic. It was, indeed, at this point that "the government began to lose all possibility of conquering the social cushion constituted by the middle class".[71] On 6 January 1972 the chamber of deputies listened to Tohá's belligerent defence and promptly suspended him only to find that the same day Allende moved his friend to take charge of the ministry of defence. Yet this was a Pyhrric victory for the president. Prats correctly noted that "the opposition has obtained the great advantage of coming together politically, overcoming profound differences of the immediate past and has forged an iron parliamentary front that will be in a condition to block and reject every legal initiative emanating from the government".[72]

The growing consolidation of the right was also music to the ears of those standing to the left of the government. After Castro's departure, *Punto Final*, speaking for both the MIR and the left wing of the socialist party, which had been disgusted by the discretion with which the visit had been handled, called followers to arms: "We must pass to the offensive." Not only should both agriculture and industry be transformed. But, it demanded, "Liberate the means of communication (press,

---

[68] Fuentes, *Memorias*, pp. 109–10. Several months later *El Mercurio* published the related documents obtained from Patricio Cueto Román, a militant from communist youth.

[69] *El Siglo*, 5 December 1971.

[70] *El Mercurio*, 22 December 1971.

[71] "Chile: El juego de la pera madura", *Panorama* (Buenos Aires), 30 August 1973.

[72] Prats, *Memorias*, p. 245.

radio, cinema, television etc.) from the domination of the bourgeoisie and imperialism."[73] By March, military intelligence (SIM) had uncovered the existence of a clandestine paramilitary organisation of the MIR in Antofagasta, Santiago, Concepción and Temuco.[74] And on a visit to Havana in January 1972 leading figures from both communist and socialist parties – Jorge Montes, Samuel Riquelme, Arnoldo Camú and Ariel Ulloa – stated in an interview: "In Chile for the short or medium term the issue is between fascism or socialism. Now there is no room for any other type of compromise political solutions. And we are convinced that this is a struggle we are going to win."[75] Yet instead of reaching out to the middle class, which the communist party proposed, albeit to a limited degree, and which even hostile embassies expected them to do, the socialists instead increasingly argued that they should move ahead to revolution at a more rapid pace. If they had thought about it historically and internationally, they would have understood that they were in a position not unlike that of Germany at the end of 1932 or Spain in the first half of 1936. Unfortunately Chilean exceptionalism militated against such comparisons. "Both extremes want quick solutions," noted the British embassy, "not excluding the use of force if necessary, and both moderate groups have to make periodic tactical concessions in order to avoid their rank and file being attracted away by extremists."[76] In parenthesis, however, it is worth noting that the communist leadership were never entirely of one mind in these matters. Corvalán held the line between the more appeasement-minded wing led by Millas, while the more traditional harder line found its voice in Teitelboim who, in the New Year, declared that the *via Chilena* did not necessarily exclude the use of force. "It remains to be seen", the Brazilian ambassador noted, "whether the appeal to violence contributes to speeding up change or brings the armed forces, who have up to now held themselves apart, directly into the game."[77]

---

[73] Leader entitled "Socialismo para aplastar al fascismo", *Punto Final*, 21 December 1971.

[74] Prats, *Memorias*, p. 256.

[75] Interviewed by the Cuban periodical *Bohemia*: Chile. *Archivio Ministerio de Asuntos Exteriores (MAE). Memorias de Embajada. 1972. Cuba. Embachile. Ofic. Ord. R.* Juan Enrique Vega (Havana) to Ministry (Santiago), 18 January 1972.

[76] "Chile: Annual Review for 1971", 12 January 1972 – *FCO 7/2210*.

[77] Câmara Canto (Santiago) to Secretary of State (Brasilia), 10 January 1972: *MRE. Ofícios Recibidos. Chile. 1972.* vol. 1.

At El Arrayán near Santiago the leaders of UP held a series of three meetings from late January through the first week of February 1972. *El Siglo* had greeted the New Year celebrating nationalisation of the mines, the expropriation of more estates in one year than ever before, the 12 percent growth in industrial production, the reduction in unemployment, the daily milk allowance to children (actually begun under Frei), the increase in school rolls, the payment of social security to the elderly and the sick. But it also issued some words of caution that the communist party had long been pressing on Allende in private. Here all the emphasis was upon not "widening" but "deepening" change and upon much greater consolidation before further advances – corruption, bureaucracy and low productivity of labour were key concerns.[78] Communist anxieties were evidently more than justified by the shock of two by-elections. On 16 January the christian democrat Rafael Moreno defeated socialist deputy Héctor Olivares, winning a seat in the senate previously held by the PS – that of O'Higgins and Colchagua; and the candidate for the PN, Sergio Diez, defeated UP candidate María Elena Mery, taking a seat in the chamber of deputies for rural Linares, with backing from the christian democrats. *El Mercurio* put the successes partly down to the women's vote. Both reversed losses of 1971 at the expense of UP.[79] Similarly in local elections the peasantry turned out in number for both the PDC and PN. And what was so disturbing was that these UP losses occurred largely in areas that had undergone agrarian reform. It was also the case that Mery's manifesto called for expropriation of land without compensation and without allowing the owners to hold on to their other property to which they were normally entitled. These positions had been heavily attacked by the PCCh, the *API* and the dissenting radicals under Bossay.[80] Corvalán explained:

> These peasants were discontented because, having received land, they had insufficient help from the *Instituto de Desarrollo Agropecuario* or from the state bank; attempts were made to impose upon them rigid schemes of organisation of property and production; the question of property title was

[78] "Profundizar en 1972 los avances de 1971", *El Siglo*, 2 January 1972.

[79] "Repudio campesino a la UP", *El Mercurio*, 17 January 1972.

[80] Joaquim de Almeida Serra (Santiago) to Secretary of State (Brasilia), 28 December 1971: *MRE. Oficios Recibidos*. Chile. 1971. vol. 8.

not resolved; and they did not agree with the indiscriminate seizure of estates that some groups of the extreme left were putting into effect. They felt insecure as to whether the lands that had been assigned to them were definitely their own.[81]

The UP's El Arrayán meetings thus opened in unpropitious circumstances on 31 January. A further sign of trouble appeared on 2 February. Mauricio Junk of the radical party, now minister of mines, spoke out on the importance of embedding the advances made within a legal framework. Socialist deputy Mario Palestro attacked him for making the statement, using the specious grounds that the minister was not a politician but a specialist. On Palestro's view the government should "take off the white gloves of democracy and put on boxing gloves".[82] At the closed meeting many issues arose. The first to be disputed was agrarian policy: socialists wanted expropriation of all properties above 40 hectares and to "accelerate and radicalise" the revolution in the countryside. This was successfully blocked for the time being. Second, battle was joined over the formulation of a single line to win over the middle classes. The third dispute was over the MIR: the communists failed to obtain outright condemnation, though the MIR's positions were criticised implicitly. Moreover it was agreed that negotiations should be opened with them in the course of February with a view to ascertaining terms for joint action and acceptance by the MIR of UP tactics. For the MIR to be included in UP, all partners would have to agree. On the fourth issue, of christian democracy, the parties split predictably. On one side were the communists, the PIR and the *API* (social democrats), on the other the PS and the christian left (IC). The former argued that on selective issues the UP programme and the programme on which Tomic stood for election coincided; UP should strive for agreement on these matters, "win over certain strata and isolate the main opponents of the anti-imperialist democratic change". Because the PS and IC objected, the proposal was shelved *sine die*. Fifth, it was argued that the PIR, MAPU and the PSD (social democrats) were trying to roll back the UP's programme, and that the radicals were playing the role of the protector of middle-class interests. The last topic of debate was parliamentary reform: on 3 June 1971 at the

[81] Corvalán, *De lo vivido*, pp. 136–7.
[82] *La Tercera de la Hora*, 3 February 1972.

third plenum of MAPU, general secretary Rodrigo Ambrosio had declared that "The next battle must be the elimination of the two-chamber Parliament and its substitution for a Single Chamber."[83] However, as a result of the recent by-elections losses, the UP leaders at El Arrayán decided not to go for a plebiscite for a unicameral parliament.[84]

The declaration that closed El Arrayán on 8 February roundly condemned many obstacles to efficient production – including bureaucracy, sectarianism, dishonesty and the like – but it failed to meet the core of PCCh and PIR concerns. The only area that these were joined was in emphasising the importance of small and medium-sized farmers – 40 percent of the rural population – and safeguarding them from expropriation.[85] Properties of between 40 and 80 hectares, forming 30 percent of Chilean agriculture, were not to be seized in the foreseeable future, according to the vice-president of the PIR.[86] In a separate declaration, originally confidential but unaccountably and officially released to the public, the PS boasted of its success *vis-à-vis* its partners and rivals: "The justice of the party's positions has once and for all been recognised with respect to not holding back 'to consolidate the process', but to deepen it, aggressively confronting the resistance of the bourgeoisie." Specifically the PS had, first, won the argument that "a conciliatory face" should not be shown to the right, and, second, avoided domination by social democrats. It also claimed credit for rebuffing PCCh and PIR attempts to lay the blame on the MIR. Nothing in the socialist statement indicated real willingness to meet middle-class anxieties.[87]

Despite the efforts made at El Arrayán, UP remained rent by disagreement over strategy and tactics, just as the opposition was beginning to find some coherence. The key differences remained: whether to adopt a more realistic economic policy; whether to negotiate with the more moderate

---

[83] Huidobro, *Decisión*, p. 43.

[84] "Zu den Ergebnissen der internen Beratungen der Unidad Popular en el Arrayan". These details were obtained by the East German embassy, probably from both the socialists and the communists – GDR embassy (Santiago) to Berlin, 11 February 1972: *AA*. Ministerium ... Abteilung Lateinamerika. C33354.000001.

[85] "Unidad Popular (Comité Nacional): La Declaración de El Arrayán", 9 February 1972: Farias, *La izquierda chilena*, pp. 1976–93.

[86] *El Mercurio*, 8 February 1972.

[87] "Partido Socialista (Departamento Nacional de Educación Política): La tesis del partido y la Declaración de El Arrayán". Documento confidencial interno. *Discusión*, 21 February 1972: ibid., pp. 1994–2006.

elements of the opposition; and how to respond to the activities of the MIR. The struggle between communists and socialists, between consolidation versus acceleration, thus continued unabated. And the damaging practice of the *cuoteo* – party patronage in businesses appropriated by the state – continued as before. Moreover cabinet changes reflected the ascendancy of the Altamirano wing of the PS. Hernán del Canto, defeated in the Valparaíso by-election and hardliner of the left, was appointed minister of the interior.

The economy remained critical. Corvalán arranged lunches at the communist central committee building where the PCCh leaders concerned directly with economic matters – Millas, Zorrilla, and José Cademártori – sat down and thrashed out the issues.

> We always concluded with the adoption of agreements that restricted Pedro's [Vuskovic] voluntaristic decisions. He greeted them without any great objection, but generally did not carry them out because they were superseded by new moves of his own, which took him even further from the line that was being drawn.[88]

The removal of Vuskovic in the cabinet reshuffle on 17 June did not effectively change anything, however, since his replacement, Carlos Matus, was a great personal friend of his predecessor,[89] who continued to exert influence from the sidelines and as deputy head of the presidential economic committee, which co-ordinated policy. The communists were therefore not surprised when, in December, Vuskovic – always represented as independent and a "technician" – applied to join the socialist party. He even let it be known that he had presidential ambitions for 1976.

Meanwhile opponents on the right launched a campaign to forestall the electoral process by direct action. On 4 March a secret meeting was held between the PN and PyL to launch anti-government operations under the banner "Solidarity, Order, Freedom", a slogan reminiscent of that used in Brazil in 1964 for the overthrow of Goulart: "God, Fatherland, Family".[90] A week later UP launched a prosecution of Jarpa for inflammatory

---

[88] Millas, *Memorias*, pp. 70–1.
[89] "Confidential": a note by H. A. A. Hankey on a conversation with Directeur d'Amérique at the Quai d'Orsay Saint-Legier, formerly ambassador to Santiago, 14 June 1972: *FCO 7/2208*.
[90] Zorina et al., *Uroki Chili*, p. 314.

declarations. Then on 13 March the streets of Santiago witnessed violent confrontation between PyL and the government's supporters. Walls appeared daubed with the spiderlike insignia of PyL, accompanied by the threatening slogan "*Ya viene Djakarta*" (Djakarta is on its way – a reference to the coup in Indonesia that wiped out the commmunist party in 1965). At a meeting of senior officers five days later, Prats found supporters of the government outnumbered by those backing the opposition. On 19 March, however, a ray of hope appeared. At a meeting of the *consejo nacional*, the chairman of the PDC, Renán Fuentealba, attacked the government on the grounds that the president's words did not square with the actions of his subordinates and that democratic forces were inadequately represented in office. He did, however, echo the persistent refrain of the PCCh leadership by calling for dialogue with the government on specific items. This call was fiercely attacked in the opposition newspaper *El Mercurio* on 21 March as appeasement of the left. *El Mercurio* told the opposition not to await the congressional elections in a year's time, but "to act today with intelligence and courage". "The Chilean Government seems to have moved sharply to the left again," the British ambassador noted, "and to have abandoned the attempt to obtain the cooperation of the centre which was agreed at the UP meeting at El Arrayan."[91]

Fragmentation of UP unity and growing coherence between elements of the opposition resulted largely from the behaviour of the MIR and Allende's unwillingness to act effectively to restrain them. One instance of this was the election of the rector of the Universidad de Chile, a position that had fast become of great symbolic significance. In order to beat Edgardo Boeninger Kausel, the favourite of the right, Allende secured the candidacy of Felipe Herrera Lane for UP. Herrera's merit as a means of dividing the right from the centre was that he had presided over the World Bank in Washington for many years (he brought in Orlando Letelier in the mid-sixties) and was thus a respected member of the establishment who could win votes from democrats of left and right. Just as the campaign took off, however, word came in that Allende's nephew, Andrés Pascal, had announced his own candidacy in the pages of *El Rebelde*, which he edited for the MIR. The split in the vote on the left effectively assured Boeninger's victory early in May.

[91] Hildyard (Santiago) to Hunter (London), 14 April 1972: *FCO 7/2212*.

Some observers saw the government as relentlessly moving towards suffo-cation of capitalism and democracy. In the words of the British embassy:

> Politically the ruthlessness and sectarianism of the UP parties, the illegal takeovers of farms by extremists in the countryside with the acquiescence of the authorities ("the workers' Government cannot oppress the workers"), the intervention or take-over of key industries by dubious legal procedures, and the pressure on non-UP organisations and communications media have alienated whole sectors of the population, and have eventually pushed the Christan Democrats into definite and determined opposition.[92]

This image is one of greater repression. The other side of the coin portrayed a régime fast losing its grip on the situation. By June it seemed to French diplomats that UP "now was not fully in control of events outside Santiago itself".[93] This was particularly true of the region to the south of the capital. Former foreign minister Valdés pointed out that "Very little was coming from the large belt of land in the south where farms had been taken over by the extreme socialist groups ... and this area was virtually outside the control of the Government; not even the police could operate there."[94] Indeed, the communist senator Volodia Teitelboim told the British ambassador, within the hearing of Corvalán, "that the horse needed to be calmed down" and that the jockey should keep it "on a tighter rein".[95] Either way the conclusion amounted to the same:

> Many Christian Democrats now think that a major confrontation is inevitable in the not too distant future. They share the view of the Right wing that whatever the President may say, or whatever short-term tactical concessions he may make, he is being pushed inexorably towards a totalitarian State which he would be unable to control whatever he himself might want.[96]

---

[92] Hildyard, "Impressions of Chile under a Government of Popular Unity": *FCO 2/2212*.

[93] Former ambassador to Santiago Saint Legier, Directeur d'Amérique at the Quai d'Orsay, 14 June 1972: *FCO 7/2208*.

[94] At lunch with A. Hankey, 6 April 1972, enclosed in Hankey to Sir Leslie Monson, 12 April 1972: *FCO 7/2212*.

[95] Hildyard (Santiago) to Hunter (London), 5 April 1972: ibid.

[96] Hildyard, "Impressions of Chile under a Government of Popular Unity", 17 March 1972: ibid.

After considerable effort the christian democrats finally obtained a further commitment from the president to deal with the MIR's illegal behaviour, but its value was in doubt. "He has, of course done this before, particularly in September last year", the British noted, "and nothing seemed to change."[97] The issue of control extended into government itself.

The PIR was the least likely member of UP. The CIA in the person of Keith Wheelock had attempted through subsidy to block the radical party's drift leftwards at the June 1967 party conference but failed. Worse still from the US viewpoint, at the radical party conference in July 1969 the dissentients (backed by the CIA) were removed from the leadership.[98] More recently the PIR, formed in August 1971, from the more moderate wing of the radical party, had acted as go-between on behalf of UP in talks with the christian democrats. Now, on 7 April 1972, when UP failed to follow through on what had been agreed, the PIR resigned from the ruling coalition. Senator Alberto Baltra, the PIR's leader and until recently a regular at the UP leadership meetings, "confirmed that Allende is less and less in control of the situation, particularly of the economy". Baltra continued:

> Allende is the spokesman, trouble-shooter, and peace-keeper, but although he has an extraordinary capacity for appearing to be well-informed, even in matters of detail, he only really concerns himself with short-term tactical issues. In a sense there is no real Government; the various parties or personalities (eg Vuskovic) push their own policies while Allende smooths out differences. In crunches he takes the short term view and appears unwilling or unable to stand up to the left.[99]

The communist party leadership frequently spoke of a crisis within the UP leadership. The Soviet ambassador in Santiago considered "the unity of the Chilean working class in the form of unity between communists and socialists is at present insufficient to meet the harder and more

[97] Hildyard (Santiago) to Hunter (London), 11 May 1972: ibid.

[98] "Political Action Related to 1970 Chilean Presidential Election", Memorandum for the 40 Committee, March 1970: *NARA. Chile Declassification Project. NSC.*

[99] Hildyard (Santiago) to Hunter (London), 20 April 1972: *FCO 7/2209.*

complicated demands required by the class struggle".[100] The problem, as the communists saw it, lay in the fact that the socialist party tolerated within its ranks people who were also members of the MIR. Corvalán told the Italian communists that the "socialists have more than flirted" with "groups of the 'left' … by which they have been extensively infiltrated".[101]

The deputy general secretary of the communist party, Victor Díaz, was pleased that "The Unidad Popular Government's measures have substantially weakened the position of the financial oligarchy and the large landowners; however," he warned, "they have not yet been defeated." Moreover, nationalisation of US copper assets brought down upon Chile an international boycott by the Paris Club of the major Western states which jeopardised an already vulnerable foreign exchange position. In the face of these difficulties, disunity within UP only made matters worse. "The key problem for Unidad Popular", Díaz said, "is the Socialist Party. One wing supports the UP government, the other, however, supports the MIR ultra-left group. The MIR", Díaz emphasised, "in particular sets the middle classes against the government, and these tendencies are gaining the support of the majority of the Socialist Party."[102]

The communist party thus found itself – on the departure of the non-Marxist radicals of the PIR – the more conservative element within the governing coalition. Problems were compounded in that Castro, now deeply sceptical of UP's attempts to win over the left of the christian democratic party, was aiding and abetting the MIR in taking direct and violent action in the field. Díaz reported:

> President Allende himself has already protested against this: that the Cuban comrades have behind his back reached confidential agreements, which publicly compromise the government and place it in a difficult position. (Shipments of weapons etc.) The Cuban comrades support left extremist groups which took part in bank raids.[103]

---

[100] Memorandum by Markowski, head of the international relations division of the SED Central Committee apparatus, "Zur gegenwärtigen Lage in Chile": *SAPMO. Sozialistische Einheitspartei Deutschland.* Zentralkomitee, Internationale Verbindungen: DY/30/IV.B 2/20. Information Nr.75/72 für die Mitglieder und Kandidaten des Politburos, 6 July 1972.
[101] *Archivio PCI.* Esteri. Cile. 046.189–199.
[102] SAPMO. "Zur gegenwärtigen Situation in Chile. Gespräch des Genossen Hermann Axen mit Genossen Victor Diaz, stell. Generalsekretär der KP Chiles, und Genossen Luis Barria, Mitglied des ZK der KP Chiles": *SAPMO* … Information Nr 90/72 für das Politbüro, 31 July 1972.
[103] Ibid.

Part of the background to Cuban behaviour may be found in US defense intelligence agency testimony before congress in late September 1972. The DIA asserted that "Castro has lost some patience with Allende's slow pace". It continued, matching the tenor of reports given in East Berlin by the Chilean communist party: "Although Castro and Allende are close friends, Allende feels that the Cuban has sometimes overstepped his authority in Chile."[104]

Events were running well beyond Allende's ability to control them. On 10 August Prats, in receipt of alarmist information from military intelligence, the SIM, that such groups as the MLN (Movimiento de Liberación Nacional) and the Movimiento 16 de julio on the extreme left were acquiring an insurrectionary character, arranged a long meeting with Allende. Prats updated the president on this apparent threat, adding that he did not know whether his most incorrigible enemies lay with the opposition or "within the Unidad Popular parties themselves".[105] Allende's astonishing response, according to Prats, was to "complain bitterly about the incredible mistakes committed by politicians and civil servants, for whom he had to take responsibility, faced with an implacable opposition".[106] The Foreign and Commonwealth Office in London noted that "It was thanks above all to the influence of the left-wing leadership of the Socialist Party that [Justice Minister] Manuel Sanhueza [Cruz]'s attempt to reach agreement with the Christian Democrats over the Constitutional Reform Bill broke down."[107] The Hamilton-Fuentealba bill had attempted to limit the extent of government control over the economy. Its rejection by the left had precipitated the departure of the PIR from government. Though not as active as Castro would have liked, Allende's tolerance of the extreme left seemed over-generous to many.

---

[104] Testimony of Paul Wallner, Western Area Analyst, Defense Intelligence Agency, 26 September 1972: *Soviet Activities in Cuba – Hearing before the Subcommittee on Inter-American Affairs of the Committee of Foreign Affairs, House of Representatives, 92nd Congress, 2nd Session*, Part 3 (Washington DC 1972), p. 9.

[105] Prats, *Memorias*, p. 281.

[106] Ibid.

[107] Note from Stephen Clissold, Foreign Office Research Department, 8 November 1972: *FCO 7/2209.*

6

THE MIDDLE CLASS STRIKES

Y con Nixon de fondo principal
se lanzaron al Paro Patronal.

Pablo Neruda[1]

An item central to UP's Basic Programme was the liberation of Chile from "subordination to foreign capital".[2] In the narrowest sense of alienating foreign direct investment at whatever cost, UP succeeded. But, in the wider and more critical sense of removing Chile's need for external financial assistance, the régime failed. This was partly the result of events entirely beyond reach: the world price of copper dropped disastrously. It was also, however, the consequence of conscious policy. By expropriating the copper assets of the Kennecott Corporation without compensation Chile precipitated the decision by a Paris court on 30 September 1972 to seize one and a quarter million tons of copper bound for Le Havre. All of a sudden the valuable West European market for Chile's main export closed. Allende also refused net recompense to any US multinational expropriated, reportedly when he discovered that a trusted ally on the compensation committee had been bribed by ITT to the tune of $500,000.[3] It was also certain given past practice – let alone the views of Nixon and Kissinger – that Washington would deny the

---

[1] "And with Nixon behind it, the bosses' strike was launched" – "Incitación al nixonicidio y alabanza de la revolución chilena": Neruda, *Obras Completas III*, p. 735.

[2] "Programa Básico de Gobierno de la Unidad Popular", 5 September 1970: González and Talavera, *Los mil días*, vol. 2, p. 956.

[3] This point was made by former ambassador Korry in an interview: Palast, "A Marxist threat to cola sales?"

régime any assistance. Damage was also self-inflicted because mis-management of the economy made a bad situation worse. By December 1972, when Allende visited Moscow in search of immediate assistance, the black market escudo-dollar rate had plummeted to 290–300/1, as against the official rate of 46/1.[4] A key point in the Basic Programme was that "The rise in the cost of living is a fire raging in the homes of the people and for the housewife in particular."[5] Yet as even Corvalán acknowledged, in August 1972 "the cost of living rose as much as or more than in the first seven months of the year". He added, ominously: "If at that time there had been a reactionary government, the people would have brought it down."[6] At issue were not only white goods but even basic foodstuffs. A devastating attack on the hypertrophy of the state in the government's agrarian reform was delivered by MAPU general secretary Jaime Gazmuri: the *asentamientos* were undercapitalised and badly run; no serious attempt was made to recruit non-Marxist agronomists to help the collective farms; and small farmers were provided with no security to encourage investment. Yet the state was omnipresent. Gazmuri condemned

> ... the high level of bureaucratisation that has accompanied and is accompanying the development of the process ... State institutions have been seen bursting out in every direction, whether in the application of the means of expropriation, in the organisation of the area reformed, in the management of the process of production in the countryside, or in the implementation of the alliance with middle and small proprietors.[7]

By the end of August 1972, in order to undermine the now-thriving black market, the government raised prices on bread by 180 percent, on beef by 230 percent, on mutton by 160 percent and milk and milk products by 140 percent, on basic household products by 260 percent and on clothing by 160–190 percent. It is therefore not surprising that the country was very soon paralysed by vociferous resistance and, increasingly, also civil disobedience from a burgeoning opposition. Corvalán later told the Italian

[4] Chancery (Santiago) to London, 29 December 1972: *FCO 7/2209*.
[5] Programa Básico: González and Talavera, *Los mil días*, p. 949.
[6] Eduardo Labarca's interview with Corvalán, December 1972: reprinted in idid., vol. 2, p. 1161.
[7] Interview: *Punto Final*, 10 October 1972.

communists: "A part of the middle class and the lumpenproletariat do not, of course, accept this state of affairs; they respond with exasperation and could become an instrument of reactionary groups."[8]

The assumption had been that, whatever measures the régime took to destroy private sector incentives to act as the engine of economic growth, investors would somehow continue to sustain the health of the economy until their companies were nationalised. UP thus deceived itself as to the reality of what it was doing and the consequences therefrom. Miscalculation extended to the conduct of foreign policy. At the same time as the government switched its posture from multilateral co-operation within the Organization of American States and under the umbrella of Washington to fully fledged co-operation with the communist bloc, it denounced the "imperialist powers" (which included potential friends in the social democracies of Western Europe) and rejected any agreements that "limit ... sovereignty" and any aid with political strings. As rhetoric, such words were immensely satisfying to unreflecting leftist sentiment; as policy, however, they caused considerable and unnecessary damage. "They said that we were going to be isolated", Allende had remarked on 4 November 1971.[9] He had no idea then how true this was to be.

The United States played a double role in securing the weakening of the Chilean economy. When Stanford professor Richard Fagen arrived in Santiago for research in February 1972, he was surprised by how openly US officials paraded their activities in undermining the Allende regime. Fagen recalls that "a U.S. Foreign Service officer – an acquaintance of mine – got in touch with me and said that the U.S. Embassy in Santiago had succeeded in infiltrating all parties of the Popular Unity coalition, but that it had not yet managed to infiltrate the Movement of the Revolutionary Left [MIR] ... " Ever anxious to find a route into the senior ranks of the MIR – possibly through Fagen's university and other contacts – the official bragged about the role of various agents under diplomatic cover and told him that one-third of the embassy personnel were officers of the CIA. "The incident is a measure of how blatantly the U.S. Embassy operated during that period", Fagen

---

[8] *Archivio PCI.* Esteri. Cile. 046.189–199.
[9] Allende, *Obras*, p. 143.

states.[10] Indeed, intelligence sources later told the *New York Times* that "The people within the Embassy felt that they were engaged in a kind of warfare, the people either were with you or against you when it came to Allende." These sources added that "There were a lot of people in Santiago on the far right who were essentially dedicating their lives to the overthrow of Allende – it was like a holy war. These people were increasingly seen at the embassy in 1972 and 1973."[11]

The CIA station in Santiago, headed by Raymond Warren[12] since Hecksher's departure after Allende came into office, did not lack experience in economic destabilisation. The agency had long played a role within the international trades union movement. To combat Soviet dominance of international labour organisations through the World Federation of Trades Unions (WFTU), the Americans had set up the International Confederation of Free Trades Unions (ICFTU) in 1949. It also worked through International Trade Secretariats (ITS) which represented particular branches of industry worldwide. All this was done through the AFL-CIO, headed by two leading anti-communists, George Meany and ex-communist Jay Lovestone. In Latin America the AFL-CIO also operated through ORIT – the Organización Regional Interamericana de Trabajadores (originally the Confederación Interamericana de Trabajadores) – which also worked as a vehicle for the CIA.[13] The controlling body for the AFL-CIO was its Committee of International Labor Affairs. Co-operation with the US government was close. It is therefore entirely inaccurate to talk of CIA infiltration of the US labour movement. They were invited in. The labor attachés at US embassies – who were occasionally also from the CIA – reported both to the department of state and the AFL-CIO international department. A further body was created in 1961 after the failure of the Bay of Pigs invasion as a response to Castroite infiltration of the Latin American labour

[10] "The Intrigues Before Allende Fell", *Los Angeles Times*, 6 October 1973.

[11] *New York Times*, 20 September 1974. These sources were reported by Seymour Hersh.

[12] *AA*. Bestand Ministerium für Auswärtige Angelegenheiten der DDR. 000001. C 3352. Abteilung Lateinamerika. Felipe Suarez, "Consideraciones sobre la situacion en Chile", November 1974. A veteran of Guatemala (1954) Warren was also named in the *Washington Post*, 17 September 2000.

[13] This much is apparent from former ORIT official Fanny Simon's visit to Santiago in April 1973, which resulted in a report that had nothing to do with labour but everything to do with Allende's need for a military government. See her report of 17 April 1973: *NARA*. Department of State: RG 59, LAB 3-3, ORIT, Box 1383.

movement. This was the American Institute for Free Labor Development (AIFLD), administered by William Doherty, who on 12 June 1964 acknowledged its role in training Brazilians who helped overthrow President João Goulart in the coup earlier that year.[14] Doherty had also aided in the downfall in 1964 of Marxist leader Cheddi Jagan of British Guiana by backing a prolonged general strike lasting seventy-nine days, which crippled the economy. Some £100,000 was dispensed to strikers in this tiny colony by CIA agent Howard McCabe from a Georgetown hotel.[15] The *Washington Post* reported a few years later that Doherty "is said to be closely acquainted with CIA operations" – which was about as explicit as it could be.[16] AIFLD was set up partly because of the ineffectiveness of ORIT. Its operations were "the result of several years' study and planning".[17] The board was chaired by J. Peter Grace, president of W. R. Grace and Co., which owned large tracts of Chilean industry. But, as a former CIA officer explains, "Business leaders are front men on the Board of Directors so that large sums of AID [US Agency for International Development] money can be channelled to AIFLD."[18] Initial funding came partly from the Kaplan Fund (a known CIA route) through the Michigan Fund, one of the Delaware corporations that channeled money for the agency. Such trades union operations in the Third World were initially managed at the CIA by Thomas Braden, later by Cord Meyer.[19]

The effectiveness of these operations in Chile up to the election of Allende should not, however, be exaggerated. Previous attempts to create rival institutions to the communist-dominated CUT had always failed. ORIT was weak; so was AIFLD. Its formal role was to train foreign trades unionists in American values to keep them from communism. It thus formally buttressed US foreign policy in the region. AIFLD had been in Chile since 1964 and decided to suspend in-country training after Allende won the elections in 1970. Instead the United States began bringing

---

[14] *Los gremios patronales*, ed. D. Aron et al. (Santiago 1973). This booklet appeared in Santiago on the weekend of 21 July, evidently a product of government intelligence sources (at least, so the US embassy believed). See *NARA*. Department of State, Chile, RG 59, LAB 13 CAN to LAB CHILE, Box 1394. They were relieved that nothing more compromising appeared.

[15] *Sunday Times*, 16 and 23 April 1967. Some of this information came from an MI6 officer.

[16] *Washington Post*, 23 February 1967.

[17] Agee, *Inside the Company*, p. 243.

[18] Ibid., p. 244.

[19] *Washington Post*, 23 February 1967.

Chileans over to AIFLD at Front Royal in Virginia, seventy miles due west of Washington DC. In respect of organised labour, the Americans were remarkably unprepared for what was to follow in Chile; but they soon made up the distance.

At the CUT elections (31 May – 3 June 1972) the socialists were relegated to third place by the PDC. The Italian communist party, reflecting the views of the PCCh, said the results "have sounded an alarm bell".[20] The vote did not indicate a shift to pro-capitalist sentiment; it did, however, highlight opportunities for using elements within the labour movement to undermine the government. Strikes in the transport sector began very soon thereafter. US labor attaché Robert O'Neill took note. The CUT itself represented only 20 percent of Chilean workers and these tended to be the most skilled and therefore the better paid. The prospects for exploiting the shift in opinion away from UP (the extreme left were annihilated in the elections) appeared good. O'Neill looked forward to the prospect of better-paid workers reacting against urging from the government that they restrain their demands and against the extreme left accusing them of being an elite. "This resentment could build," he commented, "with sufficient help from extremists' attacks, to a point where the workers in copper, ENAP, CAP, LAN, as well as Maritime unions, Communications, Banks, and some public sectors could initially form a block within CUT to defend their positions and eventually be the basis for a break-up of CUT. And what would CUT be without these sectors?" His conclusion for AIFLD was that it "will continue to stress contacts in the above sectors, utilizing union-to-union trips and Front Royal courses for younger leaders".[21] This paid off when tensions increased through that winter.

The work of the United States was made easier by the fact that instead of moving further to the centre and engaging christian democracy, the socialist party instinctively pushed UP in the opposite direction. At a closed plenum of the PS central committee that met from 4 to 10 July the PDC proposal for the Hamilton-Fuentealba bill defining the proportions of private, mixed and state ownership within the economy was decisively

[20] *Archivio PCI.* Esteri. Cile. 801. "Note sull'America Latina", July 1972.

[21] O'Neill (Santiago) to Jesse Friedman, director regional/sur, AIFLD: *George Meany Memorial Archives* (Maryland). RG18-0101. International Affairs Department, Country Files, 1969–1981. 5/16. Chile.

rejected. This bill had originally been presented to the Senate on 20 October 1971.[22] Allende responded by vetoing the bill – a veto that, without two-thirds of the vote in congress, the PDC was unable to override. Moreover negotiations with the christian democrats were broken off and it was decided to hold a plebiscite on the most important economic issues. Worse still from the viewpoint of relations with the centre and right, Altamirano announced that "in the course of the revolutionary process, the parties participating in it have the right to break any laws effective in the country".[23]

On 5 July, a PN resolution in parliament succeeded in ousting the minister of the interior, Hernán del Canto, as being responsible equally for illegal land appropriations and for allowing a customs exemption for a weighty shipment from Cuba of thirteen crates described in the manifest as works of art. The president's explanation never sounded plausible. It soon emerged that these were armaments.[24] Worse news followed. On 19 July more than thirty members of the MIR and others including known members of the PS and a member of the presidential bodyguard GAP were arrested, *inter alia*, for a series of robberies of banks and shops. On 27 July regional organisations of the PS, MIR, MAPU, the radical party and the left christian democrats in Concepción announced the creation of a "People's Assembly" that would counter "the bourgeois and counter-revolutionary parliament" and called for an all-out strike across the province in protest against the "maneouvres of the reactionary majority in congress". Once again, led by the PS and the MIR this much-publicised initiative showed a degree of interchangeability between the two organisations that was bound to reinforce the drift of the PDC further to the right. It was therefore condemned by the PCCh in no uncertain terms, a stance the MIR predictably described as "absurd".[25] But in this case the communists were closer to Allende, who also criticised this untimely move. The president reminded all militants in UP that they had a responsibility as protagonists in the revolutionary process. He "rejected any attempt at outlining spontaneously parallel tactics". Nothing better suited the

---

[22] González and Talavera et al., *Los mil días de Allende*, vol. 2, pp. 988–90.

[23] Zorina, *Uroki Chili*, p. 331.

[24] After the coup the list of the contents was found in the flat of "Coco" Paredes, formerly director-general of police detectives, at Torre 18 Remodelación, San Borja, apartment 13.

[25] Ibid., p. 334.

"enemy" than "diversionary displays" from within UP, as they would broadcast any act of indiscipline to distort the image of government policy: "The enemy studies our weaknesses and exploits them", he said. Instead Allende wanted the focus to be on winning the general elections for parliament in 1973, which "will enable us to press forward with the institutional and legal changes indispensable to rescue the country from underdevelopment and put an end to the blocking power of a revanchist opposition that protects the interests of reaction and helps favour the plans of imperialism".[26]

On 4 August the expulsion of thirty-three members of the PS for simultaneously belonging to the MIR showed a new determination to get to grips with the problem. But the PS and Allende personally lacked the ability because in the last resort they lacked the will to take the kind of measures that would put an end to uncontrolled activities on their left.

Of course, not all the apparent provocations actually originated with the MIR. Black operations long effected by the CIA and their allies were not unknown. On 4 August, for instance, police forces raided an encampment of the poor organised, as they invariably were, along military lines at Lo Hermida, where barricades had been set up in north-eastern Santiago.

The police came in search of a member of the MIR, Héctor Prieto Callupil. The raid turned into a veritable battle, with the result that one of the occupants died.[27] In total eleven were also wounded and 160 arrested. This was described by the leaders of the encampment as a "massacre",[28] an exaggeration repeated in *El Rebelde*,[29] and in a leaflet also produced by the MIR,[30] despite the fact that half the wounded were policemen.[31] MIR militants promptly demanded that Eduardo ("Coco") Paredes and Carlos Toro, director and deputy director of police detectives, be dismissed. Ironically years later it was discovered that the leader of the encampment, "comandante" Raúl, was none other than Osvaldo ("*El*

[26] *La Nación*, 1 August 1972: González and Talavera, *Los mil días*, vol. 2, pp. 1136–40.

[27] Prats, *Memorias*, p. 280.

[28] "MIR: Mensaje de los pobladores de lo Hermida a los pobres de todo Chile", 8 August 1972: reprinted in *Estudios Públicos*, pp. 457–64.

[29] *El Rebelde*, 26 September 1972.

[30] *Lo Hermida: la cara más fea del reformismo*. This was published on 20 August 1973. For more, see E. Condal, *Il Cile di Allende e il ruolo del* MIR (Milan 1973), p. 77.

[31] For the government's account, see *El Siglo*, 6 August 1972: González and Talavera, *Los mil días*, vol. 1, pp. 424–7.

Guatón") – "Fatso" – Romo, a member of the army who had infiltrated the MIR as an *agent provocateur*; he later became a known torturer for the DINA.[32] From the viewpoint of the United States and the hard right this incident could thus be chalked up as as yet one further catalyst speeding Allende's ultimate downfall. The Chilean communist party certainly had its own suspicions at the time, given "comandante" Raúl's call on parliamentarians on the left and the right to accuse Paredes and others of unconstitutional behaviour, an issue taken up with some force in the CIA-supported *La Segunda* and *El Mercurio*.[33] "The incidents at dawn yesterday", wrote the communist daily *El Siglo*, "also reflect with clarity once again the objective coincidence between the positions of the extreme left and the right. The objective common to both is to attack and attempt to destroy the image of the government."[34]

On 21 August 1972 a strike was called by shopkeepers as a result of the death of one of their number when the government requisitioned his premises; that day a riot in the south resulted in thirteen people dead and six seriously injured. Minister of economics Matus appeared on the radio and demanded that shopkeepers open their shops or face requisition by the government. Those shops that resisted the representatives of the Dirección de Industria y Comercio (DIRINCO) were duly seized. Over one hundred people were arrested in street protests. After dinner at minister of defence Tohá's with Altamirano and foreign minister Almeyda, Prats – reflecting recent heated exchanges with fellow officers – emphasised the seriousness of these armed confrontations. He told Altamirano the armed forces believed "he was the éminence grise of the extreme Left", an accusation Altamirano of course denied.[35] The government responded to the strike by forcing open twenty shops that had been closed; in the ensuing fracas seventy arrests were made. Some 95 percent of shops had participated in the strike. On 26 August Altamirano further raised the political temperature by announcing: "The government has suggested and continues to suggest that the reactionaries do not want civil war, and therefore has asked us to restrain workers,

---

[32] Óscar Soto, *El Último Día de Salvador Allende* (Santiago 1999), p. 74. Also a point footnoted in Zorina et al., *Uroki Chili*, p. 335.

[33] See, for instance, the editorial in *La Segunda*, 5 August 1972: González and Talavera, *Los mil días*, vol. 1, pp. 420–3.

[34] *El Siglo*, 6 August 1972: ibid., vol. 1, p. 425.

[35] Prats, *Memorias*, p. 283.

peasants and the young. We cannot any longer restrain ourselves and, if reaction tomorrow turns one hundred people out onto the street, we will turn out a thousand."[36] Three days later the president placed Bío-Bío province in a state of emergency as a result of a strike prompted by government closure of a hostile radio station. From congress came news that a bill introduced by senator Juan de Dios Carmona (PDC) handing the military control over armaments of a certain calibre had been approved in committee. In the same spirit Corvalán wrote to the president on 31 August warning that increasing street confrontations had to cease, and that "provocateurs from the far Left" had to be restrained.[37] Prats, too, had taken to cautioning Allende that matters might get out of control – but not so much through UP tolerating the antics of the MIR, as through a speeding up of the nationalisation programme (which is precisely what the PCCh was doing). "This", in the judgement of Prats, "generates new resistance on each occasion that progressively reinforces the opposition all the more to the point at which they enter a one-way street with no democratic way out."[38] No one could say they had not been forewarned. The PCCh was, as ever, more alert to the danger than the others. Teitelboim told Adam Watson, formerly ambassador to Cuba: "the folly of appealing to force was that the Left didn't have the force".[39]

The month of September 1972 began with demonstrations by teenage schoolchildren organised by PyL setting up barricades at crossroads in sections of the capital, and with a warning from the government of a so-called September Plan to launch a coup by means of growing unrest. But instead of reaching out to the more moderate elements within the christian democratic party, which would have been consistent with his belief that UP had reached the stage of an "anti-fascist struggle",[40] Allende delivered a two-hour speech on the anniversary of his election condemning the extreme left and insisting upon a peaceful settlement of differences, but simultaneously calling for a new constitution – which the PDC did not want. "No longer can the situation persist wherein the opposition has a majority in congress at a time when the greater part of the Chilean

---

[36] Zorina et al., *Uroki Chili*, p. 338.

[37] Ibid., p. 339.

[38] Prats, *Memorias*, p. 285.

[39] *Listener*, 27 September 1973.

[40] A term he used at the seventh congress of the communist youth organisation on 9 September.

people supports the government, Allende said."[41] A week later he followed this with a bill for a unicameral parliament which he presented to the leaders of the UP coalition. This was hardly going to win over his opponents, and he may well have moved in this direction to neutralise opposition within the socialist party to other, more urgent choices. For he told Corvalán and Altamirano that they faced three options: carrying on as before, but only with complete consensus within the coalition; or allying with the PDC on mutually agreeable terms; or, bringing the military into the cabinet.

It should have been evident that inclusion of options two and three were largely, if not entirely, designed to force adoption of option one. Altamirano predictably rejected the last two options "categorically", whereas Corvalán typically asked to refer them to the PCCh political committee.[42] Within the political committee Millas was the most favourably disposed to the christian democrats. But Corvalán's view as expressed to the Soviet ambassador on 13 September showed the limits of what they would accept. He "considered that a part of christian democracy speaks in favour of collaborating with Unidad Popular, but the majority of the party is taken with the spirit of revenge".[43]

The military option was no accident. In this increasingly febrile milieu, on 8 September general Alfredo Canales Márquez had told rear-admiral Horacio Justiniano Aguirre that within two months a military coup would take place; that if a general did not lead the movement, a colonel would; that within the air force the generals did not think the government could continue, etcetera. Justiniano reported this to admiral Montero, who passed it on to Prats, who in turn told Tohá and thus it reached Allende.[44] A week later the MIR leadership announced over the radio that part of the September Plan involved armed action by both PyL and the national party's paramilitaries, Rolando Matus, who, under the guise of MIR militants, would attack the homes of officers and soldiers as well as military and police buildings to provoke a coup. After confirming the facts of the conversation with Justiniano, on 21 September Prats asked Canales to resign and not without reason. Even the Americans fully accepted that

[41] Zorina et al., *Uroki Chili,* p. 340.

[42] Ibid., pp. 340–1.

[43] Conversation with Basov, 13 September 1972: *Estudios Públicos*, no. 72, spring 1998, p. 441.

[44] Prats, *Memorias*, pp. 289–90.

Canales "was generally acknowledged to be the leader of the military coup plotters".[45] And the Foreign and Commonwealth Office in London noted that "at one time – before Prats secured the dismissal of the right wing general Canales – the Brazilians seemed to have been in touch with that general and to have been considering providing at least logistical support for a subversive movement from bases in Bolivia".[46]

The Chilean government was thus highly sensitised to attitudes within the armed forces. More worrying still, *El Mercurio* indicated that the christian democratic right would, under certain conditions, welcome the armed forces as the saviours of the country:

> The constitutional principle that directs the conduct of the armed forces is that they are essentially unquestioningly obedient. This means that they must loyally carry out the instructions of their hierarchical superiors in the sphere in which they are competent and that they may not intervene in the game of day-to-day politics [*política contingente*].
>
> While the actions of the government remain free from any reproach for unconstitutional behaviour, obedience and professional non-participation in politics do not present problems in either theory or practice for the fighting services. Difficulties arise when there are risks that the constitution is being overridden, whether as result of individual actions of those governing, or in consequence of the virulence of a revolutionary process that is aimed precisely at destroying the existing order. In this latter case the constitutionalist doctrine of unquestioning obedience of the army is in force with as much strength as ever, on condition that the true doctrine of the army is not confused with a lack of personality in command and with indiscriminate submission to possible arbitrary behaviour emanating from the government.

It is easy to see where this line of logic was leading. "It is not enough that the armed forces recuse themselves from questioning, that is from not intervening in day-to-day politics, but precisely that their spirit of loyalty to the Constitution should not be utilised in order that they remain inactive while the other principles ... are violated."[47]

[45] "Memorandum for the 40 Committee", 13 October 1972.
[46] Note by Clissold, 13 April 1973: *FCO 7/2410*.
[47] "La doctrina del ejercito", *El Mercurio*, 24 September 1972.

Conflict appeared imminent. "Every kind of arms is stored in the homes of the middle class and the city aristocracy", Prats noted, while PyL were organising the defence of residential districts – *Proteco* – against the possibility of looting by "uncontrolled mobs".[48] The state of alarm among those with property – particularly in prosperous suburbs like the Barrio Alto in Santiago – was at its height. In *El Mercurio* Orlando Sáenz Rojas, president of the industrial organisation Sofofa and member of the "invisible front" and leadership of Patria y Libertad, denounced the new Millas–Matus economic leadership as no better than that of Vuskovic – worse indeed, signifying "an intensification, if that is possible, of aggression against the private sector". "If countries can go broke," Sáenz intoned, "we have to say that ours is broke."[49] But the problem went far beyond this.

The character assumed by the protest movement indicated outside involvement and extensive financial support. The United States did not invent the crisis. But the crisis gave Nixon and Kissinger the hope they needed that finally Allende might be crushed. The prospect now opened of adding elements from the Chilean industrial and service sectors of the economy "to support the over-all covert political action programme". "The private sector only recently has become alarmed and started to resist in an organized way", Kissinger was told on 20 September; "CIA thinks that support and encouragement of the politically-oriented activities of the private sector might be a significant adjunct to the current main effort of direct support to opposition parties."[50] "What we were really doing", recalled a CIA official, "was supporting a civilian resistance movement against an arbitrary government. Our target was the middle-class groups who were working against Allende."[51] The view expressed by Australian journalist Robert Moss, himself closely aligned to the right, left no room for doubt as to how Allende was seen: "The process of nationalisation that is going on in Chile is concerned with power, not with socialism or economic reform."[52] The power struggle was primary.

---

[48] Prats, *Memorias*, p. 287.
[49] *El Mercurio*, 4 September 1972.
[50] "Memorandum for Dr Kissinger" from Rob Roy Ratliff, "Financial Support for the Chilean Private Sector", 20 September 1972. *NARA. Chile Declassification Project. NSC.*
[51] *Time*, 30 September 1974.
[52] "Allende's Chile", *Encounter*, August 1972, vol. xxxix, no. 2, p. 78.

The first stage, not long after the national party called for civil resistance, was a strike called by León Vilarín, a former militant of the socialist party and now president of the national association of truck-owners, the Confederación Nacional de Dueños de Camiones de Chile, followed by other small businesses. Vilarín, who had known Allende for thirty years, is reported to have been advised by Emmanuel Boggs, former head of AIFLD in Chile.[53] Vilarín later told Italian journalist Maurizio Chierici that he had received funding from "North American trades union associations".[54] They were by no means the only source of support. *Time* magazine later cited CIA sources to the effect that "Laundered CIA money, reportedly channeled to Santiago by way of Christian Democratic parties in Europe, helped finance the Chilean truckers' 45-day strike, one of the worst blows to the economy."[55]

Until early October the PDC was still counting on the forthcoming congressional elections in March 1973 as the means of reining in UP and had not yet entirely given up on the hope of diluting, if not reorienting, government policy. But government resistance to pleas for greater moderation drove the christian democrats further towards the national party, which was itself hand in glove with the United States. The PCCh was correct, at its central committee plenum from 30 September to 2 October, in signalling the collapse of support for the government among the middle classes and the importance for UP of winning over medium and small proprietors.[56] As a consequence Corvalán was talking to Fuentealba of the PDC in an effort to agree the limits of state appropriation. And Allende, having seen Canales readily removed, seemed steadfastly confident that the worst possible outcome was inconceivable. "The *coup d'état*", he told an Italian journalist, "is a plant that cannot germinate in Chile. Granted, there are some groups in conspiracy. But you have been here several weeks and will have seen the combative spirit of the people and its resolve not to allow seditious adventures to prosper; you will also have been able to evaluate the stance taken by our armed forces."[57]

---

[53] Information obtained by the MIR: *Punto Final*, 11 September 1973.
[54] Chierici, "Undici Settembre", p. 40.
[55] *Time*, 30 September 1974.
[56] Zorina et al., *Uroki Chili*, p. 342.
[57] *Corriere della Sera*, 3 October 1972.

But such optimism was almost immediately thrown abruptly into doubt. On 6 October the first clear signal for action came when Francisco Bulnes declared in the senate "the opinion of the National Party: that this government has become illegitimate".[58] On the right wing of the PDC, Patricio Aylwin also aligned himself with this position. But it was the PN that held the initiative. As its leader Jarpa subsequently revealed: "We had a strike department which encompassed bankers, private employees, public employees, shopkeepers, truck owners, agrobusinessmen, lawyers and doctors ... "[59] In such circumstances it must have been impossible to distinguish between CIA funding for the national party proper and for the conduct of the strike.

Mobilisation had spread across the board. Inspired by broadcasts on 22 August, from PyL's radio station, Radio Agricultura, the middle-class housewives who had filled the streets at the end of Castro's visit the previous year now reappeared at exactly 10.00pm each night banging their pots and pans for fifteen minutes of protest. Radio Agricultura was soon shut down on government orders. But that did nothing to quell discontent; rather the reverse. Outside the Bernardo O'Higgins military school in Santiago housewives pelted cadets with grains of wheat and rice, shouting, "*Gallinas!*" (chickens). Foreign correspondents soon discovered that street rioters were being hired at a rate of 300 escudos a day (a dollar at the current rate). As part of its *Proteco* programme PyL issued a guide for community protection that contained advice more appropriate to insurrection. "Try to surround your enemies," it suggested, "firing without pity."[60] When Allende had delivered a speech in September warning of a plan to paralyse the country by means of a transport strike, the pro-opposition *Economist* magazine – employing Robert Moss, who spent an unusual amount of his time with PyL – had mocked the claim. But a truck strike involving 12,000 owners (out of a national total of some 50,000) duly began for an indefinite period at midnight on 10 October. The spark for the walk-out was the announcement on 7 October by the state production corporation (CORFO) that the government would set up a pilot scheme for a state-owned road haulage system in Aisén, southern Chile. That this was not

[58] *El Mercurio*, 7 October 1972.
[59] Onofre Jarpa, *Confesiones*, p. 174.
[60] *Time*, 9 October 1972.

just idle speculation was borne out when a little over a week later economics minister Matus told the journal *Ercilla* that "Transport is far too valuable to remain in private hands. In order to build socialism, the means of transport have to be socialised."[61]

The régime thus played directly into the hands of the right, and the United States. As state department intelligence acknowledged without access to all of White House activities, "The manner in which the situation has evolved suggests that there was some pre-planning and an orchestration of support by elements not immediately concerned with the transportation industry, primarily business and professional groups."[62] Allende reacted promptly by arresting the leaders of the strike, and within two days the government had promulgated a state of emergency in the twelve provinces of the centre and south of the country, from Valparaíso to Bío-Bío. On 13 October the chamber of commerce called on all shops to close as the strike spread to other unions and professional associations. The centres for retail distribution set up and controlled by the parties of the left, known as JAPs (*juntas de abastecimiento y precios*), announced that they reserved the right to force shops open. On 14 October Allende stated over the radio that he was prepared to release those arrested and return requisitioned lorries provided work was resumed, at the same time warning that this was his last step before taking the most extreme measures.[63] On 15 October the PDC's *consejo nacional* responded by pledging its support for the strike and called on the population "to mass mobilisation". A war of nerves was now fully engaged. On 16 October students, doctors, technicians and bank employees walked out, followed by dentists, lawyers, merchant seamen and even private school pupils. The railway line from Santiago to Valparaíso was sabotaged, as was the line between the capital and San Antonio. By 21 October an estimated two-thirds of farm walkers had also downed tools.

"Chile will not be paralysed", the president solemnly intoned.[64] To no avail. A close friend subsequently reported that "when the political crisis started, Allende reconciled himself to the immediate possibility of being

---

[61] Zorina et al., *Uroki Chili*, p. 344.

[62] "Chile: Major Challenge to President Allende", Intelligence Note, Bureau of Intelligence and Research, 18 October 1972: *NARA*. Department of State: RG 59, Lab 6-1 Chile.

[63] Zorina et al., *Uroki Chili*, p. 344.

[64] *Las Noticias de Ultima Hora*, 13 October 1972.

overthrown and assassinated".[65] The political thrust of the strike was from the outset self-evident. "The role of the opposition has now changed", *La Prensa* declared on 16 October; "It has now gone beyond the bounds of congress." A memorandum from the US state department noted: "Truckers' grievances with the Allende government (over such issues as freight rates and the scarcity of spare parts) formed the *ostensible* [author's italics] basis of the trucking strike which began last week in southern Chile and has spread to the more populous central zone."[66] On 21 October Allende convened a meeting with Tohá and the heads of the various armed forces: Montero (navy), Ruiz (air force), Sepúlveda (carabineros) and Prats (army). Allende proposed that they join the cabinet and the following day he clarified to Prats that the aim was to frustrate those behind the strike who were counting on a coup.[67] Allende had to wait further for a positive response. But it was a clever move, given the view from the opposition. On 24 October the West German ambassador had a meeting with Jarpa who said "that a solution to the domestic political problems is only thinkable with the help of the military. He wants responsibility before long laid upon the Chilean generals ... " Jarpa went on to ask the ambassador what the Federal Republic's opinion would be of a "military dictatorship" in Chile (he received a negative response).[68]

Prices rocketed as goods failed to reach their destination. The price of potatoes, for instance, had risen from 2 escudos in 1971 to 50 escudos.[69] The government had little alternative but to take the offensive; it requisitioned those companies producing necessities that had joined the strike. *Dirinco* seized trucks and handed them over to workers to break the strike and took charge of distribution of goods, which inevitably led to political favouritism. A manifesto from "socialist workers" issued by the PS on 23 October openly spoke of a "rationalisation of distribution by

---

[65] Told to Hugh O'Shaughnessy, "Supper with Allende as crowds riot", *Observer*, 29 October 1972. The informer was possibly Olivares.

[66] "Memorandum for Mr. Henry A. Kissinger, The White House – Subject: Situation in Chile", 16 October 1972: *NARA*. Department of State – RG 59, Lab 3-2 Chile, Lab 6-1 Chile, Box 1395.

[67] Prats, *Memorias*, p. 304.

[68] Lahn (Santiago) to Bonn, 24 October 1973: *AA*. Bundesarchiv. Politisches Archiv. Bestand 33. Band 69. Betreff Chile 1972.

[69] "The October Strikes in Chile" – Hildyard (Santiago) to the Secretary of State (London), 28 November 1972: *FCO 7/2209*.

class criteria".[70] When Sáenz and others from Sofofa came to see Prats to complain, they were told bluntly that they took a "calculated risk" by joining a political strike.[71] But the government was soon forced to back away from one unpopular measure of censorship by releasing radio stations from nationwide military control. Moreover, it accepted Carmona's law for the control of armed groups, whose cutting edge would obviously be directed at the MIR in order to appease the PDC and the military. It was duly promulgated on 22 October. Middle-class housewives were cleaning out whatever shops were open and jeering at troops, calling them *chocolatines* (chocolate soldiers). Peasants joined construction workers in their display of anger at the government. The streets were veiled with the acrid smoke of tear gas which greeted rioters and demonstrators, along with *guanacos* – water-cannon – named after the lamoid that spits when annoyed. Civil disorder was fast becoming a way of life for many, including those who had hitherto considered themselves respectable society. The social contract was breaking with alarming and seemingly unstoppable rapidity.

If this alone were not problem enough, the strike had already cost the country more than $170 million.[72] It had to be ended before the economy bled to death. When on 20 October Allende broached once more the idea of drawing the military into government, he was again rebuffed by the leaders of the main parties to the coalition.[73] The sense of urgency was apparent now to all but the diehard. In the next few days several railway lines were sabotaged; landowners attacked a convoy of twenty-three tractors en route to spring sowing; in the Prado tunnel between Santiago and Valparaíso, lorries breaking the strike were fired upon; and the premises of the communist party were attacked in Santiago and Punto Arenas, along with those of the socialists in Antofagasta. Behind-the-scenes negotiations with the strikers were broken off on 27 October when political demands were made of the government to rescind changes made to the economy and society since 1970. The following day the national party responded by calling on the leaders of congress to declare parliament entirely independent of government. Although not publicised at the time,

[70] "¡Para avanzar hay que destruir el poder burgues!", Manifiesto de los trabajadores socialistas, Santiago, 23 October 1972: printed in a Socialist Party pamphlet entitled *Resolución Política del Congreso de La Serena*, which of course contains much more than that.
[71] Prats, *Memorias*, p. 305.
[72] *Economist*, 11 November 1972.
[73] Zorina et al., *Uroki Chili*, p. 347.

it emerged that top officers of the air force were tied to pro-coup elements in the army, including the recently retired general Canales. The key point of contact, according to Argentinian sources, "was Brigadier-General Francisco Herrera, linked to the fascist movement Patria y Libertad via its treasurer, Miguel Ubilla Torrealba, a man who, in turn, did not worry too much about concealing the ties he had with the Central Intelligence Agency of the United States (CIA)".[74]

Opposition to incorporation of the military into the government had been strongest among the socialists. The communists initially objected, as did MAPU, but Allende insisted that Chile was heading for civil war, and that by drawing in the military, they could lessen that possibility. The PS central committee insisted that they would leave the cabinet, though not UP, if Allende went ahead. They were still discussing the matter in plenum on the evening of 1 November when word came from Allende that he was proceeding with the idea. The socialists were thus left with the choice of acceptance or deserting the cabinet.[75] Since 4 November was the deadline for signing up candidates for the March elections, Allende effectively had them boxed in.[76] "We are not going to leave the government because this will mean provoking its fall", the central committee resolved.[77] Yet even in these desperate circumstances it is asserted that Allende's position won out by only one vote.[78] The PCCh was more positive. Indeed, interviewed by the Italian newspaper *Il Giorno* on 2 November, Corvalán stated that "the reorganisation of the cabinet is to be understood as an instrument, which, together with the fighting potential of the proletariat, guarantees the continuation and deepening of the revolutionary process". A month later he echoed his belief that incorporation of the military created "an unbreachable dam against sedition. It suffices to recall that it dealt a mortal blow to the political strike begun by the truckers."[79] But it was also "organised in agreement

[74] *Panorama* (Buenos Aires), 13 September 1973.
[75] "Partido Socialista: Informe del Comité Central al Pleno de Coya", November 1972: reprinted in Farias, *La izquierda chilena*, p. 3547.
[76] As ever well-informed, Miguel Enríquez outlined this in his speech to the MIR Central Committee on 3 November: ibid., p. 3460.
[77] "Partido Socialista …": ibid., p. 3551.
[78] "The October Strikes …"
[79] Corvalán's interview with Eduardo Labarca, December 1972: reprinted in González and Talavera, *Los mil días*, vol. 2, p. 1158.

with Christian Democracy and had as its basic objective (for the PDC at any rate) the impartiality of the parliamentary elections of March 1973; impartiality that was fundamental for the opposition".[80]

The military were sworn in on 2 November. The effect was immediately positive within the PDC. Tomic, for the party's centre left, had already suggested that only parliamentary elections could express the will of the people. The PN took an entirely different view, of course. This meant Allende's tactic had succeeded. A split now re-emerged on the right. In addition to Prats at interior, admiral Ismael Huerta Díaz became minister of public works and transport; brigadier-general Claudio Sepúlveda Donoso of the air force became minister of mines.[81] The CUT was also put into government, with its secretary-general, Rolando Calderón Aranguiz, at agriculture and its president, Figueroa, at labour. The former was a curious choice, since Calderón was a known extreme leftist within the PS, close to both the MIR and Cuba; although he had once been a protégé of Altamirano, Calderón now regarded him as too moderate. Calderón had pioneered *tomas* (land seizures) – via the Confederación Campesina Ranquil and the Federación Campesina e Indigena de Chile; he had trained as a guerrilla in Cuba, and he had subsequently been active in setting up a guerrilla training camp at Guayacan.[82]

The conclusion has to be that Allende was, once more, safeguarding the interests of the revolution while appearing to appease the right. It was also at this time that Fernando Flores Labra of MAPU, an Allende loyalist regarded by many as a communist, took the economics portfolio. This was prelude to a move by Prats to end the strike by the promise of compromise and the nullification of measures of expropriation taken during the conflict (which promise was subsequently reneged upon). On 5 November the cabinet was presented with a declaration from the government to the strikers "ordered by comrade Allende and elaborated by four ministers, without consulting either the leaders or the leaders of the socialist party".[83] General Prats, whose nickname fast became "Tapa" (lid) because he was a source of restraint, read it over the national radio network. On the

---

[80] Tomic, "Aclaraciones sobre ciertos hechos históricos", *Chile 1970–1973*, p. 196.

[81] Prats, *Memorias*, p. 310.

[82] S. Clissold to Miss Rycroft (Latin American Department), Miss Allott (IRD) and the Permanent Under-Secretary's Department (which handles MI6), 8 November 1972: *FCO 7/2209.*

[83] "Partido Socialista ...": Farias, *La izquierda chilena*, p. 3548.

following day the leaders of the Comando Nacional de Defensa Gremial declared an end to the three-week strike, which had by then spread to middle-class professional associations and other trades unions. On 7 November Allende – almost overcome at having escaped the very worst and with his famous *muñeca* once again vindicated – boasted to the Colombian ambassador: "Have you ever seen a more subtle wrist than mine?"[84] Yet by his action Allende had effectively recognised the armed forces as the third estate (after government and opposition). That this should have caused concern is evident from the British ambassador's assessment of the balance of opinion within that estate: "Certain generals," he noted, "some middle-ranking officers, and quite substantial sections of the rank and file, particularly in the Army and Air Force, favour the UP." But, he added, "the majority in each sector almost certainly favour the Opposition, and Right-wing Nationalist tendencies are strong, particularly among the middle-ranking officers and the NCOs".[85]

Significant though the support for the strikes might have been, the sober assessment in Washington was that although this wave was "the most serious challenge to Allende to date … it is not likely to topple his government".[86] A compromise was therefore not unexpected. The only note of dissent was that sounded by Altamirano, who insisted that those responsible for the strike receive punishment. He also warned that failure to act would merely produce "a transitory truce, while the enemies of the people heal their wounds, but it would mean an inevitable future confrontation".[87] The central committee plenum of the socialist party met on 10–12 November and reasserted the need "to advance without compromise", after which Altamirano argued for sustaining the momentum against striking businesses. Here he sounded his most anarchistic note: "One cannot construct a new society without destroying the old and, from an ideological viewpoint, until the ashes of the latter have been cast to the winds." He reasserted "the necessary priority of destroying the economic bases in which bourgeois power is established". And in a transparent reference to the recent strikes, he asserted that

[84] As reported by the British ambassador, Hildyard, to London, 28 November 1972: *FCO 7/2209*.
[85] Ibid.
[86] "Chile: Major Challenge to President Allende", Intelligence Note, Bureau of Intelligence and Research, State Department: *NARA*. Department of State: RG 59, LAB 3-2 Chile to LAB 3-2 Col, Box 1395.
[87] Radio broadcast, 7 November 1972: *Las Noticias de Ultima Hora*, 8 November 1972.

"If the bourgeoisie itself abandons its legality when it is convenient, a revolutionary can have no reason at all that induces him to fear and respect it."[88] He also boasted to the Cuban daily *Granma* on 25 November: "Our party is creating throughout the country communal committees which are taking control over the distribution of products and the business of transportation, and leading the fight against speculation. These organisations", he promised, "will ultimately have to become the embryo of independent people's power."[89]

These were what became known as the *cordones industriales*. They were very much a socialist party experiment, distinctive from their predecessors, the UP committees at plant level that had been set up to secure the new government and which very much involved the communist party and the CUT. The *cordones* were based on the trades unions collaborating at local level – without official CUT approbation – as a first line of defence to protect enterprises taken over by the state. They were not organs of massed worker participation, but essentially involved "those linked to [political] … parties".[90] Each *cordon* had its own well-defined jurisdiction, and within it an assembly was formed of delegates from enterprises within the locality. They were not directly elected but were sent in by the trades unions from the various plants. What gave the *cordones* status was the strike of October 1972. MIR activist Mario Olivares, working at Easton Chile, part of the Vicuña Mackenna *cordon* in Santiago, describes the *cordones* as "embryonic organs of power, local power". Not everyone agreed, however, that they should be so. The PCCh, sections of the PS, MAPU and IC "saw it basically as an apparatus of local power but not to the extent of bringing into question the state apparatus itself".[91] What they could all agree upon, during the October strike and thereafter as the black market seized the economy by the throat, was that the *cordones* should provide an alternative and sympathetic provision of goods to the local working class. But what of course attracted the most attention were the higher political ambitions and what they augured for the supporters of the existing socio-economic order. "In this sense," one former activist recalls, "the cordones had acquired

---

[88]   *Punto Final* (supplement), 13 February 1973.
[89]   Zorina et al., *Uroki Chili*, p. 353.
[90]   Testimony of activist José Moya, who worked at IRT in Santiago: Gaudichaud, *Poder Popular*, p. 124.
[91]   Ibid., p. 171.

a political relevance and an image of political power far beyond that which really existed."[92] The right never had to look far for confirmation of its deepest anxieties. Yet at local level among the *cordones*, sentiment was very different. PCCh militant Juan Alarcón describes their reaction to the truckers' strike: "There was great support for the people's government – there always was – but we felt the power there: we felt that we had a people's government, that we had a workers' government but yet we did not hold power, they [the truckers] were still more powerful than ourselves."[93]

Washington's belief at this stage was that the "opposition is not, and probably cannot quickly become, organized in any systematic way to seize power from the government on its own, but can only hope that its manifestations of massive protest will oblige the military to take over and dictate a turn-around in the government's political-economic program".[94] Here the hand of the United States had scarcely been invisible. In the *Observer*, Hugh O'Shaughnessy annoyed the Foreign and Commonwealth Office in London by pointing out from Santiago: "Amid all the political speculation, one big mystery remains. Who is paying for the present strikes and why have so many dollars started floating around on the black market?"[95] Professor Richard Fagen noted: "Those of us living in Santiago were amazed at the seeming ease with which tens of thousands of persons without visible income – and without savings because of the inflationary spiral – were able to support themselves. The dollar rate on the black market dropped, indicating that fresh sources of currency were flowing into the country. It was everyday speculation in Santiago, both on the Right and Left, that the United States was funding the walkouts".[96] It is striking that in his memoir the then US ambassador Nathaniel Davis is entirely silent on this subject. The biographer of the head of the western hemisphere division at the CIA, Tom Shackley, tells us on the basis of interviews with those serving under him, that the station in Santiago was "given $100,000 to distribute to anti-Allende business organizations".[97] This would not have included AIFLD funding.

[92] Pablo Muñoz testimony: ibid., p. 318.
[93] Ibid., p. 103.
[94] *NARA. Chile Declassification Project. NSC.* Memorandum for Henry Kissinger, 16 October 1972.
[95] "Crunch week for Allende", *Observer*, 22 October 1972.
[96] "The Intrigues before Allende Fell", *Los Angeles Times*, 6 October 1974.
[97] Corn, *Blond Ghost*, p. 251.

The former head of covert operations at the CIA, Ray Cline, was by 1972 in charge of intelligence and research at the state department. That meant he dealt with the 40 Committee as the right-hand man of the under secretary for political affairs. During the period between April 1972 and December 1974, up to 40 covert operations were agreed to by the committee "without a single meeting". Instead written submissions would be taken and a vote garnered by telephone.[98] This procedure will have encompassed the latter stages of the covert activities against Allende. Cline subsequently acknowledged that CIA efforts to oust UP "included the direct financing of a number of anti-Allende trade groups and labor unions, including truckers". Although both the state department and the CIA were dubious of the value of the operations, the White House "decided to push the program".[99] Furthermore, US intelligence sources later told the *New York Times* that the majority of the $8 million allocated for CIA covert operations in Chile in 1972 and 1973 did not, as claimed, go to support the press, but went instead to provide means of support for those on strike against the Allende regime. "Among those heavily subsidized, these sources said, were the organizers of a nationwide truck strike that lasted 26 days in the fall of 1972 ..." All of this, it was asserted, was approved by the 40 Committee.[100] However, it failed in its primary objective, outwitted by Allende.

In the aftermath of the strike, on 30 October the general secretary of the Chilean government, Hernán del Canto, handed the East German ambassador a secret estimate formulated by the US embassy in Santiago. Summed up by ambassador Spindler, the document drew three conclusions about recent events: first, the "aim of the operation was not attained (from which it is obvious that they had the overthrow of the Allende government in mind)"; second, the attempt "to split the working-class" and "subordinate the army to the interests of the USA" and "prop up an anti-national alliance" had failed; and, third, the "revolutionary process in Chile runs more deeply than hitherto suspected".[101]

In London at the Cabinet Office, charged with the joint intelligence assessments, Lord Gordon-Lennox scheduled for discussion at the

---

[98] Testimony of James Gardner: *US Intelligence Agencies and Activities*, p. 827.
[99] *New York Times*, 17 October 1974.
[100] Ibid., 20 September 1974.
[101] Spindler (Santiago) to Axen (Berlin), 30 October 1972 – *SAPMO*. DY/30/IV B 2/20 259.

intelligence group the "possible reaction of the United States Government to events in Chile if they became convinced that Chile's slide into the Communist camp was irreversible by peaceful means, or on the point of becoming so". "I suppose", he wrote, "that some elements in the US Administration, under a President much fortified by a recent electoral success, might take a more hawkish attitude than at present?"[102] This soon proved a prescient observation. But Allende was too buoyed up by his tactical victory to notice what had become plain to others. It appears that in perpetually pirouetting between various forces, Allende now calculated the need to lean further to the left. The defeat of what proved to be the first of several military coup attempts had left him blithely optimistic that the opposition was much less powerful than expected. This mood of intoxicating elation was doubtless strengthened by news of the US embassy's secret verdict already cited. This may have prompted a dour fatalism among some in Washington. But Nixon and Kissinger were not so resigned, and they were the only ones that counted.

Allende's starry-eyed mood was fully shared by Corvalán when the latter visited East Berlin on 23–27 November. Outlining the apparent fact that US interests and domestic reactionaries had failed in September to bring down the government "with the help of a group of military officers" led by Canales, Corvalán went on to boast that "a considerable blow had been delivered against reaction. This government held a gun to its chest and within forty-eight hours the strike had ended."[103] In contrast Corvalán's presentation of Chile's economic position was gloomy indeed. On the eve of Allende's official visit to Moscow the following week in search of financial assistance, Chile needed a further $100 million in credit to offset its foreign exchange deficit for 1972. But the question was also what would happen when the copper embargo was extended. In Moscow Corvalán had already talked with Viktor Kirilenko and Boris Ponomarev for five hours, and for a further three hours with general secretary Leonid Brezhnev and Ponomarev, who headed the

---

[102] Lord Gordon-Lennox to John Robson, Latin American Department of the Foreign and Commonwealth Office, 27 October 1972: *FCO 7/2209.*

[103] *SAPMO.* DY/30/IV B2/20 259 Information Nr. 121/72 für das Politbüro. Betrifft: Gespräch des Ersten Sekretärs des ZK der SED, Genossen Erich Honecker, mit dem Generalsekretär des ZK der KP Chiles, Genossen Luis Corvalán, am 24.11.72 im Hause des ZK.

party's department dealing with fraternal parties. Corvalán claimed agreement that "in the event of a broader copper embargo from the USA, the Soviet Union and the other socialist countries can buy Chile's copper". Corvalán also raised the idea of covering a $220 million deficit for 1973 half from Russian coffers, the rest from other members of the Soviet bloc. General secretary of the East German communist party Erich Honecker was not very forthcoming, however, pointing out that the GDR alone gave North Vietnam $100 million in aid per year and had extensive commitments elsewhere in the world.[104] Anxiety would indeed be expressed in London that blocking Chile's access to loans might drive it into the arms of the Soviet bloc.[105] But the British government need not have worried.

Corvalán's unsuccessful visit to East Berlin should have alerted Santiago to the likelihood that Allende's visit to Moscow that December in expectation of financial assistance might also prove futile. It was understood even by outside observers that "Since Allende came to power the Russians have seemed most reluctant to become too involved in the country whose Government they do not control and [which is] about as far from the Soviet Union as one could get."[106] The Russians were forewarned that UP was a chaotic mess. A succession of UP delegations had arrived in Moscow with no prior co-ordination or notification – which infuriated the Chilean embassy – in stark contrast to the rigid regimen for Russians visiting Santiago (whether under ambassador Alexeev or his successor Alexander Basov), whose schedules were all tightly planned by the Soviet embassy.[107] The fact that the Allende delegation of eighteen was unaccountably swollen by an additional forty-one accompanying the team, including spouses,[108] illustrated Allende's inability to exert his authority to streamline his own administration; it was a symptom of the very problems that the Russians were being asked to help solve.

[104] Ibid.

[105] Note by Hankey, 12 December 1972: *FCO 7/2410.*

[106] Robson (Foreign Office) to Lord Gordon-Lennox (Cabinet Office), 29 November 1972: *FCO 7/2209.*

[107] See the despatch complaining of this practice sent by the Chilean embassy to the Ministry, 18 November 1971: Chile. *MAE. Memorias de Embajada. 1971 – Embajada de Chile en Rusia. URSS, Embachile Moscow. Of. Conf. R.*

[108] Mano Valenzuela (Cabinet, Dirección General, Santiago) to Embachile, 17 November 1972: *Chile. MAE. Memorias de Embajada. 1972. URSS. Embachile. Moscu. Ofic. Conf. D.*

A total of $80 million was needed to meet Chile's requirements to service short-term credits due a group of Latin American countries on 5 January, merely for the first quarter of 1973. The UP delegation was badly fractured: not just between specialists and the rest, but also politically between members of the communist party and some of the socialists who were strongly anti-Soviet.[109] To ease the negotiations communist party secretary Corvalán and Figueroa of the CUT had further separate conversations with their Soviet colleagues. But there was little understanding between Chileans and Russians. The officials from Gosplan appeared to talk another language, and not just Russian, which was impossible to interpret to the other side. Moreover, all the Chileans appeared to share doubts about the potential applicability of Soviet technology to Chilean conditions. That was why previous and substantial credits already granted Chile by Moscow – some 200 million roubles – had gone almost entirely unused. This lack of take-up puzzled the Russians as to why the Chileans were asking now for 240 million roubles. But it was the dollar credit that was crucial. Allende's arrival on 6 December settled nothing. The president of the Soviet central bank told the delegation that Moscow was unable to meet their needs.

Allende was "dejected", the delegation demoralised. Even party-to-party contacts through Corvalán yielded nothing.[110] Allende then obtained a meeting with Brezhnev, as a result of which discussions with Gosplan reopened. How was the debt to be repaid? The Chileans responded: through copper exports. To which the Russians retorted: "and why does the USSR need copper, when we have invested extensively in the copper mines of Siberia and we have sufficient for domestic needs?" The Russians then asked for projections of the Chilean balance of payments. They also wanted to know why more credits were needed when Chile had used only one percent of previous credits granted. An embarrassing exchange then occurred as the problems of technological compatibility were raised.[111] Finally, the Russians caved in and offered $45 million. That was as far as the Soviet leaders were prepared to go. Desperate still to forestall default, Allende asked to see Brezhnev once

---

[109] Gonzalo Martner, *El Gobierno del Presidente Allende 1970–1973: una evaluación* (Chile 1988), p. 222.

[110] Ibid., pp. 223–4.

[111] Ibid., p. 225.

more, but the general secretary was hospitalised after a heart attack. At the reception before his departure, Allende buttonholed the other Soviet leaders but to no avail. The UP minister of national planning, Martner, recalls: "Allende was worn out and withdrew along with Ernesto Torrealba and myself. He asked to rest in a small room, where tired and full of sadness, he raised many things from which I remember that he said 'never have I gone to such lengths … and we have not resolved the principal issue, the ALAC [Latin American creditors] will declare us insolvent and this is the end …'"[112]

The contrast between the parsimony with which the Soviet Union treated Chile and its profligate treatment of unreliable Arab allies such as Egypt and Syria was striking. But the latter were beneficiaries of arms sales on credit which did not go through normal financial channels in Moscow but were handled directly by the ministry of defence and its subordinate industries (with Brezhnev's permission, of course). The Soviet Union's handling of Cuba's problems was on another scale entirely. The Chileans could not help but compare their position with that of Cuba. Granted, when the head of Gosplan, Baibakov, had visited Havana in April (1971) his hosts were treated to some tough talking on the subject of economic management.[113] Yet, as the Chilean embassy in Moscow discovered, the Soviet Union granted Cuba credits at no interest to cover its balance of payments deficit from 1973 to 1975, with repayment to begin only in 1986 and extended over twenty-five years. The same applied to debts outstanding to Moscow since the Cuban revolution.[114]

In retrospect, the impact of larger forces on Soviet policy became clear to those in Chile. Chonchol later noted that when Cuba first received Soviet largesse, intense rivalry prevailed between Moscow and Washington, Cuba being a vehicle for Soviet expansion in the hemisphere.

> At the time of the appearance of UP the situation had changed. We were witness to a degree of rapprochement between the Great Powers. Peaceful co-existence was entering a phase of intense diplomatic and economic

[112] Ibid., p. 226. For a similar account, see Corvalán, *De lo vivido*, pp. 144–7.
[113] "Annual Review for 1971", 1 January 1972, from the British embassy in Havana: *FCO 7/2260*.
[114] Mario Darrigrandi (Moscow) to Ministry (Santiago), 12 January 1973: Chile. *MAE. Memorias de Embajada. 1973. Rusia. URSS. Embachile. Moscu. Ord. R.*

activity with a view to normalising relations between the United States and the Soviet Union and to finding for each the means of respecting the sphere of influence of the other.[115]

Clearly Moscow shared Kissinger's view that spheres of interest were best respected – Cuba excepting – even if areas beyond remained fair game. The lack of realism displayed by Allende can only have reinforced that resolve. "The Soviet Ambassador says sadly that the Chileans have been making all the mistakes which the Russians made in the early days of their revolution", the British noted.[116]

Frustrated and depressed, Allende left the snows of Moscow for tropical Havana, arriving on 11 December. Here the contrast with the bleak Moscow meetings could not have been greater. Greeted in friendship, he was driven in an open jeep by Castro through the port of Matanzas. Both then took a yacht out of Varadero in an ostentatious display of close co-operation; symbolically, though, Castro was up at the wheel and Allende was below decks in charge of the engine. In the elusive language of the Chilean chargé d'affaires – desperate not to offend by being too honest – the president "probed the nuances of difference between the two revolutionary processes" in lengthy conversation with Castro.[117] This brief reference belies the importance of what took place. In fact, Allende had become increasingly frustrated by Castro's increasingly heavy-handed interference in Chilean internal affairs as UP failed to follow through on its success in beating the strike. Allende now succeeded in persuading his friend to draw back, the effects of which were visible to US intelligence by the New Year. DIA analyst Paul Wallner later told a congressional committee that "Cuban support to Chilean terrorists included training in Cuba and Chile, provision of security and insurgency advisers, and arms shipments reported as late as January of this year [1973]."[118] The clear implication of this assessment was that these activities ceased as of the end of January. Allende therefore won an important argument with Castro – at least for the time being.

---

[115] Jacques Chonchol, *Chili: de l'échec à l'espoir*, ed. T. Nallet (Paris 1977), p. 100.

[116] 13 March 1973: *FCO 7/2410*.

[117] Gonzalo Rojas (Havana) to Ministry (Santiago), 20 December 1972: Chile. *MAE. Memorias de Embajada. 1972. Cuba. Embachile. Ofic. Conf. R.*

[118] Testimony, 31 October 1973: *United States and Chile*, p. 160.

To sympathetic eyes – even from a great distance – UP was into uncharted waters on course for disaster. Foreign minister Almeyda visited China at the beginning of 1973 and was taken aback by his conversation with wily prime minister Chou En-lai when outlining what progress Santiago was making towards its economic goals, a preliminary to requesting aid. According to Almeyda:

> Contrary to those in Chile who were criticising the Government for not accelerating the pace of development, under the slogan "advance without compromise", Chou En-lai reckoned that the power available to the government in all its forms – political, social and military – was insufficient to take risks beyond a certain limit. He even believed that this limit may have already been exceeded. The rear, to use his words, was exposed, and the vanguard ran the risk of becoming isolated from the rear by an attack on its flanks.[119]

Not only were the armed forces a problem; so was the economy, which was in dire straits and would require sacrifices to sort out. "He warned, on the other hand, that the Chilean people did not appear to be aware of the situation; badly oriented by a programme which was purely one of making claims … " Chou went on:

> … Chairman Mao has said that things could work out or not work out, and one has to foresee other possibilities. You have outlined to me a policy for emerging from the crisis that the country faces, especially with reference to the financial situation and the balance of payments. If it works out, that's fine. But, if this policy does not work out, what are you intending to do?

At this, Almeyda belatedly realised just how precarious Chile's situation actually was. And the Chinese had no intention of providing any assistance of substance. In the follow-up letter to Allende written on 3 February, Chou bluntly drove the point home: "what is fundamental for developing countries is to base everything on one's own resources, that is to say, adopt self-reliance as the principal means, and external assistance as a complementary measure".[120]

---

[119] Almeyda, *Reencuentro*, p. 184.
[120] For the full text see ibid., pp. 186–8.

The Chinese were not alone in this opinion. In Algeria president Boumediene had reached identical conclusions. And in Moscow that spring, KGB chief Yuri Andropov asked the head of his information and analysis branch, Latin Americanist Nikolai Leonov, whether it was worth granting aid of $30 million to enable Chile to finance further imports. Leonov has recalled how difficult it was to give an honest response, but that:

> A business-like discussion of every aspect, domestic and foreign, of the political situation in Chile led to the conclusion that the Allende government had neither the means nor the will to alter the fundamental tendencies active in the country and destroying little by little the basis of society. As a result of these tendencies the government was doomed and its overthrow merely a matter of time. And $30 million was in no way going to change the situation and could just delay the denouement for a certain, quite short period of time.[121]

At times it must have seemed that the only people who did not appreciate the significance of what was happening were at La Moneda in Santiago.

---

[121] Nikolai Leonov, *Likolet'e* (Moscow 1995), pp. 125–6.

7

THE HIDDEN HAND MOVES

… our hand doesn't show on this one …

Nixon to Kissinger,
11.50am, 16 September 1973[1]

A great deal hung upon the results of the congressional elections, forthcoming in March 1973, since the contest for the presidency would not take place until September 1976. Incorporation into the cabinet of the most senior officers guaranteed for the opposition that the ballot would take place; for UP it assured that elections could take place in safety. While the outcome still lay in prospect, more moderate elements within the opposition could hope that overwhelming victory by them would block and perhaps even turn the tide of revolutionary change. For the socialists, communists and their allies an enhancement of the UP's vote would confirm the revolutionary course through to the autumn of 1976 – provided, however, the economic crisis could be solved in the meantime. Failure by UP would inevitably split the governing coalition, which was already divided over the management of the economy and the speed of advance. Failure by the PDC would drive christian democracy towards the right, the national party and malcontents within the military; and, behind them all, into the hands of the United States.

The PCCh were not optimistic. To Corvalán the strike of the middle classes was scarcely a surprise given rapid inflation, shortages of goods, the revelation that militants of the PS were engaged in military training, and the "disastrous" activities of the extreme left. Relations between

[1] Telcon, 16 September 1973: *NARA*, published on the GWU, National Security Archive website.

communists and socialists were not good. Moreover the "lack of minimal understanding between Altamirano and Allende" meant no meeting of minds. Corvalán did not think the PDC had any illusion it could win the forthcoming elections, but neither did he think the left could attain a majority in congress.[2] And from the viewpoint of those who wished to lower the revolutionary profile of the régime, the second congress of MAPU was a devastating setback. There on 3–8 December 1972 the more moderate leadership of Jaime Gazmuri was supplanted by the extreme left under Garretón, former undersecretary for the economy. The main task, in his mind, was "the establishment of a truly proletarian revolutionary party".[3] The defeated faction then set up a more moderate party, the MAPU Obrero Campesino (MOC). The drift further to the left now seemed unstoppable. "It is now clear", the British ambassador reluctantly acknowledged, "that President Allende is prepared to go the whole way to a fully centrally planned economy."[4]

The communists were, however, now slowly applying the brakes. On 14 January 1973 Millas, as minister of economics, put to congress a bill legitimising the takeover of 93 enterprises and proposing nationalisation with compensation of 49 more; he also suggested returning to their private owners 123 enterprises, including those requisitioned in October,[5] and setting up a special committee to decide which other companies of strategic importance required state ownership. These proposals were backed by his own party, the PCCh, the radicals and the military ministers, and were clearly intended in a spirit of compromise with the more moderate christian democrats in mind. Teitelboim expressed best the long-held communist position that christian democracy could be broken by deft exploitation of its warring factions. The PDC, he said, is

> … an amalgam, a "multi-class" party … we are helping along a struggle between those who entirely side with the right, within the framework of a reactionary strategy that points to civil war, and those who do not want this. We do not put everyone in the same bag. And our stance can influence the

[2] Conversation with Soviet ambassador Basov, 13 September 1972: *Estudios Públicos*, p. 442.

[3] Zorina et al., *Uroki Chili*, p. 354. Guillermo Garretón is now a wealthy businessman: *Qué Pasa*, 5 September 2003.

[4] Chile: Annual Review, 8 January 1973: *FCO 7/2409*.

[5] For the lists of companies: *Las Noticias de Ultima Hora*, 29 January 1973: González and Talavera, *Los mil días*, vol. 1, pp. 586–7.

PDC itself because it is an oscillating force without a fixed centre. We must not do anything that facilitates its betrothal to the right.

In particular, Teitelboim argued, two groups had separated from christian democracy since 1970 "and no one is to say this will not continue. If they had had a bridge open to the base of the PDC offering an alternative that did not involve ceasing to be christians or converting to Marxism, the drain from the catholic base towards Unidad Popular would in our opinion have been all the greater."[6] That draining would require reaching out to the christian democrats at all levels. Radomiro Tomic was thus correct in later claiming: "I lived the process in person and believe that its substance can be summed up in one sentence: the strategy of Unidad Popular *was never to collaborate with Christian Democracy*, but to divide it and to destroy it."[7] But the strategy – although obviously damaging to the PDC – none the less aroused the wrath and opposition of Altamirano and Garretón, now acting in tandem. During an interview straight after the March elections Altamirano was asked whether he denied all possibility of opening negotiations with christian democracy. His firm response was "Absolutely yes."[8] The push to the left was still far stronger among socialists than the attraction of the centre. On 24 January the MIR and the PS had exchanged letters agreeing the terms on which they would present a united front at the forthcoming elections.[9]

The splitting of the left at the ballot for the health workers' federation (FENATS) early in 1973 – the socialists and communists on opposite sides – which resulted in a victory for the christian democrats should have amply demonstrated the consequences of adopting such a line.[10] Yet it failed to have a salutary effect. What the socialists, MAPU and the MIR regarded as a government attempt to appease the bourgeoisie now prompted outright confrontation within UP. On 26 January the PS political committee rejected Millas's proposals and suggested that their representative at the ministry of economics, an under-secretary, resign, which he duly did. Allende hurriedly backtracked in a letter to the PS

[6] Interview with *Politique-Hebdo*, June 1972: reproduced in Condal, *Il Cile*, pp. 96–7.
[7] Tomic, "Aclaraciones … ", p. 198.
[8] Also reproduced in Condal, *Il Cile*, p. 114.
[9] Zorina et al., *Uroki Chili*, p. 359.
[10] *Las Noticias de Ultima Hora*, 19 March 1973.

political committee and said the companies listed by Millas for restitution would not necessarily be returned to their owners.[11] Even after, on 8 February, Corvalán replied positively to a letter from Altamirano to halt the polemics, Altamirano and Garretón together publicly attacked the Millas proposals at a meeting of trades union activists four days later. Indeed the socialist party organised a number of meetings throughout the country to do the same.

The opposition, which already controlled congress, were more optimistic than the PCCh about the forthcoming elections. Believing 60–70 percent of the population to be against UP, Frei told West German diplomats that "the opposition reckons on an overwhelming victory".[12] The results thus came as a surprise. On 4 March UP gained only 43.39 percent of the vote (1,589,025), a drop from 49.74 percent in the local elections a year before. The opposition electoral front, the *confederación democrática* (*CODE*), won 54.7 percent of the vote (2,003,047) and thus continued to be able to deny the government legislation based on socialist aspirations despite UP's acquisition of two new senators and six new deputies. "Opposition leaders were uniformly optimistic about the probable outcome of the congressional elections." The US government had reported that CODE's failed expectations were attributable to "how important the 'class struggle' has become to Chilean low income groups which have identified with the Allende government. Economic problems are a burning issue for the opposition's electorate, but less so for the Chilean lower classes, including newly enfranchised illiterates who are apparently convinced that Allende will eventually improve their lot." The United States realised that CODE had underestimated the impact of votes of 18-to-21-year-olds. Faulty opinion polling that had predicted more than 60 percent of the vote going to the opposition also played its part. The US government, which had thrown in at least $1,627,666 to support the opposition (not counting contributions from business), was inevitably disappointed too.[13]

---

[11] *Las Noticias de Ultima Hora*, 30 January 1973: reprinted in González and Talavera, *Los mil días*, vol. 1, pp. 587–8.

[12] Lahn (Santiago) to Bonn, 25 September 1972: *AA*. Politisches Archiv des Auswärtiges Amt. Bestand 33. Band 639. Betreff Chile 1972.

[13] *NARA Chile Declassification Project*. *NSC*. "Outcome of 4 March 1973 Chilean Congressional Elections".

The elections proved the turning point at home and abroad. At home they meant that the christian democrats had lost a chance to overthrow the government because two-thirds of seats in the senate were required to do this and had not been won; but lost too was any hope of the ruling coalition that its revolution could be completed unhindered: the opposition still had seats sufficient to have ministers condemned and dismissed and to challenge the legality of various executive orders. The stalemate tended to strengthen the two extremes of the political spectrum: neither for their differing reasons was prepared to wait any longer. Disappointment also exacerbated the impatience of the military and further undermined confidence in the economy. The constitutional order began to disintegrate as a consequence.

Though on the left as well as the right the results were greeted with dismay, Altamirano issued a characteristically defiant statement: "There has not been and will not be a change in government, nor alterations that do not advance with compromise to the conquest of power and the construction of socialism."[14] But to the realist the prospects for the revolution now looked distinctly bleak. The best that could be said of the electorate came from Teitelboim: "they voted with their heads against their own stomachs".[15] The economic crisis was indeed driving many into the hands of the extreme right, and the "socialists tend to confront economic problems by treating them as pre-eminently aspects of the political struggle" rather than in their own terms.[16] In agriculture conditions had worsened because the government ceased its predecessor's practice of allowing *asentamientos* to go private, with the result that uncertainty removed incentives for investment.[17] Private sector figures on agricultural production estimated output for 1972–73 as down 22 percent on the previous year; wheat production fell a colossal 34 percent. These were the worst figures in living memory, with the exception of the drought of 1969–70.[18] In the economy as a whole, the World Bank estimates inflation to have risen between 27 and 35 percent in 1971, the money supply having increased by 114 percent.[19] The difference between

[14] *Las Noticias de Ultima Hora*, 9 March 1973: González and Talavera, *Los mil días*, p. 600.
[15] Quoted by Pajetta of the PCI: *Archivio PCI*. Estera. Cile. 046.189-199.
[16] Noted by Pajetta, ibid.
[17] Levy et al., *Chile: An Economy*, pp. 68–9.
[18] *Bolsa Review*, vol. 7, no. 82, October 1973, pp. 494–5.
[19] Levy et al., *Chile: An Economy*, p. 70.

the two was apparently accounted for by a decrease in the velocity of circulation caused by the hoarding of cash. Wages had risen appreciably, particularly for the lower paid, even allowing for the erosion due to inflation. And as wages and salaries rose so profits declined.[20] Despite falling revenues from copper exports – the real price dropped to $49.3 from $64.1 (1970–71) – the government had held the exchange rate constant until December 1971 and tightened controls on imports for other than the public sector. Copper exports were also held back by the loss of managerial and technical expertise after nationalisation, even after the price rose exceptionally high in the first quarter of 1973. The most alarming sign, however, was the increase in food imports by 43 percent in real terms, while capital goods imported dropped 15 percent. This was reflected in the balance of trade: a surplus of $95 million (1970) turned into a deficit of $90 million, leaving a total shortfall of $205 million.[21] 1972 had seen a breakdown in control over state enterprises and the public sector as a whole. Production was stagnant, even though unemployment continued to fall. The World Bank's adjusted price index shows inflation rising in 1972 as high as 145.6 percent (as against the official figure of 77.8 percent). The difference was largely to be accounted for in the government measuring the prices they themselves set which, with goods in short supply, led to black market retail prices that were not recognised in UP statistics. This was critical. That year the black market rate of exchange reached ten times the official rate; rising to a colossal 40:1 in the following year. Consumer loans were being paid at from 74 to 254 percent.[22] The damaging effect on living standards of the least well-off arose in part from the fact that the wage and family allowance adjustments made by government matched the official price index, not the real rise in prices, even if the goods sought could not be obtained on the open market.[23] The World Bank summed up the situation for the citizen in the following terms:

> The massive wage and salary adjustments of January 1971 resulted in a quick and considerable improvement in the real earnings of workers in the lowest

[20] Ibid., p. 71.
[21] Ibid., p. 72.
[22] Ibid., p. 77.
[23] Ibid., p. 78.

pay brackets. These gains rapidly began to fade away, however, as inflation accelerated. Despite the increasing frequency of adjustments, by the third quarter of 1972 the real minimum wage had fallen below the average level of 1970, and by the third quarter of 1973 it had fallen to or below the levels of the mid-1960s. In the meantime, smaller nominal adjustments were applied to the white-collar minimum salary; by the end of 1971, its real value had already fallen below the 1970 average, and it declined steadily thereafter.[24]

Had social welfare provision compensated by raising the living standards of the population as a whole, the burden would have been easier to bear. But when one looks at components such as rates of infant mortality (health) and literacy (education), what catches the eye is the continuity of progress between Chile under Frei and Chile under Allende, rather than any marked improvement from 1970 to 1973. Infant deaths per year stood at 29,394 in 1965, for example, dropping gradually each year to 20,750 in the election year of 1970. Thereafter they continued to fall slowly to 19,271 in 1971, rose slightly to 19, 752 in 1972 and fell again to 18,029 in 1973, the year of the coup. They also continued to drop thereafter under Pinochet.[25] Similarly with literacy: educational enrolment grew steadily under Alessandri in 1960 from 1,506,287 through to 2,523,605 in 1970, and therefore continued the slight upward climb to 2,836,470 in 1971, 2,985,455 in 1972 and 3,101,195 in 1973, falling off slightly thereafter under Pinochet.[26]

Sustaining support for UP even among its core voters, whose standard of living had initially risen appreciably at the onset of the administration,[27] was thus in jeopardy. When one goes on to consider those elements in the population already opposed to UP from the skilled working classes and the middle classes, it is easy to see how sullen suspicion was to balloon into overt hostility.

[24] Ibid., p. 79.

[25] Markos Mamalakis, *Historical Statistics of Chile: Demography and Labor Force*, vol. 2 (Westport/ London 1978), p. 44. There is a general belief that the absolute levels are overstated because of the means of garnering the figures, but the methodology is the same throughout, so the relative differences are accepted to be valid.

[26] Ibid., p. 165.

[27] US ambassador Korry, for example, stated in July 1971 that 90% of all Chileans were now better off than before: *United States and Chile*, p. 9.

Yet hotheads within government followed Altamirano in pressing ahead with socialism of the most radical kind. Everyone agreed that education had long been an area in need of reform. Now on 9 March the ministry issued proposals for "A Unified National School System" – Escuela Nacional Unificada (ENU) – in the same terms as the decree for democratising education that had already been rejected by the comptroller general (Controloría General) which, together with the supreme court, acted as legal guardian of the constitution. These proposals aimed at substituting for "an educational system which is authoritarian, competitive and traditionalist, destined to produce uncommitted and egoistic individuals focused on their own personal success" a system that instilled "skills, concepts, habits, opinions, attitudes and values favourable to collective labour". The proposals would "contribute to the harmonic development of the personality of the young in the values of humanistic socialism".[28] The least that could be said of this objective was that it represented a clear threat to those who favoured religious education or freedom from indoctrination into socialism. It breached article 10 (clause 7) of the statute of constitutional guarantees agreed between the PDC and UP that had enabled Allende to take the presidency. The statute had explicitly provided that the national education system would be "democratic and pluralist and will not have an officially partisan orientation".[29] Given that the new proposals were scheduled for consideration by congress – in which the opposition had a veto – their form and content were ineptly conceived and were bound to raise rather than lower the political temperature. Matters were not helped when, in the face of intense criticism from both the episcopacy and the opposition, education minister Jorge Tapia Valdés defiantly stated that "to oppose the *ENU* is to render oneself guilty of deepening the educational crisis … and to place oneself in opposition to the country". He went on: "the decision has been taken: this is not the moment to doubt for one second that the reform will go ahead … the legitimacy, the legality of the reform … means that the months ahead are simply for making the *ENU* a reality and putting it into practice in June and the beginning of the second semester".[30] By April, however, the

[28] González and Talavera, *Los mil días*, vol. 2, pp. 1217–32.

[29] "Ley Num. 17.398": ibid., vol. 2, p. 976.

[30] *El Mercurio*, 6 April 1973: ibid., p. 616.

government had taken fright and quietly shelved these controversial proposals for another year.[31]

Within government the PCCh as usual had its ears closest to the ground. It reluctantly but realistically concluded that to all intents and purposes the entire experiment of Unidad Popular stood in jeopardy unless drastic corrective measures were taken. Corvalán had had in mind an unusual solution ever since the inclusion of Prats and his fellow officers in Allende's cabinet. In December 1972, when asked whether the presence of the military in government would prove temporary, he had answered: "The possibility is not discounted ... that it might have to continue beyond March and that the collaboration between military and civilians in the government could be turned into a further peculiarity of the Chilean revolutionary process."[32]

That was not to be the case, however: communist influence within government had waned considerably since the heady days of the previous autumn. On 2 March, two days before the elections, Allende spoke to the commanders-in-chief and told them he intended to make changes to his cabinet whatever the results might be. On 27 March he announced a new team that excluded the military, on the grounds that their inclusion had originally been motivated by the need "to ensure respect for order and authority, to assure public order and in general guarantee democratic development in all national activity". He none the less continued to talk vaguely about measures to ensure that the armed forces become more integrated in the development of the country; whatever that might have meant.[33] Allende may not have known that in the run-up to the elections opposition had been strongly expressed within the council of generals against remaining in government. Only three – Guillermo Pickering Vásquez, Hermán Brady Roche and Mario Sepúlveda Squella – backed Prats in favouring a continued presence. Prats none the less prevailed with the proviso that Allende moderate the régime's behaviour.[34] For the communists, Corvalán continued to press for a quasi-military solution to the country's growing problems. Once again, he assumed Chile could

[31] Chancery (Santiago) to London, 4 May 1973: *FCO 7/2410.*

[32] Corvalán's interview with Eduardo Labarca, December 1972: González and Talavera, *Los mil días,* vol. 2, p. 1159.

[33] *Las Ultimas Noticias,* 28 March 1973: ibid., vol. 1, pp. 610–11.

[34] The source for this was Robert Moss, who invariably turns out to be correct. Noted by Clissold, 13 April 1973: *FCO 7/2410.*

defy political practice common elsewhere. But he had not counted on the rigidity of Allende's convictions.

No one doubted that what Allende was attempting for Chile would have to fit formally within the constitutional framework he had inherited, though he was subjected continuously to pressure for revolutionary solutions, as with the educational reform. A CIA report on the elections of March 1973 referred to Allende's preference "to win through legalistic methods".[35] In May, for example, the president sought to avoid calling a state of emergency as recommended by the military; and in a discussion of the prospects for unseating the government, and who would or would not support such moves, the CIA was forced to the conclusion that the army's generals were "not openly against Allende".[36] In this they were disappointed, but not nearly as much as their counterparts from the Pentagon.

The US service attachés in Santiago and the military advisory group (milgroup), had long been pressing Washington for dramatic action to force a coup in Chile.[37] Moreover businessmen such as Hernán Cubillos Sallato – himself an ex-naval officer, close to the United States, and described by Robert Moss as in touch with the entire opposition – were anticipating the need for a coup. In conversation with Murray Hunter, head of the Foreign and Commonwealth Office Latin American department, Cubillos "forecast a steady resistance to legislation by constitutional means would culminate in a confrontation which by implication would let in an armed forces régime. He said several times that he did not think Allende would last until 1976."[38] But US ambassador Davis was much opposed to any such move, as were many in the CIA already troubled by Lyndon Johnson's brazen invasion of the Dominican Republic in 1965[39] and haunted by the lingering spectre of Vietnam. Senior figures in the agency were more inclined to wait it out, assuming UP would discredit themselves and ultimately step down in despair. The

---

[35] Report, 2 March 1973: *NARA. Chile Human Rights Abuses Special Search.* CIA Directorate of Operations Documents, Box 3.

[36] Ibid.

[37] Personal information from an authoritative source (A).

[38] Hunter's record, 18 April 1973: *FCO 7/2410.*

[39] David Phillips, in charge of the Chile task force and later head of the western hemisphere division of the CIA, said he was "shocked and disturbed" at the Dominican Republic invasion: D. Phillips, *The Night Watch* (London 1978), p. 222.

attachés, however, found a strong echo in the White House, where Nixon and Kissinger both had become obsessed lest the Watergate scandal cripple US authority abroad. After the March ballot, as yet unnamed officials now concluded that "a political solution to the Chilean problem has become more doubtful in terms of the 1976 presidential election".[40] For a while two options had been aired. A memorandum for the chief of the CIA's western hemisphere division in mid-April 1973 pointed out that "any action program must be designed either to provoke the [Chilean] military into action or to strengthen the democratic parties sufficiently to enable the opposition candidate – probably Eduardo Frei – to defeat the UP in 1976. The Santiago Station's recommendation … is essentially to proceed full steam ahead along both of these tracks."[41] The author of the memorandum thought the two options contradicted one another: "a policy designed to provoke a military coup in the next six months to a year must seek to increase political tensions and to intensify economic suffering, particularly among the lower classes, so that a feeling of national desperation will impel the military to move".[42] Yet propping up the constitutional opposition would give hope and relieve these pressures, lulling optimists into believing that in 1976 they could still jettison UP.

As bureaucrats must, the official chose to square the circle in order to meet the recommendations of the CIA station and the stance of the White House.

> This course would call for maintaining support for political parties at a minimum level while seeking to develop the conditions which would be conducive to military action. This course would involve large-scale support to the [deleted], the militant elements on the PN, and, possibly, to [deleted]. It would be … designed for implementation within a fixed time frame, perhaps six to nine months, during which time every effort would be made to promote economic chaos, escalate political tensions, and induce a climate of desperation in which the PDC and the people generally come to desire military intervention. Ideally it would succeed in inducing the military to take over the government completely …[43]

---

[40] Quoted but unattributed in an anonymous (after deletion) document destined for the chief of the CIA western hemisphere division, 17 April 1973: *NARA. Chile Declassification Project. NSC.*
[41] Ibid.
[42] Ibid.
[43] Ibid.

Into these calculations came plausible news of a sharp reorientation in PCCh policy towards an authoritarian solution based on the incorporation of the military fully into government. Some in Washington and Santiago were now champing at the bit. US ambassador Davis, however, "gave instructions to the U.S. Mission staff that no one was to involve himself in coup plotting or in conversations on the subject that could be construed as encouragement".[44] But his predecessor had issued the same orders and with precisely the same ineffectual result. In the utmost secrecy president Nixon had already taken a crucial decision on covert action, circumventing the 40 Committee and the ambassador both.[45] "It is true that during the Nixon Administration the President and the CIA bypassed the Committee on sensitive topics, notably the campaigns to 'destabilise' the regime of Chilean President Salvador Allende in 1973", recalls former state department under-secretary for political affairs (and member of the committee) Alexis Johnson.[46] Nixon decided go one step further than a *golpe seco* or *golpe blando* – which would just ensure a military majority in cabinet. He moved instead directly towards a full military coup, the "Brazilian" option of 1964 – *golpe negro*. As in that instance, the United States would prepare the ground and do everything short of seizing power themselves. The coup would be effected from the Pentagon, using DIA and naval intelligence working with and through the Chilean armed forces.[47] The director of the CIA was so instructed by the White House.[48] And for this purpose it was essential that the CIA station in Santiago should disengage from operational contact with the Chilean military: first, so that the embassy (especially ambassador Davis) would have absolutely no knowledge of what was to take place; and, second, in order that no clear paper trail would exist that might later implicate the US government (the Watergate scandal of 1972 had reminded the White House of the paramount importance of discretion). By the end of May, Washington had instructed the Santiago CIA station to cease any operational contacts with the armed

---

[44] N. Davis, *The Last Two Years of Salvador Allende* (Ithaca 1985), p. 348.

[45] Testimony from source (A), off-the-record in Washington DC.

[46] U. Alexis Johnson, *The Right Hand of Power* (New Jersey 1984), p. 347.

[47] Testimony from source (A). For a distant echo – Gabriel García Marquez, "La ultima cueca feliz de Salvador Allende", 10 October 1980, in Witker, *Salvador Allende*, p. 197. This is also the thrust of the story told in T. Hauser, *Missing: The Execution of Charles Horman* (London 1982).

[48] Testimony from source (A).

forces in Chile. "In short," the new chief of the western hemisphere division David Phillips recalled, "the CIA Station Chief was ordered to do the best he could on forecasting a coup from the margin of any plotting and to avoid contacts or actions which might later be construed as supporting or encouraging those who planned to overthrow Allende."[49] A crucial link instead was forged with the Chilean navy. "The real co-ordination and planning of the coup took place in Valparaíso", Prats later told journalist Marlise Simons.[50] The US naval mission stood a few hundred yards down the road from Chilean naval headquarters, on Prat Street. Captain Ray Davis was nominally head of mission but he doubled as head of the military advisory group (milgroup); operational control thus fell to his deputy, lieutenant-colonel Patrick Ryan, US marine corps. Communications from Washington were channeled through the US navy's secure network running along the Pacific coast to Valparaíso.[51] Thus the ambassador had no access to incoming and outgoing traffic regarding preparations for the coup.

The deception worked. Indeed, mainstream CIA officers were left baffled in trying to decipher the reasoning behind what was formally a decision not to back a coup since they had concluded that both the military and the christian democrats were "steadily moving toward some kind of military intervention". Thus these perplexed officials had to "assume HQS decision to proceed in manner described … reflects, among other things, a lack of solid evidence that armed forces prepared to move in decisive manner against Allende regime and that opposition, especially PDC, would support such a move".[52] But news of the decision and its timing did very soon leak out. During the turbulent hearings held not long after the coup by the house subcommittee on inter-American affairs in late September 1973, a succession of officials, including assistant secretary of state for inter-American affairs Jack Kubisch and deputy assistant secretary of state (and former deputy chief of mission in Santiago) Harry Shlaudeman, categorically denied any US involvement in the coup. Kubisch, whether from genuine ignorance or just an excess of zeal, also insisted "there was no financing, for example, to the truckers'

[49] Phillips, *The Night Watch*, p. 238.
[50] *Sunday Times*, 27 October 1974.
[51] See, also, *NACLA's Latin American & Empire Report*, 1974, vol. VIII, no. 6, p. 15.
[52] Heavily censored CIA document of 2 May 1973: *NARA. CIA Chile III.*

strike".[53] This we now know to be completely untrue.[54] However, subcommittee chairman Dante Fascell had come into possession of some unusual detail. Even with security deletions and the chairman's use of the hypothetical, the record shows he had a rough idea of what had taken place. "In other words," Fascell is recorded as saying after a deletion in the text, "that leads me to believe that if there was a clandestine operation by the CIA in Chile since May of this year that the authority for that emanated from some place else [other than the 40 Committee], and you did not have the opportunity to either approve or disprove [reject]?"[55] Moreover, in early September the MIR leader, Miguel Enríquez, was in possession of information that senior naval officers, including vice-admiral Merino and rear-admiral Pablo Weber Munich, had been preparing a coup since the month of May.[56] And Prats later testified that Merino "had maintained continuous contact with the American military attaché just before the start of the coup d'état".[57] At the hearings chaired by Fascell, congressman Donald Fraser cut in: "Mr Secretary, what I wanted to ask you follows the inference one gets from the exchange you had with the chairman, that there were clandestine activities by the CIA during this period, whether you approved of them or not …" Fascell also stated that he had "heard all kinds of rumors about how the AFL-CIO fomented all these strikes in Chile", which, of course, Kubisch denied.[58] It has to be remembered that hitherto officials were simply unaccustomed to being interrogated on the issue of covert operations in open session, whether or not they knew answers to the questions fired at them.

When the incoming British ambassador, Reginald Secondé, called to present his credentials at La Moneda in mid-May, he found Allende "tense". Yet, noted Secondé, "He seems determined to push through his political ideas in the belief that the practical problems will somehow fall

---

[53] Testimony, 25 September: *United States and Chile*, p. 134.

[54] Fully confirmed by another authoritative source off the record (B).

[55] *United States and Chile*, p. 147.

[56] *Las Noticias de Ultima Hora*, 4 September 1973: González and Talavera, *Los mil días*, vol. 2, p. 840.

[57] Told by Prats to a journalist from Radio Hilversam not long before his assassination: *Le Monde*, 9 October 1974. This was to be an unattributed background briefing but was released after the assassination.

[58] *United States and Chile*, p. 156.

into place."[59] It was this, and the belief within the leadership of the PCCh that Prats had voted communist in March – "of General Prats our comrades proudly say, telling one not to repeat it, that he had voted communist in the elections"[60] – that prompted Corvalán to broach the idea of a coalition between the military and the parties of the working class. Prats was central to this plan. "There seems no doubt", London noted, "that Prats does now have very close and friendly links with the Chilean CP, particularly with Volodia Tietelboim [sic]. [Robert] Moss says that he has made no secret in private conversation of his admiration for the Party, and particularly for its discipline and organisation."[61] This illustrates the enigma that the general presented. Senator Raúl Morales Adriasola commented that "Prats is a mystery as much to ourselves as to Unidad Popular".[62] Months after the tragedy had drawn to a close, Allende aide Joan Garcés revealed something of what Prats had told him that illustrates deeper motives during this troubled period. Initially Prats had spent his life just earning a living. But he did not wish to "tie" his hands "because perhaps one day I could in some way contribute to the betterment of my country. I believe," Prats continued, "without wishing to sound presumptuous, that to remain loyal towards Dr Allende I must not follow a predetermined path."[63] This was the language of a political aspirant, not a serving officer. His opponents noted with interest that, in substituting for the president when Allende was out of the country, he had a photograph taken of himself in the presidential sash.

That Prats likely as not voted communist will have rung alarm bells in Washington, and anything Moss knew, Washington also no doubt knew. The CIA argued that whereas prior to May 1973 the communist party was very much on the side of "gradual and continual consolidation of political power" – that is, maximum moderation – it was now protesting against government weakness in dealing with the right. In late May, for example, the PCCh warned its members against the dangers of another general strike and expressed the hope "that the government adopts a more energetic attitude against those who once again embark on the path of

[59] Secondé (Santiago) to London, 14 May 1973: *FCO 7/2410*.
[60] Pajetta, 18 September 1973: *Archivio PCI. Segreteria. Prot. 2072/S*.
[61] Clissold, 13 April 1973: *FCO 7/2410*.
[62] Yofre, *Misión Argentina en Chile*, p. 207.
[63] *Le Monde*, 5 October 1974.

disobedience". As if to underline the problem, PyL issued a declaration following its congress in Temuco stating that "the future of Chile depends on the course and direction that our armed forces resolve to take". Should the armed forces "resolve to act in defence of our integrity as a nation, there does not exist an armed paramilitary power capable of confronting them".[64] It was surely also assumed that to act decisively would require the exercise of force. On 11 June communist leaders decided the political situation was critical, agreed upon more offensive tactics, and began making provision for the possibility of violence.[65] Joaquin Peña, head of the communist party's paramilitary organisation, started work on an underground network in the event of civil war. The PCCh was looking for a way out that would protect the attainments of the revolution and sustain the left in power until a further advance could be safely contemplated. Regarding the means to this end, however, the communists were remarkably flexible.

In Peru "progressive" generals were making a revolution. Could not Chile do the same with its "progressive" generals? Only three years before, nothing could have been further from Corvalán's mind, though others in the leadership such as Teitelboim always took a more generous view of the military's potential. Italian communist Pajetta, talking to leaders of UP in early June, was baffled by the way in which the Chilean comrades and Allende talked about the army "as though it were a neutral force, as though to say it is a social force that does not, however, feel the influences of social processes".[66] In fact PCCh thinking went a good deal further in its assumptions. On 20 June the East German politburo received an update on Chile. What Corvalán had told Allende was that "The leadership of the Chilean CP is of the opinion that the development process on the part of the UP government can go no further. The only possible way out … is the creation of a mixed government of representatives of the working class and the military."[67] But Allende was not prepared to play fast and loose with constitutionality on this order of magnitude, regardless of the fact that the right was

[64] Both quoted in Câmara Canto (Santiago) to Secretary of State (Brasilia), 24 May 1973: *MRE. Oficios Recibidos*. Chile. 1973. vol. 5.
[65] Report from CIA Station (Santiago) to Washington, 25 July 1973: *NARA. CIA Chile III.*
[66] 18 September 1973: *Archivio PCI*. Segreteria. Prot. 2072/S.
[67] "Betrifft: Gegenwärtige Lage in Chile". Information Nr. 41/73 für das Politbüro": *SAPMO*. SED.ZK. International Verbindungen. DY/30/IV.B 2/20.102.

increasingly willing to do so. Bearing all this in mind, the KGB, after analysing the latest information from stations in New York and Washington, and then Havana, reached the certain conclusion that a coup from the right was not only inevitable but imminent.[68]

As early as 6 June Allende told a meeting of the UP leadership that the government had evidence of a revolt from the right expected within three months.[69] As if confirming these fears, on 22 June the leadership of the PN – bent on a military régime – published an advertisement in *El Mercurio* claiming "the Allende government is unlawful and must be replaced". This prompted an intemperate and foolish government request to judge Raúl Moroni that he close the paper for sedition for a period of six days, only to have the instruction overturned at higher level. The constitutionalist opposition was no less depressed than Allende. Frei's Fabian tactic of awaiting the "ripe apple" – *la pera madura* – that would fall into his hands of its own accord by 1976 tested the patience of the right. Leading figures such as senator Patricio Aylwin lamented the fact that "instead of readying themselves to seek a path of understanding with those always so disposed within christian democracy, they [UP] pressed on with their offensive towards the attainment of 'total power' to which they aspired without pretence".[70] Two senior christian democrats visited the United States at US government expense in early June: Juan de Dios Carmona, the author of the law against the holding of arms, which was implemented almost exclusively against the left, and Andrés Zaldívar, no less a diehard.[71]

At home the economy, which Allende neither understood nor sought to manage personally, was heading for the edge of a cliff. Even the infinitely patient Corvalán had all but given up sounding the alarm on this subject. When they met early in June 1973, Pajetta was taken aback in his conversations with Corvalán by

> the way in which he spoke of the absence of an economic policy, of a planning policy, of the arbitrary nature of interventions in individual directions and of the intervention of workers in every individual enterprise in confrontation with their own management. But I recall being struck by

[68] Nikolai Leonov in interview: "El General Nikolai Leonov en el CEP", *Estudios Públicos* (Santiago), 73, summer 1999, p. 74.
[69] Zorina et al., *Uroki Chili*, p. 377.
[70] Aylwin, *Reencuentro de los Demócratas*, p. 24.
[71] Prats testimony to the Radio Hilversam correspondent: *Le Monde*, 9 October 1974.

his attitude almost of resignation, I would say; just as when he had spoken of the same question with respect to the countryside.

Here, especially, the chaos was most evident. Corvalán had said: "we know that what we have destroyed was a rotten system [*un sistema infame*] but which worked; and we have substituted a situation that we have not succeeded in mastering".[72] This was a stunning admission of failure.

The elections had resolved nothing. At mines like El Teniente production had slumped with the loss of qualified managers. The arrival of a few Soviet specialists had changed nothing substantially for the better. Kennecott had trained 400–500 Chileans, of whom 140 were lost by July 1971. At that time US ambassador Korry testified:

> You have government officials going to the mines and saying all the supervisors are so-called mummies ... and telling the workers: "You will be running the mine."
>
> So the discipline and the hierarchical structure in the mines have deteriorated. A great many of the supervisors say this is the kind of life they don't want to lead under any conditions. They just take their retirement pay and go.[73]

By early 1973 relatively well-paid copper miners at El Teniente were striking at a cost of $30 million in foreign exchange earnings[74] and, ironically, with the staunch support of the PDC. Once again the United States lurked in the background. At Front Royal, Virginia, Jorge Castillo, on the staff of AIFLD in Chile, had the previous summer been asked by his superiors to provide a list of suitable trades union leaders in the copper and steel industries; this he duly did.[75] Castillo was then in the urgent business of opening a dialogue with non-communist and non-socialist trades unions. In 1972 grants had been given to leaders of the railway workers.[76] CIA money found its way towards various causes, all unremittingly hostile to UP on a scale from psychological warfare to outright terrorism. Students, led by PN extremists (the Roland Matus

[72] Note of 18 September 1973: *Archivio PCI*. Segreteria. Prot. 2072/S

[73] *United States and Chile*, p. 20.

[74] The government estimate: Zorina et al., *Uroki Chili*, p. 382. US sources suggested more than double.

[75] Jorge Castillo to William Doherty for O'Neill, 19 August 1971: *George Meany Memorial Archive*, RG 18-010. International Affairs Department. Country Files, 1969–1981. 5/15. Chile.

[76] McLennan to O'Neill, 2 May 1972: ibid. 5/16. Chile.

Brigade) and PyL, were out on the streets colliding with the authorities. To opposition eyes, the process of appropriating private property was continuing relentlessly at the same alarming pace as before. And to the dismay of the MIR the military had begun raids in search of arms caches at a rate of at least three a week, resulting in seventy-five operations between 23 July and 5 September.[77]

Raúl, cardinal Silva Henríquez, was urgently contacted twice by Allende in the hope that his friendship with senator Patricio Aylwin, president of the PDC, and other leading christian democrats as well as the prestige of the church could persuade them into an understanding with UP. Not that Allende himself lacked PDC friendships, but they were concentrated on the left of the party, who were in the minority once Aylwin became party president. And Allende's relationship with Frei had never recovered from the dirty tricks employed in the election of 1964 – further testimony to the president's difficulty suppressing his emotions. A proud man to the last, Allende was too conscious of the prestige of office to concede a public appeal for help. A go-between of some independent authority was more acceptable. The cardinal was given to understand on both occasions in May that "Allende knew that the situation was headed for disaster and wanted help to escape this critical juncture."[78] On the first occasion the president warned of civil war; on the second Allende caught the cardinal moments before dining with Frei and asked him to convey Allende's wishes to have a *tête-à-tête* with Frei. "The second time in a fortnight", Frei reflected pensively.[79] Yet Allende was notoriously artful and not about to sell out his position readily.

Sympathetic onlookers from abroad found Allende's entire approach bewildering. The president liked to deal with and through top people. When journalist Rossanda probed him about the apparent absence of mass participation in Chile, she was perplexed by the extraordinary reply – more reminiscent of Eastern Bloc régimes than those in the West – "We can mobilise the masses when we want."[80] He somehow expected that they would turn out on demand. And this was not Indonesia, Allende

---

[77] Raúl Silva Henríquez, *Memorias*, vol. 2 (Santiago 1991), p. 249. Also speech by Altamirano, 9 September 1973: González and Talavera, *Los mil días*, vol. 2, p. 1277.

[78] Silva Henríquez, *Memorias*, p. 249.

[79] Ibid., pp. 251–2.

[80] Rossanda, "Successi, limiti e scogli", p. 185.

insisted. "Do you believe that the workers would allow industries to be taken from them? And the peasants the land?" Yet when challenged that miners on strike did not regard the mines as theirs but as belonging to the state, he refused to acknowledge what soon became an obvious truth.[81] The Italian communist Pajetta later reflected: "The position of General Prats and the cardinal primate were … of course important, but also important were the forces that had been subjected in these years not only to the jolts of the policy of nationalisation but to the ruinous economic situation."[82]

Allende scarcely reassured Frei. First, the government had no control over the hotheads; second, the attitude of UP's leadership, including that of the president, was ambivalent; third, there was no guarantee that any gesture of rapprochement would be reciprocated.[83] Behind every statement lay deep-seated mistrust. The very personal attacks on Frei in the pro-UP press – even from the government's official daily *La Nación* – that followed both the revelations of the CIA aid to his campaign in 1964 and his indiscreet remarks to US officials in October 1970 further alienated him. To his consternation they did not cease even after he assumed presidency of the senate in May 1973. The atmosphere worsened still when striking miners marched in the streets of Santiago and clashed with the police over successive days. Bernardo Leighton of the PDC left told Prats in mid-June that Frei was intransigent in opposition to talks with UP.[84] Likewise Garretón for MAPU took the same attitude *vis-à-vis* the PDC.[85] Moreover attempts to persuade Prats to accept the defence portfolio and admiral Raúl Montero Cornejo and general César Ruiz Danyau to head other ministries came to nothing.[86] This did not prevent Allende from surprising everyone by raising the matter again at his official residence Tomás Moro on 23 June but without even specifying the offices to be held. Once more Prats said that without a truce between government and opposition the idea was unthinkable.[87] Allende had as a preferable alternative sounded the UP leadership on the idea of a referendum to

---

[81] Ibid., p. 188.
[82] Note: *Archivio PCI*. Segereteria. Prot. 2072/S.
[83] Silva Henríquez, *Memorias*, p. 252.
[84] Prats, *Memorias*, p. 408.
[85] Ibid.
[86] Ibid., p. 409.
[87] Ibid., p. 410.

settle the division of the economy in terms of three types of ownership: private, public and mixed. But they refused to accept the proposal. Meanwhile the PCCh opened a campaign under the slogan "No to civil war" which led many – including the cardinal – to believe that the communists had no confidence in winning.[88] Indeed, PCCh politburo member Teitelboim, who dealt with military matters, had already pointed out that "if we have to fight against the entire army, the whole of the right and the whole of the centre" there was little chance of victory. "For this reason we cannot and must not provoke a collision."[89]

Sensitive to criticism but woefully indifferent to the sensitivities of others – not least the doubting centre – UP continued to act with high-handedness against its opponents. The government gave every appearance of ruling by raw emotion rather than considered reason. As already noted, on 22 June, at the request of the executive, a judge had ordered *El Mercurio* to be closed. This was only one instance. Barely a week would pass without further rounds of ammunition being handed gratuitously to the opposition by thoughtless measures of repression. From the right the writer Martín Cerda delivered in *Las Ultimas Noticias* a particularly biting and damaging diagnosis of a public relations disaster:

> The factious spirit has always been a logical sequel of the failure of revolutionary utopianism … When, these days, the central offices of the Catholic University are stoned, the TV installations of the University of Chile are destroyed, an attempt is made to silence the daily *El Mercurio*, chaos reigns, thuggish behaviour and terror walk the streets, Parliament and the judiciary are threatened, nonsense is talked in public calling those who think differently anti-patriotic, fascists or counter-revolutionaries, this is not the shadow of Rosa Luxemburg, or dialectical thought, or the humanist hope of a classless society, but the odious spectre of Stalin, the grotesque lesson of Castro and the factious spirit of those who now occupy the stage of our country.[90]

Tactically the military uprising on 29 June came as no surprise. On 25 June the authorities arrested a group belonging to the paramilitary Roland

[88] Ibid., p. 256.

[89] Interviewed by *Politique-Hebdo*: reproduced in *Il Cile*, p. 98.

[90] "El espíritu faccioso", *Las Ultimas Noticias*, 29 June 1973: reprinted in González and Talavera, *Los mil días*, vol. 1, pp. 709–10.

Matus brigade of the national party in Chillán and uncovered an arms cache. They also found that a member of the PyL leadership, lawyer Miranda Carrington, who was connected to the CIA, had told supporters that "day x" for a coup was scheduled to be 27 June.[91] According to the army's subsequent official report on the plot:

> It was discovered on 26 June and was due to take place on the following day, on the understanding that the president would be at Tomás Moro until the evening. Two officers of the 2nd tank regiment were in touch with Patria y Libertad at middle level; three meetings were held. At the last, which took place on Sunday 24, the top leadership of this movement participated.[92]

A year before, on 10-11 June 1972, the political commission of PyL had held continuous meetings chaired by leader Pablo Rodríguez after his return from the United States.[93] It concluded that the "only possible way out was a coup d'état". But it also envisioned that the armed forces would have to carry it out.[94] However, when two conspirators – captain Sergio Rochas Aros and lieutenant José Gasset Ojeda – came calling, PyL leaders had difficulty taking them seriously, since the idea that the small number of troops proposed could seize the presidential palace and prompt a nationwide uprising seemed farcical.[95] Pablo Rodríguez could not make up his mind. He was in a sense a victim of the White House decision to and to leave the CIA station in the dark. He had no idea of the scale of the intended coup. From his limited vantage-point he saw the conspirators as both crazy and brave; then he labelled them *chocolatínes* (chocolate soldiers).[96] But, once embroiled in negotiations, PyL found it impossible entirely to extricate themselves.

The plan, described later by the army, was that "five tanks, under the command of a lieutenant, would assemble at Tomás Moro. They would capture the president and hold him in the Santa Rosa barracks [the unit's

---

[91] Zorina et al., *Uroki Chili*, p. 380. Also, testimony from Joan Garcés dated 7 November 1973, dateline Paris: J. Garcés, *El estado y los problemas tácticos en el gobierno de Allende* (Buenos Aires 1973), p. 40.

[92] Quoted at length in "Chile: El juego de la pera madura", *Panorama* (Buenos Aires), 30 August 1973.

[93] Fuentes, *Memorias Secretas*, p. 137.

[94] Ibid.

[95] Ibid., pp. 268–79. José Gasset is wrongly identified as Guillermo.

[96] Ibid., pp. 272 and 279.

base]; five tanks would start by seizing La Moneda. Patria y Libertad would provoke riots from the evening of the 26th." But the idea, in this report, that PyL could assure the participation of other units and branches of the armed forces was pure wishful thinking – whether on the part of the *chocolatínes* or the military investigators. PyL had pressed the conspirators repeatedly as to how exactly other units would follow suit. Anyway, as the report continues: "A Patria y Libertad contact called one of the officers involved at 6.00pm on the 26th, telling him 'no go.'" Moreover the general commanding Santiago army garrison, Mario Sepúlveda Squella, warned the officers involved that they were being watched. However, they continued their suspicious activity. On the morning of 27 June an official investigation began, and that evening one officer was arrested and held incommunicado in the ministry of defence guardhouse. Still the plot continued.

On the evening of 28 June regimental commander colonel Roberto Souper Onfray – a cousin of MIR's Miguel Enríquez on his mother's side – told officers that he was to be relieved of his duties the following morning. An officer told the others that a coup was planned and ready to be delivered, which prompted dissent and no agreement. Between 3.30 and 6.00am, however, two lieutenants raised officers from their sleep and told them they were under orders to obey the commanding officer's orders. At 7.10 the regimental commander met his officers, thanked them for their participation and took charge of a tank. Dissenting voices had no effect.[97] The coup was put down with ease but with twenty-two people dead and fifty wounded within merely four hours. As a precaution the government asked for but failed to receive permission from congress to declare a nationwide state of siege. Allende called on the workers to occupy the factories and announced that "if the coup comes, the people will be given arms."[98] That day some 250 premises were occupied and the *cordones industriales* sprang into action around the city. Meanwhile the PyL leadership fled to the Ecuadorian embassy whence they issued misleading declarations announcing themselves to be the inspiration for the putsch but – equally erroneously – declaring themselves betrayed.[99] The day won, Allende succeeded in persuading reluctant and embarrassed

[97] *Panorama*, 30 August 1973.
[98] Silva Henríquez, *Memorias*, p. 258.
[99] Prats, *Memorias*, p. 422.

commanders-in-chief to appear on his balcony while he improvised to the multitude of triumphant UP supporters below; in the fevered atmosphere of the moment, this gesture further enraged hostile officers, particularly, but not solely, in the navy.

The putsch could easily be dismissed as a Chekhovian tragi-comedy. Yet its consequences were serious. For the uprising triggered direct action from the left and the extreme left to defend the régime and thereby accelerated the process of radicalisation; in so doing it necessarily struck further alarm among the property-owning and middle classes. On the day of the *tanquetazo*, as it became known, some 30,000 small and medium-sized enterprises were rapidly snatched by the left.[100] Later the government said it would return all except those of significance to the country's economy or those owned by people who had fled from them, or people accused of sabotage or of supplying the black market.[101] Given the ease with which the organized left could classify the expropriated under one or other category and with no effective judicial authority to challenge them, the attack on private property was clearly still proceeding apace, rendering worthless recent reassurances to small and medium-sized enterprises. The extent of government non-compliance with instructions from the courts was already such that pre-putsch – on 1 June – the Supreme Court had written to the president to demand something be done, only to receive a verbose and legally unsubstantiated argument that the executive should choose when to enforce the law according to circumstances.[102] The post-putsch sequestrations exacerbated an existing conflict. Thus when on 1 August a civic front of professional organisations was set up, the christian democrats made four demands, one of which called for the restoration to their owners of factories and farms seized on and after 29 June.

Another important consequence of the *tanquetazo* was that it gave military conspirators a clear view of UP capabilities. Pinochet later recalled: "the Marxists had revealed their dispositions, their action posts in buildings, the industrial cordons surrounding the city. It was also possible to see what organization the groups had and how the extremists

---

[100] Zorina et al., *Uroki Chili*, p. 380.
[101] Decision by the president's council on economic questions, 14 July 1973: ibid., p. 385.
[102] For the exchange of correspondence: González and Talavera, *Los mil días*, vol. 2, pp. 1232–62.

would act in a similar situation."[103] Vice-admiral Ismael Huerta noted that when the tanks came out, people did not fill the streets to stop them. "They were things that we took into account", he recalled.[104]

The US government was surreptitiously involved in the putsch. And this US involvement, as first projected, completely circumvented normal channels; not merely ambassador Davis, most of the 40 Committee, and the CIA at Langley (excepting of course director Colby and deputy director lieutenant-general Walters) but also the chief of station in Santiago were cut out of the circle of knowledge as well as of decision. The White House had counted on the first, second and fourth divisions of the army, as well as sections of the other services including the carabineros. But they failed because the third division in the capital was pro-UP, and military intelligence had detected the plot in advance. This necessarily created a major problem for the extraction of those in the field when everything went awry. In desperation the White House turned to Britain's MI6, which obliged by sending in a small SAS team to exfiltrate US assets in early July.[105] Since January 1972 David Spedding had been head of the MI6 station in Santiago under diplomatic cover, latterly as first secretary. It is almost certain he must have known of the operation, even if he did not inform the ambassador, as protocol normally dictates. This degree of separation obviously created high risks for all, especially the United States; it was highly unorthodox and therefore infuriated old hands when they discovered its existence, but it was a policy sustained through to September regardless.[106]

If anything confirmed the need for tight US control and management of a Chilean coup, the earlier failure of the *tanquetazo* did so. US defence intelligence later reported that "At that time many Naval officers were ready and willing to join in with what they thought was an attempt at a coup. The Air Force officers were also ready to join."[107] Senior officers in the navy had reacted to the mutiny by insisting on the need to ensure unity within the service from top to bottom and close co-ordination with the army. Vice-admiral Huidobro, commanding Chile's marines, hurried

---

[103] Pinochet, *The Crucial Day*, pp. 95–6.

[104] Quoted in Carvajal Prado, *Téngase presente* (Santiago 1994), pp. 172-3.

[105] Personal information from an authoritative source (C).

[106] Personal information from an authoritative source (A).

[107] "Events Leading up to the 11 September Military Coup in Chile ... ": *NARA*. Department of Defense Information Report, 29 October 1973.

to Santiago to investigate the circumstances surrounding events, meeting senior naval officers at the ministry.[108] Evidently as a result of his report back to Valparaíso, "Senior Naval authorities (NFI) managed to convince their personnel that this was not the moment for a move." But, as US observers noted, "The event and its failure within four hours, gave many a deep sense of frustration and disappointment. It also left many members of the Navy with an increased willingness to move at a later date."[109] Indeed, the Argentinian military attaché reported that

> Days later in my presence, together with my wife, in the course of a dinner with naval officers and their wives, one of them called her husband a 'queer' [*maricón*] and refused to let him come home. The officer had to sleep at the Naval Club. Another, boiling with greater indignation, declared a 'sex strike', on the argument that if he wanted to be a man in bed he first had to be a man in the street.[110]

Not that nothing was done. Huidobro recalls:

> In Santiago an event had occurred of the utmost significance. For the same reason, and completely spontaneously, the generals of the air force who were gathering in their headquarters in the same building in the ministry of defence, assembled at the location of the meeting of admirals, where a conversation arose that showed a convergence of views and the determination finally to put an end to the situation which was driving the country over a cliff.[111]

Therefore on 30 June both Montero for the navy and Ruiz for the air force asked for a meeting with Prats, which took place that evening. Two others joined them. One admiral present openly expressed the view that young officers were in sympathy with Souper's putsch.[112] But Prats prevailed upon them to be patient and agree merely to press the government for a political truce which would mean it sharing power and for alleviation of the economic crisis. Head of army logistics general Oscar

[108] Huidobro, *Decisión Naval*, pp. 126–7.
[109] "Events … "
[110] Quoted in Yofre, *Misión Argentina*, pp. 359–60.
[111] Ibid., p. 128
[112] Prats, *Memorias*, p. 423.

Bonilla Bradanovic reported that the christian democrats were willing to reach agreement with Allende, though only on the basis of a mixed civilian–military administration which would exclude UP. That evening senior officers from the three services met without Prats.

The fundamental problem for the conspirators was that no coup could succeed without the army – and the army, true to its Prussian roots, was rigid in respecting seniority and hierarchy. The officers who gathered that evening included Pinochet, Bonilla (a close friend of Frei's), and Sergio Nuño for the army; Patricio Carvajal Prado, Hugo Cabezas and Ismael Huerta for the navy; and Gustavo Leigh, Claudio Sepúlveda, Augustín Rodríguez, Nicarnor Díaz, and Francisco Herrera for the air force. They discussed the entire scene, political and economic. Their working premiss was made up of three parts: unity between the services, all other forces should be disarmed, and members of the fighting services should in no circumstances fire upon one another. This effectively meant that were a coup launched, none would oppose, but equally that any coup had to be agreed between the services. Given prevailing opinion, this gave the army a veto. They arranged a further meeting for 2 July.[113] Meanwhile a meeting by Prats with Altamirano and others from the PS brought agreement no closer. At a further gathering, with Allende and Tohá along with the other commanders-in-chief, Prats put forward the proposals he had hammered out with the commanders-in-chief. No decision was taken. The CUT leaders then came to see Prats and expressed the workers' wish to defend the government against a coup alongside loyal members of the military.[114] Enríquez made the same offer on behalf of the MIR.[115] It was hard for anyone to know exactly where loyalties lay. Many had their suspicions.

Alarmed by the *tanquetazo* and alert to rumours of what was now afoot among senior officers, the communist party was by no means alone in pressing for an immediate purge of the officer corps of all three services. Millas, for one, did not deny that Prats played a decisive role in suppressing the revolt. But he was not alone and certainly not incorrect in finding "suspicious the behaviour of the head of the air force César Ruiz Danyau and of the carabineros José Maria Sepúlveda and in Valparaíso something

---

[113] Huidobro, *Decisión Naval*, p. 128.

[114] Prats, *Memorias*, p. 424.

[115] Pascal, "El Mir", Part 4.

strange was apparent in the navy …"[116] As a result Victor Díaz, the under-secretary general of the PCCh, entrusted Millas with the task of suggesting to Allende and Prats an immediate purge from the officer corps of unreliable elements.[117]

The president, however, proved very reluctant to grasp this particularly ugly nettle. He focused instead on accelerating an understanding with the christian democrats. In a surprise move Enríquez came to warn Prats of the disloyalty of general Bonilla. He also said that former minister of defence Sergio Ossa, liaising between the PDC and junior officers, had expressed the view that the commander-in-chief could not command the loyalty of these men, the opinion being almost unanimous that he should retire.[118] The commander-in-chief knew a lot of this to be true. It did not, however, rouse him to action. His self-absorption was doubtless intensified by personal humiliation in a much-publicised incident at the hands of an indignant middle-class housewife. Alejandrina Cox stuck her tongue out at him in stationary traffic, a harmless if juvenile act that in the febrile atmosphere that clouded Santiago along with the winter fog prompted him to draw his pistol on her. Somehow the press were on the spot. Nothing better illustrated the tightly coiled tension in the country. This incident had occurred the day before the *tanquetazo*. Knowledge of his personal unpopularity within the ranks thus "merely served to accen-tuate" Prats's sense of "bitterness" and "isolation". There was little point in passing information concerning disloyalty on to military intelligence (SIM) – though he did so – because "for several months it only worked on information that touched left extremism, but showed no interest in extremist movements on the right". Proof enough lay in the fact that the SIM had not warned of the links between the recent mutiny and PyL, though they were doubtless known.[119] Indeed, as we will see later, elements within SIM were now working hand in glove with the United States. Furthermore, whatever happened, Prats – like his predecessor – ultimately felt greater loyalty to the army than to government, since he refused to risk an "institutional schism" come what may. In any circumstances this amounted to an extraordinary abdication of a commander-in-chief's

---

[116] Millas, *Memorias*, p. 357.
[117] Ibid.
[118] Prats, *Memorias*, pp. 432–3.
[119] Ibid., p. 434.

responsibilities to an elected government, but it was entirely consistent even with the views of the deceased general Schneider and the traditions of the officer corps. It effectively meant that Allende could not purge disloyal officers. Unable to act, the president characteristically shut his eyes to what was happening: he refused to meet officers and NCOs who had information about coup plotting. Colonel Ominami, head of the arsenal at El Bosque air base, contacted Laura Allende to report that pro-UP officers were being purged. He asked to see the president but was refused. Similarly general Alberto Bachelet and other pro-UP officers discreetly called for action against those conspiring, but they too were refused access to Allende.[120] On 19 July Allende, under enormous pressure, un-characteristically vented his bitterness at Prats's reluctance to remove senior offices with clearly hostile political positions; yet he did nothing to remedy the situation.[121]

The hopes and expectations barely a month before that the PCCh had placed in the incorporation of a pro-UP officer corps into government had thus proved misjudged, to say the least. Now the sense of alarm within communist ranks was palpable. Teitelboim told Hermann Axen, charged with the international relations of the East German communist party (SED): "It is known that the USA, above all the CIA, has planned an operation 'Djakarta', resulting in the mass liquidation of Communists, or some variant thereof."[122] After workers took control of factories during the uprising of army officers on 29 June, the communists had "demonstrated their unwillingness to return the bulk of factories and industries seized". This represented a "shift to more extreme tactics, includ-ing preparations for violent action", in the words of the CIA station in Santiago, which also reported the distribution of arms to PCCh members who responded to the call to join the "equipo" (security team).[123] Instructions from the Santiago regional committee of the PCCh to its cells on 30 June called on members to "get hold of a firearm", and that, in the event of a confrontation, a "highly specialised PCCh team will

[120] Pascal, "El Mir", Part 4.

[121] Prats, *Memorias*, p. 441.

[122] Axen's record of the discussion, 9 August 1973: *AA*. Abteilung Internationale Verbindung – DY/30/IV. B 2/20. 257.

[123] A photocopy of the instructions reproduced in *Libro Blanco del cambio de gobierno en Chile 11 de Septiembre de 1973*, p. 48.

physically liquidate leaders of the opposition …". The CIA station concluded: "Thus, Allende, the consummate politician who has defused the previous crises through political manoeuvres and compromise – an art in which he excels – may now find this ability to repeat past successes to be much more limited."[124] They certainly hoped so, and were not to be disappointed.

Other avenues cut off, the only alternative for UP was to reach a deal with christian democracy. Indeed, this was precisely what Prats had relentlessly and repeatedly pressed upon Allende. When on 7 July the president had expressed to Prats "his fears of a new military uprising [*una nueva asonada golpista*]" and pointedly asked whether any major military units remained loyal to the government, the response he received was not exactly reassuring. Prats instead emphasised the importance of averting a rift within the armed forces as it would provoke "a terrible civil war" such as in 1891. The general once again insisted that the possibilities of negotiation with the PDC should be exhausted. Allende responded that dialogue was "impracticable" but insisted instead that Prats talk directly to Frei.[125] The latter did not exactly meet him halfway, asserting that "one cannot exchange views when the adversary places a machine gun on the table".[126] Although neither Allende nor Frei could have known of the White House decision for a coup, both were acting as though it were a foregone conclusion. And they were right.

Thus the negotiations that did eventually take place bore an air of unreality from the outset. Moreover, even if Allende thought talks could end in agreement, his own party had no such belief because it was not prepared to make any substantive concessions including an end to seizures of property unauthorised by congress and accelerated by the putsch. The leader in *Punto Final* on 3 July expressed the views of not only the MIR but also the mainstream of the socialist party: "People's Dictatorship: The Only Remedy Against Coups d'État". It pointed out that a reactionary conspiracy had penetrated the barracks, winning over those in command of the troops. This was a warning that power of the people had to be mobilised. The bourgeoisie was actually weaker than supposed; hence the

---

[124] Report of 25 July 1973: *NARA*. CIA Chíle III. Also, the recollections of a former member of the PCCh.

[125] Prats, *Memorias*, p. 431.

[126] Ibid., p. 432.

chaotic responses in opposition to UP. What was needed was "courage and a revolutionary decision that does not vacillate in turning to the power of the working class and the patriotic and progressive sectors of the armed forces". By these means a true democracy for the workers could be established even if not for the majority of the population (a frightening prospect to most).[127] The MIR even considered whether it should go onto the offensive, act in combination with sympathetic officers and take over various military bases. But Enríquez feared UP would punish them rather than build on the advance.[128] In any case the MIR did not have the manpower and no one really knew the sympathies of the great majority of those serving in the ranks of the armed forces. PS faith in the progressive elements within the military as a weight in the final balance was equally illusory. As already mentioned, one of the by-products of the *tanquetazo* had been the mobilisation of the left into action through its paramilitary groupings based in various factories, the *cordones industriales*. After the putsch these were the focus of arms searches carried out by the military, the air force leading the way. They and the navy were the most virulently hostile to UP. It has to be remembered that the JAPs which controlled food rationing favoured socialists, the MIR and communists, and most members of the armed forces belonged to neither group. During a raid one of the air force pilots menacingly voiced a common deep-seated hostility: "If you want civil war, try something now you queers."[129]

Altamirano had told Prats on 19 July that he was happy to see UP come to terms with the christian democrats.[130] He was insincere. As Allende attempted to move closer to the christian democrats, Altamirano and the PS along with MAPU were ineluctably converging with the MIR. Unidad Popular now became a contradiction in terms. Chile was effectively gravitating inexorably towards a parallel system of power – more than merely in terms of the usual high-flown rhetoric. At Tomás Moro, just two days later, on 21 July, the commander-in-chief heard that Altamirano had quietly dropped any reference to the urgency of a dialogue with the PDC.[131] Altamirano's convictions emerged the following day during a

---

[127] *Punto Final*, 3 July 1973.
[128] Pascal, "El Mir", Part 4.
[129] "Réquiem para la 'via chilena'", *Panorama*, 13 September 1973.
[130] Prats, *Memorias*, p. 441.
[131] Ibid., p. 442.

meeting at Payita's residence, El Cañaveral. The president let the others speak. Prats has described what took place:

> The discussion is bitter, because I decide to go to the point. Altamirano maintains that, although he understands the vital need for dialogue, it will lead to the exhaustion of the political process developed by UP. Corvalán says that the economic circumstances in which the country is living leave no alternative to dialogue, but that this must evolve from UP's position of strength. Altamirano states that the position of strength must be created by the commanders-in-chief, eliminating the generals and admirals who overtly favour a coup.

To this Prats bluntly retorted that it was not the fault of the armed forces that they were now politicised to the point of mutiny; and "that it has to be understood that the armed forces feel themselves surrounded by extremes and that the prospect of a military coup is not only going to exhaust the UP's political process but wipe it out".[132]

A complete stand-off thus existed between the military and the government, with Prats pivoting somewhere precariously in between. The military were conducting raids on the extreme left to find the caches of arms that had suddenly been unearthed on 29 June, a process that was not applied to the extreme right, and that Allende was effectively powerless to stop. The *tanquetazo* had thus, wittingly or unwittingly, revealed the hand of the left and its paramilitary preparations without in any way strengthening the hand of the president; in fact the opposite seemed the case. Moreover, the distinctive positions favoured by both Altamirano and Corvalán for talks with the christian democrats were utterly unrealistic, so agreeing to dialogue in these circumstances did not add up to a great deal. Although Altamirano opposed all negotiations, Corvalán favoured them only to gain time. As the CIA station reported: "the PCCh has concluded that it needs more time to prepare its armed cadres. For this reason, it is maintaining a public posture in favor of a dialogue with the PDC."[133] And the president himself was, to say the least, ambivalent about conceding anything of substance to the opposition. When Allende died,

---

[132] Ibid., pp. 443–4.
[133] CIA Station (Santiago) to Washington, 25 July 1973: *NARA. CIA Chile III.*

a eulogy in the ultra-left Italian periodical *Il Manifesto* praised the deceased in unintentionally damaging terms: "Allende always offered a dialogue, but one has to recognise that he never conceded anything."[134] Given this stance, all negotiations appeared designed to delay the evil hour of the final confrontation.

Meanwhile, less under attack from the PCCh, the MIR – supported from the PS, MAPU and the IC – accelerated its offensive. *El Rebelde* attacked any and every compromise and called on the NCOs and ranks of the armed forces to "watch and denounce coup-makers [*golpistas*]" among the officer corps.[135] For the christian democrats, in the senate on 11 July Aylwin coldly stated that "the majority of our compatriots have lost faith in a democratic solution for the crisis in which Chile is living". He dilated on the dangers of totalitarianism from the left and warned that "the implacable onslaught of sectarianism, arbitrary behaviour, discrimination and violence are each day pushing more Chileans into thinking that only a military dictatorship can re-establish in Chile the order and authority indispensable for the salvation of our future as a nation". But he went on to insist that christian democrats were against any kind of dictatorship and ended on a conciliatory note: "while there is any possibility of overcoming by institutional means the crisis in which Chile is living, we will do our part to seek it".[136] It was around this time that a group of business leaders came to see Aylwin at the headquarters of the PDC. "Without beating about the bush they told me that they saw no other way out of the country's serious crisis than a military insurrection."[137] According to his own account, Aylwin sent them away empty-handed. A few days later the episcopacy intervened with a declaration – *La paz de Chile tiene un precio* (The peace of Chile has a price) – arguing that both sides had to make concessions and calling for a political truce leading to an eventual understanding.[138] Within twenty-four hours cardinal Silva Henríquez received a letter from Corvalán accepting the offer. Allende, however, made a public statement calling on the PDC to initiate talks but not giving any details. Altamirano

[134] Quoted by Pajetta: *Archivio PCI. Segreteria.* Prot. 2072/S.

[135] Câmara Canto (Santiago) to Secretary of State (Brasilia), 25 July 1973: *MRE. Oficios Recibidos.* Chile 1973, vol. 7.

[136] Aylwin, *Reencuentro de los Demócratas*, pp. 25–6.

[137] Ibid., pp. 27–8.

[138] Silva Henríquez, *Memorias*, p. 260.

was still blocking any movement in this direction. On 23 July Allende invited the cardinal to the presidential palace, La Moneda. Here he was briefed on the problems the president was facing within UP and his irritation with his own party. Silva Henríquez came away with Allende's expressed willingness to confront his party and the request to contact Aylwin asking him to soften his opposition and reassuring him that the appointment of the senator's friend Carlos Briones as minister of the interior was proof of his intentions.[139]

Talks on 26 July proceeded at the cardinal's residence on Simon Bolívar Street after Aylwin announced acceptance of Allende's offer. But his party had given him a rough time for conceding negotiations, fearing "that we would be victims of a new trick on the part of the government".[140] For his part Allende was in just as difficult a position. Even before Aylwin's announcement, the attempt to enlist four leading christian democrats into the cabinet – Valdés (whom Castro had suggested nearly three years before), Domingo Santa María, Tomic and Fernando Castillo Velasco – had been firmly rejected by the PDC. Worse was to follow. On 26 July Allende's naval aide, submarine commander Arturo Araya Peters, a trusted figure at La Moneda, was gunned down at his home at the hands of a team from the extreme right – the Guerrilleros Nacionalistas – by a well-aimed bullet through his thorax. The assassination further aggravated UP's relations with the navy, in particular, because one of the GAP – Domingo Blanco Tarrés ("Bruno") – was initially named as the culprit, though he had been guarding Allende at the time.[141] More importantly, as Prats later suggested, the aim must have been to cut off Allende from all knowledge of what was going on at naval headquarters.[142] Just two weeks earlier at Prats's unknowing authorisation, Merino's subordinates had completed an "anti-insurgency plan" for the navy – Plan Cochayuyo – which Merino intended to serve a purpose in the forthcoming coup.[143]

[139] Ibid.

[140] Aylwin, *Reencuentro de los Demócratas*, p. 26.

[141] Cristián Pérez, "Salvador Allende, apuntes sobre su dispositivo de seguridad: El Grupo de Amigos Personales (GAP)", *Estudios Públicos*, 29, winter 2000, p. 66.

[142] Silva Henríquez, *Memorias*, p. 261. The assassination team included Mario Eduardo Rojas Zegers, Guillermo Necochea Aspillaga, Edmundo Enrique Sebastián Quiroz Ruiz, Miguel Victor Sepúlveda Campos, Guillermo Bunster Thiesse, Carlos Fernández Farias, Juan Antonio Tacconi Quiroz, Guillermo Claverie Barbet – *Punto Final*, 14 August 1973. Also, see Avendaño and Palma, *El Rebelde*, p. 170. *Sunday Times*, 27 October 1974.

[143] Merino, *Bitácora*, pp. 206–7.

Allende was under siege from every direction, just as the White House intended. There were limits even to his capacity for improvisation, and the strain was showing. Sympathetic but not uncritical, the Italian communists lamented that "it is difficult for him to be an organiser of men and centre of activity in a modern apparatus [of state]".[144] 26 July was not only the date of Araya's assassination: it was also the day truckers resumed the strike concluded in November 1972, on the grounds that the terms promised had not since been met. In distant Greenwich, Connecticut, former CIA official Keith Wheelock – a Chile veteran (1966–69) – had no doubt what this meant. "The series of opposition-supported strikes, especially that of the truckers, seemed aimed at triggering Allende's overthrow."[145] Vilarín's union now counted 15,000 members with 40,000 lorries. The industrial stoppage well under way, Vilarín told Radio Agricultura that "the strike of those in transport will not end until such time as the Unidad Popular government resigns".[146] "Direct subsidies" were, according to US intelligence sources, "provided for a strike of middle-class shop-keepers and a taxi strike among others, that disrupted the capital city of Santiago in the summer of 1973".[147] Vilarín also subsequently acknowledged AIFLD as his source of funding.[148]

Then president of Sofofa, Orlando Sáenz recalls: "Dollars were deposited for us in five accounts we held in Europe, the USA and Latin America ... All we knew was that we had to have a great deal of money to create the conditions for a military coup. Many is the time I wondered how much of this money was from the USA. But that was not important for us. What was important was to design a system so that the donor felt safe. The five bank accounts were in two names. I was the common factor in the five accounts. To support the truckers on strike, I handed over the money to their leader Leon Vilarín and a couple of other people too. To support PyL I handed the money over to Pablo Rodríguez. In the case of the national party (Jarpa), the money passed through the hands of senator Pedro Ibañez (deceased). And, in the case of the christian democrat party, by Felipe Amunátegui. Money was also given to the strike movement via

[144] See note 129.
[145] Letter, dated 22 September 1973, to the *New York Times*, 5 October 1973.
[146] 26 August 1973: Zorina et al., *Uroki Chili*, p. 398.
[147] *New York Times*, 20 September 1974.
[148] Chierici, "Undici Settembre", p. 40.

Jaime Guzmán.[149] Almost immediately after the end of the October 1972 strike a group of trades union leaders had arrived at Front Royal, Virgina, for training at AIFLD. The course lasted from 13 November to 7 December.[150] Among them was Milenko Mihovilovic, one of the leaders of the public employees' strike.[151] In addition former strike leaders from the white-collar *gremios* attended a course on "advanced labor economics" at a university in Washington DC.[152] Jorge Guerrero, secretary of the national command for the defence of the *gremios*, was reportedly also among those invited by AIFLD.[153] It is said that additional leaders of the October strikes went to train at Front Royal at the end of February 1973.[154] Direct financial aid to the strikers was forthcoming from the CIA. Each lorry driver cost 2–3 dollars (7,000 escudos); "very cheap", noted Altamirano.[155] These subsidies were granted despite rejection of the proposal for funds by the 40 Committee at the instigation of ambassador Davis, who still believes that was the end of the matter.[156] The Russians subsequently reckoned that some $4 million went from US organisations to Chilean trades unions during the Allende period, which must, however, be an exaggeration that fails to take into account the collapse of the escudo on the black market.[157] Prats later told a journalist that ITT turned over $400,000 for the strike after a meeting with Chilean industrialists in Argentina.[158] Maintaining any secrecy in this regard was almost impossible. Truckers walked around ostentatiously with wads of notes in their pockets at a time when money was scarce. The role of the CIA was openly condemned by the CUT on 5 August.[159] And CIA agent Errol Johatan

[149] P. Verdugo, *Salvador Allende. Como la Casa Blanca provocó su muerte* (Santiago 2003).

[150] US department of labor, bureau of international labor affairs. Ron Smith to Mike Boggs (AFL-CIO). *George Meany Memorial Archive*: RG 18-010. International Affairs Department. Country Files, 1969–1981. 5/17. Chile, 1973–1974. 5/16

[151] Letter from IADSL in Chile to McLellan, Inter-American representative, AFL-CIO, 23 October 1972: ibid.

[152] *Sunday Times*, 27 October 1974.

[153] Hortensia Bussi de Allende, "The Facts about Chile", in H. Frazier, ed., *Uncloaking the CIA* (New York 1978), p. 62.

[154] Germán Marín, *Una historia fantástica y calculada: la CIA en el país de los Chilenos* (Mexico 1974), p. 161.

[155] Speech, 9 September 1973: González and Talavera, *Los mil días*, vol. 2, p. 1276.

[156] *New York Times*, 20 September 1974. Davis, *The Last Two Years of Salvador Allende*, p. 324.

[157] Tarasov and Zubenko, *The CIA in Latin America*, p. 36.

[158] This was stated in an interview with the journalist from Radio Hilversam: *Le Monde*, 9 October 1973.

[159] Zorina et al., *Uroki Chili*, p. 390.

Reinese was arrested at the Hotel Carrera carrying US dollars for delivery to the truckers.[160]

Meanwhile work pressed on towards the coup. When Araya was buried in Valparaíso at the end of July the plotters gathered, among them vice-admirals Adolfo Walbaum Wieber, Carlos Castro Madero, and Arturo Troncoso Daroch, plus two civilians – Hugo León Puelma (president of the construction workers' union) and Julio Bazán (president of the professionals' union). At this stage both Merino and Leigh saw the forth-coming coup as a brief transition to another kind of régime involving civilians: a *junta cívico-militar* on the Argentine model (*lanussisto*), not a lasting military dictatorship as in Brazil (*brasileño*).[161] This appears to be what various christian democrats had in mind.

Talks between government and opposition finally opened on 30 July, having been agreed upon only after great difficulty. Present for the PDC were Aylwin and the vice-president of the party Osvaldo Olguín, plus Allende, Briones (the new minister of the interior) and Clodomiro Almeyda (now defence minister) for the PS. The PDC proposed securing the rule of law, a guarantee for the armed forces that they held a monopoly over the use of force, an end to the seizure of property, a definition of property rights, and the formation of a cabinet including the military. But instead of tackling these contentious issues head-on, Allende suggested breaking them down for detailed consideration by separate bilateral committees. To an experienced legislator like Aylwin this looked suspiciously like a ruse to delay matters. He therefore pressed for more urgent deliberation. When Aylwin returned later in the day to talk further both Briones and Almeyda were gone. In their place sat the communist José Cademártori, the new minister for the economy. It was all too obvious by their conspicuous absence that the socialists were not serious about any talks that could resolve the differences with the opposition, though the communists were still willing. On the following day Aylwin sent Allende a letter to that effect and insisting on his original proposals.[162] As if to underline the fact that Allende had no negotiating position of

[160] *Punto Final*, 11 September 1973. An authoritative source (B) also confirms the support for the strike.

[161] *Entrevistas de Sergio Marras* (Santiago 1988), p. 130.

[162] Silva Henríquez, *Memorias*, p. 262. Also, Aylwin, *Reencuentro de los Demócratas*, p. 26. The two accounts are interchangeable since Aylwin, a friend of the cardinal, supplied the original details to him.

substance, a plenum of the PS leadership warned that the party would leave UP in the event of the christian democrats being conceded anything in the Basic Programme. Altamirano also launched into a fierce verbal attack on the armed forces.[163] Since the response sent by Allende on 2 August could not meet the PDC demands, negotiations effectively closed.

Fidel Castro had travelled a considerable distance since 1970 in respect of Chile. In contrast to his studied caution at that time – encouraged by the anti-Americanism of Tomic and Valdés still ruling the PDC – now he did not believe anything positive would come of negotiations between UP and the christian democrats. On 29 July he wrote to tell Allende that deputy prime minister Rafael Rodríguez and police chief Manuel Piñeiro would be visiting Chile briefly on the pretext of discussing the agenda of the forthcoming meeting of non-aligned countries. He went on:

> I see that you are now engaged in the delicate issue of dialogue with the DC amidst momentous events such as the brutal assassination of your naval aide and the new truck-owners' strike. I can imagine for that reason the extreme tension and your wish to gain time and improve the balance of power in case of conflict and, if possible, find a way out that allows for pressing ahead with the revolutionary process without civil war, simultaneously safeguarding your historic responsibility for what might occur. These are laudable aims. But in the event that the other party – whose real intentions we are in no condition to evaluate from here – persists in a treacherous and irresponsible policy, demanding a price that it is impossible for Unidad Popular and the Revolution to pay, which is actually entirely probable, do not for a second forget the formidable power of the Chilean working class and the vigorous support that has been offered to you at every difficult moment; it may, at your request with the Revolution in danger, paralyse those making for a coup, sustain the loyalty of the weak, impose your own conditions and decide once and for all, if it is right, the destiny of Chile. The enemy must know that you are ready and prepared to take action.

Castro once again emphasised that outward display of the will to fight was crucial to the success of UP.[164] But the offer of military assistance was

[163] Zorina et al., *Uroki Chili*, pp. 388–9.
[164] Reprinted (in photocopy) in *Libro Blanco: del cambio de gobierno en Chile 11 Septiembre de 1973*, pp. 101–2.

not accepted, though Rodríguez and Piñeiro did visit; nor was the advice, though repeated in August. The DIA in the United States gained access to this correspondence, whether before or after the coup it is impossible to say. Analyst Paul Wallner noted that "As the internal situation deteriorated ... Allende disregarded Castro's advice to consolidate his gains and eliminate the opposition."[165]

Instead Allende tried a further subterfuge by drawing in the military – hitherto a tactic much favoured by the PCCh who were, however, after 29 June now somewhat cool on the matter, at least without a thorough purge at the top of the officer corps. In November 1972 Allende had ingeniously drawn the armed forces into government and thereby outflanked the opposition. But conditions were now very different. On 3 August minister of defence Almeyda told Prats that the collapse of talks with christian democracy prompted Allende to recall the commanders-in-chief into government. Prats warned Almeyda that "in the army there is marked resistance to having itself compromised in government business".[166] But both admiral Montero and general Ruiz had already been collared, and – when faced with Allende – Prats, as so often happened, also gave way, though on this occasion with the uncomfortable after-thought that he might be the victim of "military naïveté" in matters of politics.[167] Doubts were certainly warranted, particularly given Allende's unusually candid confession that the participation of the commanders-in-chief "would be a symbol of presidential good will that *DC* could not question given its own insistence that the armed forces should take the place of most UP members of the cabinet".[168] This sounded all too like a resourceful tactical gesture designed above all to place the christian democrats on the back foot. No policy changes had been conceded to ensure the military presence and therefore nothing substantial had been conceded to buy off the PDC, let alone deepening discontent within the armed forces. And Allende's *muñeca* was a matter of notoriety; so the move was unlikely to convince those already open to doubt, let alone those bent on outright hostility. Between securing the agreement of the commanders-in-chief to become ministers and the time of their taking

---

[165] Testimony, 31 October 1973: *United States and Chile*, p. 160.
[166] Prats, *Memorias*, p. 451.
[167] Ibid., p. 452.
[168] Ibid.

the oath of office, Allende declared the confederation of truck owners outlawed for the organisation of a subversive strike, sabotage and terror. An ultimatum was issued for an end to the industrial action.[169]

It is the privilege of a statesman to pick and choose *à la carte* from advice received. It is the reciprocal privilege of the adviser to find himself, like the waiter, a mere servant excluded from the crucial decisions on which dishes are acceptable. Adviser to Allende Joan Garcés had been told nothing during the last few days as critical matters were settled by the president. His only source of information was the press – but this was enough to raise the alarm. On 8 August he sat disconsolately for at least four hours waiting to be seen by Allende, which finally he put to good use by composing a letter expressing his alarm at the recent course of events and Allende's response. Garcés was in a gloomy mood. Incorporation of the military in government carried with it "a serious risk". "What was a possibility while the cabinet was made up exclusively of civilians" – a military coup – was "converted into a certainty" once the commanders-in-chief were on board, with all that this symbolised. Delivering an ultimatum to the truckers was risky in itself, but particularly if it involved the armed forces. The previous day, Monday, had passed without any decisive action against the strikers. The same was true of Tuesday, the day of writing. "The image that appears before the country is that of a government already immobilised … if against this perspective the armed forces also find themselves equally immobilised and paralysed, this fact entails the most serious consequences." The longer the strike continued, the greater the likelihood of an insurrection. The supporters of the government were bewildered and in disarray. "Produce more. Yes of course, but the accumulated effort of several months has been eaten up, wasted in ten days of the opposition's strike. The government has found it impossible to avoid and cannot now defeat it." The civilian opposition were inevitably emboldened. Was the simple incorporation of the commanders-in-chief in cabinet likely to cause them to give up? Did it not indicate that they counted on actively mobilising "at least a sector of the armed forces"? Here Garcés turned to the experience of Spain in the mid-thirties: real enough for a child of the Franco era. Other historical examples showed that nothing paved the path to power of fascism better "than the paralysis of the liberal government in Italy and the social

[169] Zorina et al., *Uroki Chili*, p. 392.

democrats in Germany when facing serious economic and political problems created or stimulated by fascism itself". Was Chile approaching that point? "Today with the armed forces in cabinet, we are fewer steps away from this than some weeks ago." Here Garcés raised a key question that went to the heart of the prevailing assumption that Chile was exceptional:

> ... if the commanders-in-chief, the president and UP are not capable of imposing their authority in the face of an insurrection, how long can one delay middle-ranking conservative officers from feeling themselves no longer bound by their top leaders and deciding to act on their own account, isolating the high command at the summit? This is what happened one day on 18 July in Spain.

Finally, if the bourgeoisie did provoke economic collapse and the workers were "disoriented and sceptical with regard to the government" with no will to fight, then "there will be nothing to stop the fall of our government". And Garcés was suspicious of the need to create a state of emergency in various areas to cope with the strike at a time when the armed forces were paralysed when faced with signs of insurrection.[170]

Garcés's letter notwithstanding, the president instead artfully attempted to maneouvre Prats into taking the ministry of the interior – which bore the brunt of the problem of unrest. But the commander-in-chief finally stood firm and insisted on the ministry of defence. Admiral Montero readily took the ministry of finance, having turned down the foreign ministry for lack of competence. General Ruiz took public works and transport – a key position given the focus of the revival in politically motivated industrial unrest – in place of the less contentious ministry of mines. Allende also offered a ministry to the general director of the carabineros. The swearing-in took place on 9 August, but not before an unsettling meeting between the new ministers and their colleagues. Fellow generals were visibly "disconcerted". Some said that they had hoped participation in government would be on the terms Aylwin had proposed: half to two-thirds of the cabinet, the rest non-political

---

[170] Originally published in *El Mercurio*, 29 September 1973: reprinted in Soto, *El Último Día*, pp. 227–30.

elements, plus replacement of the next level of officials – the *mandos medios*. Prats explained that this would constitute a *golpe seco* – a bloodless coup d'état – which the generals were, of course, perfectly content to see happen. Ruiz had had an even harder time with his own colleagues in the air force, who point-blank objected to his taking a ministry. General Leigh – the next most senior general to Ruiz and a key figure in the conspiracy against UP – was then invited in to express his views. Leigh was insistent that participation had to be on the basis of six to nine ministries with changes, in addition, to the *mandos medios*. Prats and his colleagues none the less took the oath in the face of widespread unease within the officer corps. Allende was therefore confirmed in the false belief that there were significant elements within the armed forces upon whom he could count in the event of serious trouble. But Prats had now taken one gamble too many.[171] The day after the swearing-in, five hundred armed police, under the direct supervision, from an overhead helicopter, of transport undersecretary Jaime Faivovich – reportedly also a member of the *MIR*[172] – took all of six hours to free just three trucks held for the strike in a compound outside Santiago.[173]

Allende, now lacking substantial support in or out of government, had thus far counted entirely on his gamesmanship. He was, however, fast reaching the limits of its well-tried effectiveness. This was more apparent to outside observers than within. Three months after the coup of September 1973, Castro told the East Germans how matters had stood:

> Long before the coup we had seen that the situation was unsustainable for the Allende government. Comrade Carlos Rafael Rodríguez also asked comrade Corvalán in the summer in Chile whether, with the agreement of Unidad Popular … [there was some way] Chile could be helped. That proved impossible. The PCCh believed the situation could be rescued with PDC assistance by means of compromise. The leadership of the PS wished to employ more radical methods. President Allende trusted wholly to his own skills – that he could solve complex problems through balanced compromise.

[171] Prats, *Memorias*, pp. 456–8.
[172] Identified by the Brazilian ambassador: Câmara Canto (Santiago) to Secretary of State, 13 August 1973 – *MRE. Oficios Recibidos*. Chile. 1973. vol. 8.
[173] *Guardian*, 14 August 1973.

The Chilean comrades had a false impression of the attitude of the military leadership and no clear line on work in the armed forces. They believed in the neutrality of the armed forces and later assumed that a section of the army leadership would remain loyal to the UP government. That was a miscalculation. There were no measures taken to defend La Moneda and to defend president Allende. We were ready to defend president Allende with our forces. In our embassy in Santiago we had a large group of combat troops. We had to hand weapons sufficient for a battalion. Our troops were instructed to defend and protect president Allende once the order was given. Unfortunately Allende neglected to take such precautions.[174]

Having failed to persuade the president after the *tanquetazo*, the MIR had approached Castro with the proposal that they create armed militia. But Castro, loyal to his friend, told them to be guided in this by Allende.[175] The president would have none of it. The leadership of the socialist party therefore rashly took upon itself the job of preparing plans for preventive action to come into effect in anticipation of a coup. Pascal Allende had, since Luciano Cruz left the movement, held responsibility within the MIR for penetrating the armed forces. Humberto Sotomayor, MIR's head of security contacted Juan Cárdenas Villablanca, who headed a group of sailors bent on seizing their warship, the Blanco Encalada. A meeting was set up on the outskirts of Puente Alto. Altamirano recalls:

Some months before the coup, I was invited together with Miguel Enríquez, secretary general of the MIR, and Oscar Garretón, head of the MAPU Party, to participate in a meeting promoted by a group of non-commissioned officers and sailors. On this occasion they furnished us – with all the details laid out – the entire background to the subversive work under way. We were warned about the places, days and times of the conspiratorial meetings in which, along with senior officers of the Navy, some members of the North American naval mission had participated.[176]

[174] "Aussprache", 15 December 1973: *SAPMO* ... DY/30/IV B 2/20. 355. Recorded during a meeting with Castro in Havana.
[175] Pascal, "El Mir", Part 4.
[176] M. Brescia, "Carlos Altamirano: ¿termocéfalo o mutante?", *El periodista*, 31 August 2003; Carlos Altamirano, *Dialéctica*, p. 189.

The reaction of admiral Merino and his fellow officers to the meeting was immediate and drastic, not least because the evidence suggests that more than an exchange of information was involved, and revelations were beginning to link him and co-conspirators to the United States. Miguel Enríquez later admitted that resistance was also envisaged.[177] The Russians too learned that plans existed for action on a larger scale (see pp. 210–11). In a dramatic display of untrammelled authority, more than a hundred ratings and non-commissioned officers were arrested at various naval establishments on and off shore, including the submarine school, the naval engineering school in Valparaíso; also arrested were twenty-eight men from the crew of the *DD Blanco Encalada*, nine from the *CL Almirante Latorre*, fifteen from the *DD Cochrane*, ten from the *CL Prat*, and four from the *CL O'Higgins*.[178] On the following day arrests extended to the dockyards and arsenals (*ASMAR*) in Talcahuano. Those arrested were tortured by the Servicio de Inteligencia de la Marina (the naval intelligence service). The leaders of the cells were given particularly brutal treatment at the school for marines at Las Salinas (Viña del Mar).[179] Torture included beating, electrical shock treatment, and submersion upside-down in raw sewage. The question incessantly asked was, what did you tell these politicians? Some flavour of what could be expected should a coup succeed was not only the quality and quantity of physical abuse but also the language that accompanied it. For instance, during the interrogation naval prosecutor commander Bilbao asked how legality was to be restored when after the coup no leader of the left would survive.[180] It is claimed, apparently by Soviet intelligence sources, that a US naval attaché was connected to these events. It is also claimed that after the coup he became an adviser to DINA, Pinochet's brutal secret police.[181] Given the lack of access to the relevant archives, it is impossible to confirm this. But the treatment meeted out to mutinous naval ratings certainly fulfilled the promise of the "Djakarta" predicted by PyL and would not have seemed out of place in Vietnam. This was not merely vengeance, however; it was also a product of fear, albeit exaggerated out of all proportion. On

---

[177] Statement from the MIR Secretariat, 12 August 1973.

[178] Merino, *Bitácora*, pp. 209–10.

[179] *Punto Final*, 28 August 1973.

[180] Letter from Cárdenas and others: reprinted in González and Talavera, *Los mil días*, vol. 2, pp. 1278–80.

[181] Tarasov and Zubenko, *The CIA in Latin America*, p. 121.

10 August Merino informed Prats that a MIR cell had been discovered infiltrating the ranks and non-commissioned officers. The vice-admiral appeared seriously anxious.[182]

Any conspiracy against the upper echelons of the navy was almost bound to fail, since this was the most coherent fighting service (by virtue of life at sea) and extreme leftists in the ranks had been infiltrated. At the beginning of August PCCh leader Corvalán had been sought out by a sergeant in the marines, Cárdenas, who wanted the party to establish "a revolutionary underground organisation" in the navy. After the coup it was established that Cárdenas was connected to the CIA. On 25 August he led thirty sailors in the seizure of a radio station in Valparaíso, whence they called on all those in the armed forces to disobey their officers. The men were arrested; many other arrests then followed.[183] By such means those working with the United States could pre-emptively uncover leftist opposition within the ranks and dispose of it without restraint. It was no accident that the naval judge dealing with the mutinous ratings was Merino himself, the man who would take on leadership of the coup that overthrew Allende, the man condemned by Miguel Enríquez in a radio transmission on 3 September for his direct knowledge of "conspiratorial meetings with functionaries of the North American embassy, with politicos of the national party and senators from the PDC such as Juan de Dios Carmona".[184]

On 13 August Merino came to see Prats along with rear-admiral Carvajal Prado, chief of the national defence staff. The government had just appointed twenty-five military officers with special powers to requisition trucks and other means of transport.[185] Both Merino and Carvajal expressed their concern at the role of the armed forces in these measures. "They agreed in pointing out that the truckers' conflict is delicate because they consider that it is justified."[186] But that same day Allende called in the commanders-in-chief to ask whether the armed forces would act resolutely against the strike. He had already announced that truckers' leader Vilarín would be arrested and that if necessary he

---

[182] Prats, *Memorias*, p. 459.
[183] Zorina et al., *Uroki Chili*, p. 398.
[184] Marín, *Una historia*, p. 185.
[185] Zorina et al., *Uroki Chili*, p. 393.
[186] Prats, *Memorias*, p. 462.

himself would call for a state of siege, effectively putting the country under martial law.[187] The commanders-in-chief could have been forgiven for feeling that they had been manipulated into an embarrassing position. Their cautious response was not entirely what Allende sought: they would ensure that the armed forces would be effective but they added that Allende had to "take into consideration the fact that the strike had acquired a marked political connotation which meant that moves to intervene will be blocked not only by the resistance of the strikers but also by pressure from the opposition". Instead Prats suggested the president therefore call the leadership of the PDC and ask them to help "avert the disaster ahead". Once again, shifting the ground, Allende said he had no further to go in that direction but that the commanders-in-chief could do so.[188]

Through Leighton, Prats obtained a meeting with Aylwin. The signs were not good. At 10.15 that evening the lights went out in Santiago as a result of sabotage of power supplies by the likes of PyL, so they had to gather under candlelight in Prats's home. The discussion appeared amicable. But when Prats asked outright if the PDC in congress was willing to grant the government the right to declare a state of siege with full powers, Aylwin was "emphatic in his response: they would not concede it for any reason".[189] With PyL, on the one side, now outlawed but condemning the brutality with which the government was suppressing the truckers, and ministers José Cademártori and Aníbal Palma fulminating against the "passivity of the government" on the other,[190] what little hope of cool reason that remained was swiftly ebbing away. Moreover the small advance in understanding upon which a compromise could have been made was lost when the strikers refused to accept general Brady as the replacement for the hated Faivovich in policing the dispute.[191] And whatever support for the government that lingered among the military had all but drained away. The same was true of sentiment in the PDC.

On 14 August ten senators from the PDC issued a declaration accusing the government of violating the constitution on the grounds that Allende

---

[187] Zorina et al., *Uroki Chili*, p. 394.
[188] Prats, *Memorias*, p. 463.
[189] Ibid., p. 464.
[190] Ibid.
[191] Ibid., p. 465.

had not promulgated a law defining the division of the economy (private/ state/mixed) as approved by congress.[192] Signs of outright rebellion within the armed forces now appeared as Allende attempted to mobilise the military against the strikers. Prats was told by Merino and Carvajal that they were not minded to employ naval personnel in raids on strikers in Reñaca. "They say that the strikers have organised a 'veritable fortress' and propose that the government make a settlement and concede to the fourteen demands made by the leaders."[193] Prats found this puzzling given the extreme vigour with which raids were conducted against the left under the arms control law. But he missed the point, and this indicated that he was perilously out of touch with top-brass opinion. In fact Merino was actively and proudly protecting the strikers against militants from the MIR. On 17 August the PDC announced its support for the overtly political truckers' strike. Carvajal handed Prats for signature a telecommunications plan annexed to the armed forces' plan for internal defence (against insurgency). Carvajal congratulated himself that he had tricked Prats into signing the document without proper scrutiny by waiting until the car had arrived and Prats was hurrying to a meeting at La Moneda.[194] When Carvajal returned to his offices brandishing the signed document in triumph, "the officers waiting for me burst out into applause".[195] In retrospect commander-in-chief Prats did his best not to appear entirely unwitting. "I understand the 'double edge' of the document," he noted, "but I sign it, faced with the need to do the utmost faced with sedition en marche."[196] Matters were rapidly coming to a head, however.

That day Frei made a crucial step that looks to have been well orchestrated. "No one can deny", he declared, "that this government has brought the country to a catastrophe and now, by means of a cunning and audacious coup, uses the armed forces to take responsibility for this disaster. If you wish the establishment of peace between Chileans and an end to this chaotic situation, then you have to give the armed forces real participation in the government" – by which it soon became clear that

---

[192] Zorina et al., *Uroki Chili*, p. 394.
[193] Prats, *Memorias*, p. 465.
[194] Carvajal Prado, *Téngase Presente*, p. 49.
[195] Ibid.
[196] Prats, *Memorias*, p. 469.

he meant a military cabinet.[197] It was surely not accidental that this was the very evening general Ruiz presented his resignation as minister, which the president then insisted be accompanied by his resignation as commander-in-chief of the air force;[198] this ill-thought-out move effectively placed the most intelligent of the plotters, general Leigh, in a key position. Allende was clearly thrown by this latest blow. In front of Prats and Montero he proceeded to say that Ruiz was the only friend he had among the commanders-in-chief.[199] This was not flattery but the prelude to a bitter statement that Ruiz had now ceased to be a friend and therefore had lost his confidence, which was why he had to resign as commander-in-chief.[200] But when Allende called in Leigh, the latter refused to agree immediately to take either post. In the meantime Leigh had taken the precaution of removing the Hawker Hunter jets from air bases at El Bosque and Los Cerrillos, so he said, in case of trouble. Such apparently loyal behaviour prompted Prats to suggest that Allende should content himself with Leigh as commander-in-chief of the air force. The ministry vacated by the disloyal Ruiz was therefore given to air force general Humberto Magliochetti.[201] Magliochetti, the East German embassy reported, was believed "loyal" to the government. "He accompanied Fidel Castro during his visit to Chile and later stayed a while in Cuba after being invited there."[202]

Serious trouble now broke out. The whole purpose of giving Ruiz the transport ministry had been to neutralise him, and now he had been further alienated.[203] Instead of coming along to witness the handing over of office, Ruiz shut himself away at Los Cerrillos. Rumours then began circulating that he had been sacked – which, effectively, he had been as commander-in-chief. On 20 August out came officers' wives protesting the dismissal of Ruiz in front of the ministry of defence; the following day some three hundred then appeared outside Prats's own residence, including, to the horror and stupefaction of the lady of the house, various

[197] Quoted in *Panorama*, 20 September 1973.
[198] Prats, *Memorias*, pp. 469–70.
[199] Ibid., p. 470.
[200] Ibid., p. 471.
[201] Ibid., pp. 471–2.
[202] "Zur Situation in Chile" (Quelle: Botschaft Santiago), 21 August 1973: *AA*. Ministerium für Auswärtige Angelegenheiten der DDR. C3352. 000049.
[203] This is what Allende told Régis Debray on 19 August: Debray, "Il est mort …"

wives of active and retired army generals long familiar to them both.[204] All visitors, including Augusto Pinochet, chief of army staff, and Allende himself, were abused on arrival.

This may have proved a turning point for Pinochet, whom the conspirators had had difficulty getting on board. On 22 August UP counter-intelligence intercepted and deciphered a coded radio transmission on military matters from the right in Puerto Montt: "We are more than we thought. Little Red Riding Hood is also with us." Some thought this meant Pinochet.[205] Later that day Allende summoned a meeting of the *consejo superior de seguridad nacional* (national security council). He announced that the country faced great danger. "A military insurrection is under way and this will perhaps be the last time that we all meet together. Each must assume all their responsibilities." Those present included the heads of the three armed services. Whereas Allende had doubts about Leigh and Merino, he still trusted Pinochet.[206] Prats then summoned his generals in the vain hope that they would stand by him; they were mute in response and a delay before a final decision as to their support was called for.[207]

The following morning came news that the chamber of deputies had produced an extensive denunciation of the president that covered every misdeed that had taken place over the previous two and a half years, accusing Allende of breaching the constitution. Aylwin had personally played a part in editing the document.[208] Pinochet then arrived with the generals' response. The majority refused to sign up in support of Prats. Worse still, the two generals most opposed to a coup – Mario Sepúlveda and Guillermo Pickering – presented their resignations. Having failed to dissuade them, Prats decided to resign as well.[209] "The resignation on August 23 of Army CINC and Defense Minister General Prats removes from the armed forces the most effective opponent to coup-minded military plotters", noted a White House official. "This development in the odyssey of the Chilean military would appear at this writing to ease the way for intervention-minded officers in the Army to cooperate more

---

[204] Ibid., pp. 473–7.
[205] Garcés, *El estado*, p. 49; "Pinochet agreed not to interfere in the coup" – *United States and Chile*, p. 159.
[206] Ibid.
[207] Prats, *Memorias*, p. 484; Garcés, *El estado*, pp. 49–50.
[208] Aylwin, *El reencuentro de los Demócratas*, p. 28.
[209] Prats, *Memorias*, pp. 484–5.

actively with their coup-prone colleagues in the Navy and Air Force."[210] That day the CIA reported that the Chilean army was on a grade two alert. At one fell swoop the only real protection Allende possessed within the armed forces had fallen away irrevocably, though he did not yet know it. By the last week in August, in what Prats himself described as "a climate of psychosis",[211] Western embassies were hurrying wives and children abroad "on holiday" in mid-winter. Capturing the prevailing sentiment within government, Vuskovic confided to the outgoing East German ambassador what seemed obvious: "In the coming weeks there will be a decisive confrontation with reaction."[212]

Allende appeared in implausibly good spirits despite the crisis that was overwhelming the régime. Improvisation remained his preferred habit of work. He planned nothing beyond forty-eight hours, Debray tells us. "Familiarisation with danger ended up making him believe that one more respite would make possible a political solution." He refused to face the prospect of civil war which, Debray insists, "he judged lost, given the balance of power". Of a very different temperament, Altamirano in bleak contrast expressed himself "exasperated by Allende's shillyshallying". "The best means of precipitating the confrontation", he told Debray on 20 August, "and to make it bloodier, is to turn your back on it."[213] In this he shared completely the outlook of the MIR. And, as Pascal Allende recalls, a "revolutionary regrouping on the margins of UP seemed an imminent possibility".[214] Indeed, Enríquez had lyricised about the prospect of a "duality of power" as "the only way that permits the crystallisation of the accumulated forces that have been developing".[215] The MIR had, in the meantime, characteristically pressed hard for a "Revolutionary People's Counter-offensive" in place of Allende's policy of appeasement.[216] Unfavourable comparison was inevitably drawn between the light punishment of those involved in the

---

[210] J. Karkashian, "Subject: Chile Contingency Paper. Possible Chilean Military Intervention", 8 September 1973. *NARA*. Department of State. RG 59. Box 2196. Pol. 14. Chile to Pol. 15-1 Chile.

[211] Prats, *Memorias*, p. 454.

[212] "Zur Lage in Chile", 16 July 1973: *SAPMO* ... DY/30/IVB/20. 261.

[213] Debray, "Il est mort".

[214] Pascal, "El Mir".

[215] *Chile Hoy*, no. 59, 27 July 1973: Farias, *La izquierda chilena*, p. 4823.

[216] Miguel Enríquez, interviewed in *Punto Final*, no. 189, 31 July 1973.

June putsch and the torture to which mutinous naval ratings were being subjected.

A major symptom of the shift in power alluded to by Enríquez was use by the armed forces of raids on the left to enforce the law for the control of arms. Further menacing signs were remarked upon. The armed forces were uniformly represented as "the guarantee", according to the christian democrats. But "guarantee of what?" asked the MIR secretariat on 6 August.

> Is it a guarantee that General Manuel Torres de la Cruz raids factories looking for arms but, breaking all the rules of the law for the control of arms, allows the wives of officers to receive training in shooting? Is naval intelligence a guarantee, when its head in Talcahuano, frigate captain René Gajardo Alarcón, holds regular meetings with Patria y Libertad? What kind of guarantee is Colonel Cristián Aeckernecht, who takes part in meetings with PN deputy Patricio Mekis and with the FNPL at which they talk about future terrorist acts in Rancagua? What kind of guarantee is offered by colonel Luciano Díaz Medina, chief of staff of the general headquarters of the army's third division in Concepción, who on orders from General Washington Carrasco meets with Patria y Libertad in the offices of the third division? What guarantee is Captain of the carabineros Germán Esquivel, who with other reactionary officers created the sinister political provocation that attempted to implicate militants of the FTR, the PS and the MIR in the assassination of Captain Araya?[217]

According to Enríquez, Chile had to understand that "we are sitting on a gunpowder barrel and that there is no way out except a reactionary coup, total surrender or a people's revolutionary counter-offensive; there are no intermediate ways out, there is no possibility of conciliation or compromise deals". One of his key points was that "This is not the moment to consolidate what has been conquered" – precisely the reverse of the position readopted now by not only the PCCh, but also its fraternal parties abroad.[218]

Yet the MIR had never graduated to the status of a serious paramilitary revolutionary organisation of any size. The Italian communist Pajetta noted

[217] 6 August 1973: *El Rebelde*, no. 94, 7–13 August 1973.
[218] Speech by radio, 4 August 1973.

that "organisationally it counts for very little", though its influence was far more extensive.[219] It had no presence of any size within the trades unions. Beyond the countryside, it remained most effective as a propaganda organ exerting constant pressure on government: an important source of "political influence". Enríquez boasted that, although the MIR did not command the majority within the working class:

> ... the policies and tactics that we and the most radicalised sectors of the left advocated in 1971 (expropriation of estates of more than 40 hectares, extension of public ownership to more than ninety enterprises, workers' control in the private sector, workers' leadership in the public sector, expropriation of the Chilean Chamber of Construction, egalitarian and equitable distribution and expropriation of the large distributors, *comandos comunales* [workers' councils] and people's power, struggle against the law controlling armed groups, the right to vote of non-commissioned officers and soldiers in the armed forces and carabineros, etc.) have become the policies and tactics predominant in the heart of the working class and the people.[220]

The MIR did not, however, ever constitute an armed revolutionary vanguard that could seize power. The opposition press in late August 1973 published a leaked report on the MIR in Concepción, its spiritual birthplace and its continued stronghold. Within a city of over half a million people the MIR had only three to four hundred militants armed with some twenty rifles, twenty pistols and some hand grenades.[221] Later an extensive arsenal was found in the presidential palaces and within the *cordones industriales*, but these were predominantly socialist and communist party holdings of small arms; they were scarcely sufficient to take on even a significant part of the armed forces, possessed as they were of heavy armour.

East Germany and Allende's other allies in the Soviet bloc despaired of the deteriorating situation. Markus Wolf of East German intelligence intercepted information concerning coup preparations by the military and passed on these concerns to Allende and Corvalán. But they refused to

[219] Note by Pajetta: *Archivio PCI*; see note 134.
[220] Interview, *Chile Hoy*, no. 59, 27 July 1973: Farias, *La izquierda chilena*, pp. 4822–3.
[221] Laurence Whitehead, "Generals' strike cuts Allende's power", *Guardian*, 30 August 1973.

believe it.[222] The Cubans were active, despite Allende's reluctance to accept their reading of the situation and the offer of military assistance. On DIA estimates there were over one thousand Cubans in Chile: 250 at the embassy and the rest scattered across government as "advisers".

> About sixty or seventy were constantly travelling between Santiago and Havana, without having to pass through Chilean customs or immigration checks. The Cubans had their own communications net consisting of Motorola and Philips gear, which they used to maintain their contact with leftist extremist groups in Chile.[223]

Now, however, the Cubans were reported as exercising a restraining influence on hotheads at the top of the socialist party. In this sense something of a belated convergence had come into being between the PCCh and the Cubans. Under constant pressure from Millas, who had been pushing for a policy of "consolidation" since June 1972, the PCCh had at its central committee plenum come more fully to his point of view. Havana now took a starkly realistic stance towards the crumbling edifice of UP and the lack of any substantial alternative in the form of Altamirano, MAPU or the MIR. During a secret meeting of the ambassadors from the Warsaw Pact countries on 24 August, Alexander Basov, also a member of the central committee in Moscow, outlined the Soviet view. The Russians believed that a good "anti-imperialist-democratic programme of change" had been rushed ahead in two years before the time was ripe due to "the pressure of reactionaries and the influence of known ultra-left and petit bourgeois conceptions". Instead of stabilising advances made so that the working class became fully identified with them, even part of the PCCh had got swept along with putting the "Road to Socialism" at the centre of policy. More stability, according to Basov, was also what the "Cuban comrades" had been advising Allende and the PS leadership, to encourage the latter to adopt "a sensible and realistic position". However, "The general secretary of the PS, Carlos Altamirano, dismissed, for instance, the conception of a

---

[222] M. Volf, *Po sobstvennomu zadaniyu: Priznaniya i razdum'ya* (Moscow 1992), p. 42. The precise date of transmission is not given.
[223] *NARA. Chile Declassification Project. DOD.* Department of Defense Information Report, 29 October 1973.

revolution by stages. He wanted to force a 'decisive conclusion' by means of arms and constructed a plan for a coup from the inside, it is alleged, for 8 August in order to anticipate a military coup by right-wing officers. A group of ultra-leftist sailors and non-commissioned officers were to provide the back-up. Concrete investigations reveal that the PS together with the MIR ... with a total of over 400 men in combat were held ready. Their 'plan for insurrection' [*Aufstandsplan*] provided for the capture of strategic points, about which the PS had not made arrangements with any of its own organisations and possessed no concrete information whatever. The Cuban comrades have described it as 'playing at revolution' [*Revolutionspelierei*] without any realism."[224]

In contrast the conspirators within the armed forces were, with detailed US help, far more thorough. In mid-August a special co-ordination team for a coup was established within Chile, with delegates from each fighting service. At the committee on or around 24 August general Pinochet – up to now not the most assertive among those assembled and forever nervous about the seizure of power – uncharacteristically remarked that "the army would in fact wipe out the MIR".[225] Yet we know that "Pinochet had held the view that the military had no role in politics." The most that the Americans had hitherto been able to obtain from him was that "he agreed not to interfere in the coup".[226] As a result, CIA deputy director-general Vernon Walters, running the operation, thought little of him.[227] Meanwhile in Ecuador PyL leader Pablo Rodríguez was kept up to date on developments by the plotters.[228]

By now two periodicals subsidised by the CIA – *Sepa* and *Tribuna* – were openly calling for a military coup. Yet Allende continued to hold onto a misplaced belief in the armed forces. Although depressed that they had forced out Prats, the president was left with little recourse other than the appointment of the "fox" Pinochet, "on whose loyalty he counted since he held the confidence of General Prats". Prats had, indeed, assured him that Pinochet was prepared to force into retirement six generals

[224] "Zur Lage in Chile", 24 August 1973: *SAPMO*. DY/30/IVB/20. 261.

[225] Report from Santiago, 24 August 1973: *NARA.CIA Human Rights*.

[226] Testimony of Paul Wallner, DIA analyst, to the House of Representatives, 30 October 1973: *United States and Chile, 1970–73*, p. 159.

[227] Comments to Hernández Westmoreland, working with Walters on Chile: Chierici, "Undici Settembre", p. 40.

[228] *Qué Pasa*, 5 September 2003.

who were plotting against the government.[229] Altamirano was rightly incredulous, however. Allende acknowledged that Pinochet was, indeed, the man who had constructed the concentration camp in Pisagua on González Videla's instructions, in which communists were consigned and some shot in 1948. But what had Altamirano to say against him with respect to his current position? Nothing concrete, it turned out. Fernando Flores, who was now secretary-general of the government, also sensed that Pinochet was not to be trusted and spoke to Jaime Gazmuri (MAPU Obero-Campesino) of his anxieties; but nothing came of these concerns.[230] What both Flores and Altamirano failed to realise was that the problem was much larger than the issue of Pinochet's intentions; which, in the end, counted for nothing when pressure was exerted in combination from the navy, the air force and the White House.

By now, the end of August, Allende had decided against attending the non-aligned summit in Algeria only in part because the Chilean congress was unlikely to grant permission for his trip. The danger of a coup was all too evident. On Allende's behalf Briones held talks with Aylwin to find a way out of the impasse. He failed. Briones recalls:

> Allende, moreover, was of a mood to finish with UP because there was so much disagreement. He did not think of eliminating or liquidating UP, but wished to clarify that it was his government and that he would decide what he thought prudent even if the parties disagreed. But he was unable to do so despite making various private statements to this effect. On several occasions he said that the situation could not continue and that he would have to resign.[231]

Despite the failure of the Silva Henríquez mediation, Allende continued to believe that the way forward was working through Frei. The communists were much more sceptical, even Millas. The PCCh were convinced that "the opposition was being led de facto by Onofre Jarpa".[232] Allende insisted,

---

[229] Lillian Calm, "Memorias de Hernán Santa Cruz: revela confidencias hechas en agosto del '73 por su gran amigo Salvador Allende", *La Segunda*, 2 July 1993.

[230] Rafael Otano, "De Talca a Silicon Valley. Fernando Flores: la historia de un outsider", *APSI*, no. 432, 7 September 1992.

[231] Carlos Briones, "Desgraciadamente, Allende me pidió la carta y se perdió", *Época*, 11 September 1994.

[232] Millas, "Las dramáticas gestiones evitar el golpe de 1973", ibid.

however: "Over and above personal differences, one has to see in him the most eminent politician in the opposition, the only one who would help save the country."[233] But he was running short of trusted intermediaries. Millas was close to his cousin Juan Gómez Millas, an unconditional devotee of Frei. Could Millas approach his cousin as an intermediary to ascertain the minimal demands that could avert a confrontation? Millas went ahead and dined at his cousin's that evening; four other meetings followed. At these occasions Frei's name was never mentioned but there was no doubt between the cousins as to what was intended.

Millas's informal soundings succeeded in yielding a proposal formulated by his cousin. This consisted of a bold initiative for a constituent assembly functioning parallel to parliament and elected on the same basis as the lower house. The proposal would be subject to a plebiscite. If this were put to the people, a gathering of senior university figures headed by Juan Gómez would that same day publish a document in support and against the resort to violence. Millas's cousin gave assurances that at this stage Frei would be ready to respond instantly and positively to questions from the press, making the proposal his own.[234] The PCCh leadership agreed to this, though Allende had doubts. "This raises the problem of power", he said. "We will have at our disposal … in total less than two years instead of the three years and more that constitutionally remain of the actual presidential term" – the referendum and the time needed to get the assembly functioning would eat up what was left. This just might have averted a bloody coup, however. Allende therefore agreed to take on the challenge.[235] He then called on UP's leaders to support his call for a plebiscite.

The first week in September proved difficult, however. The socialists, MAPU and the Izquierda Cristiana all appeared ready to reject the idea, which had the backing of the communists, the PIR, the API and MAPU Obrero-Campesino. On 3 September the PDC's Tomic met the Swedish ambassador, Harald Edelstam. Tomic "said there were no prospects of continuing the dialogue with the Government and he was not intending to split the Christian Democratic Party over this. The only difference between himself and Frei was that he was willing in certain circumstances to cooperate with moderates in the Government, while Frei was not.

[233] Ibid., *passim.*
[234] Ibid.
[235] Ibid.

Tomic added that he thought the Armed Forces would move when things got bad enough and that this might be in about two months' time."[236]

In the meantime the naval conspirators were moving hard and fast to secure the resignation of commander-in-chief admiral Montero, the last obstacle within the fleet to the coup. Senior naval officers declared their lack of confidence in him and Montero was left with no alternative but to ask Allende to accept his resignation. This would normally have meant Merino's elevation as commander-in-chief. Could the appointment of a new commander-in-chief not be postponed till the end of the year, by which time the admiral was due to retire? Merino's prosecution of Altamirano and Garretón for attempting to subvert the fleet, plus his call for the detention of Miguel Enríquez, had alerted one and all to his true and uncompromising position and led leaders of the PS to call publicly for "the head of the naval judge and of all the fascist senior officers". On 4 September the press reported that the president had attempted to avoid Merino's promotion by offering the job to rear-admiral Carvajal which offer, if accepted, would have *inter alia* forced Merino's resignation. However, being one of the conspirators, Carvajal refused the appointment.[237] Allende therefore refused to accept Montero's resignation.

On Wednesday 5 September Merino decided to leave Valparaíso for Santiago by car along with Huidobro to force the issue. At the ministry Montero phoned Allende, informed him of the situation and was told that they should all come to Tomás Moro to talk about it. They arrived at around 11.00pm to find Allende "very angry, heated and in a state of great annoyance". Allende opened with a diatribe against the admirals for attempting to get rid of their commander-in-chief, insisting that this was his privilege. From then on the atmosphere deteriorated further, culminating in a blistering exchange. The president accused Merino of saying that Allende was "at war against the navy". To which the admiral recalls having retorted: "Yes, sir … we are at war with you. The navy is at war, because it is not communist and will never be communist, neither the admirals nor the naval council, nor any sailor, since we were raised in another school; we will defend it to the last, it is our life and the life of our Chile."[238]

---

[236] Secondé (Santiago) to London, 4 September 1973: *FCO 7/2411.*
[237] *Tribuna*, 4 September 1973: González and Talavera, *Los mil días*, vol. 2, pp. 844–5.
[238] Merino, *Bitácora*, pp. 217–18.

Yet the president had by no means given up. Two days later, Friday 7 September, Merino was invited to lunch alone with Allende. By then the president had fully absorbed the news that the PS was going to reject his proposals at a meeting that very day. He was in a gloomy and belligerent mood. To Merino's alarm, his own arrival was heralded by a mob of photographers. He was also lunching with Orlando Letelier, the new minister of defence, despite his understanding that the occasion was to be *à deux*. In each corner of the room where they sat for lunch, stood a guard armed with a machine gun: it was an unhappy but revealing symbol of the complete breakdown in trust between the armed forces and the administration. Letelier was dismissed for dessert and coffee. When Merino insisted that the only way to reassure the country was for the president to change the level of government directly beneath the ministers – the *mandos medios* – Allende not entirely disingenuously responded: "Look, if you wish to change someone … go and talk to Teitelboim, with Patas Cortas (Corvalán) or Altamirano. They are the ones in charge; I am in charge of nothing."[239] Merino was struck by "the absolute indifference" with which Allende responded to his string of complaints.[240] He thus came away with no resolution of the issue of Montero's resignation. The coup now *en marche*, PyL leader Pablo Rodríguez was airlifted by military helicopter from Lake Quiyelhue and brought in to the air base at Catrico.[241]

Allende spent the rest of the day at a meeting of the PS. Out of steadfast loyalty he "spent hours and hours with them, without achieving anything".[242] The discussion went on until 3.00am Saturday morning.[243] The UP leadership was scheduled to meet in the *sala de consejos* at La Moneda later that day, without Allende. Corvalán did not think it worth attending given Altamirano's fixed opposition to the plebiscite. Millas went in his place. There Anselmo Sule for the PR and Gazmuri for MAPU Obrero-Campesino, as expected, spoke in support of Allende. Rafael Tarud, speaking on behalf of *API*, delivered some dramatic news from military members who had spoken in confidence of what retired officers

[239] Ibid, p. 223.
[240] Ibid., p. 224.
[241] *Qué Pasa*, 5 September 2003.
[242] Briones, "Desgraciadamente".
[243] Erich Schnake, "Se me quedó muy grabada", *Época*, 11 September 1994.

had told them. An extremely violent coup was in preparation; the details he gave corresponded exactly to what later occurred. Millas naturally spoke for Allende in the name of the PCCh. Bosco Parra for the Izquierda Cristiana initially supported the proposals, having heard the latest concerning a coup, as did Guillermo Garretón for MAPU; but both later changed their minds when senior figures from the PS, Adonis Sepúlveda and Erich Schnake, arrived. Sepúlveda took the chair and gave the rostrum to Schnake – close to the MIR – who promptly declared that the dangers were exaggerated and that making concessions was the real menace; the socialist leadership apparently believed that the army remained predominantly in favour of the government and one could be assured they would not support a coup from the right. Indeed, Schnake suggested that in the event of the coup UP would take counter-action that would ensure the full realisation of the Basic Programme. It was proposed that the military committees of both the PCCh and PS meet to resolve their differences. This Millas resolutely opposed, not least because he knew generals Herman Brady and Raúl Benavides had access to information from the socialist military committee headed by Arnoldo Camú; the communists knew from Prats that these two generals were men of the Pentagon.

The proposal from Hugo Miranda from the PR that Allende be presented with these differences of view was overruled from the chair. Sepúlveda also refused to adjourn the meeting to resolve differences. His own proposal that they agree to the rejection of Allende's initiative was then opposed by Millas, Sule, Gazmuri and Tarud. An hour of further discussion led nowhere and the meeting folded without any agreed decision. Millas secured the first audience with Allende, but to no effect. The president had just seen the commanders-in-chief to express his dissatisfaction with a raid the air force had conducted in Summar. Neither Pinochet nor Montero had backed Leigh in this matter. But Montero did not have his service behind him and Pinochet's manner gave grounds for suspicion. Allende postponed his meetings with the socialists and the communists until the following morning, saying that after "wasting time listening to Adonis who exhausts my patience" he wanted to lunch with his family at Tomás Moro as usual on Sundays (his wife, Tencha, and daughter Isabel were back from a visit to Mexico). That Saturday afternoon was intended for a meeting with Prats, reviewing the changes in appointments made in haste by Pinochet in the past few days.[244] And the evening was devoted to Tati's birthday celebrations.

Also that Saturday, the US DIA later reported, "the Navy was prepared to initiate a unilateral coup". But rear-admiral Carvajal cancelled it "until the support of the Army, Air Force and Carabineros could be enlisted."[245] According to the DIA: "An air force plane visited all major commands in Chile that day, collecting sworn promises from all area commanders to support a coup move now scheduled for 10 September."[246] This deadline was then further delayed by the need to prepare the army.[247] When Prats had lunch with the president he was surprised at how optimistic he seemed. But this was because Allende still believed that temporising could hold off the inevitable and ultimately make it the improbable. The president told Prats that on Monday a plebiscite would be announced, which would probably be lost; yet this would be "an honourable defeat for UP, because it would express the wish of the majority of the people that would enable them to avoid a civil war". Prats listened stupefied "as though my ears had misunderstood his words. He looked at me questioningly, with his penetrating eyes."[248] Prats intervened. "'Pardon me, Mr President' – I said slowly, while Flores leaned back in his seat – 'you are swimming in a sea of illusions. How can you call a plebiscite which will take thirty to sixty days to implement, if you have to face a military coup within ten days?'" Do you therefore believe there are no loyal regiments? Allende asked "in a very different tone", adding, "Do you therefore not believe in the loyalty of Pinochet and Leigh, those I named as commanders-in-chief?" In response Prats insisted that they could be overruled by conspirators from below, since the members of the armed forces would above all seek to avoid a split that would lead to civil war.[249] That day PyL leaders Rodríguez and Eduardo Díaz Herrera were told the coup was now brought forward to Tuesday 11 September.[250]

---

[244] Millas, "Las dramáticas gestiones".

[245] *NARA. Chile Declassification Project.* Department of Defense Intelligence Information Report, 29 October 1973.

[246] Ibid.

[247] Ibid.

[248] Prats, *Memorias*, p. 509.

[249] Ibid., p. 510.

[250] *Qué Pasa*, 5 September 2003.

Knowing nothing of this, except the danger of a coup, Corvalán, Millas and Victor Díaz came to see Allende at 9.00am on Sunday 9 September for what turned out to be a three-hour meeting. Corvalán remembers that "In his [Allende's] opinion the coup was imminent. He told us this very calmly without any sign of dejection."[251] He told them he was calling the plebiscite because "he wanted to avoid a bloodbath and … he had to seek a solution".[252] Corvalán was insistent that Allende should not delay the plebiscite because of socialist party opposition. At 11.30am the phone rang and Allende's friend, journalist Frida Modak, reported on the results of a meeting at the PDC. The good news, reading between the lines, was that the plebiscite might be acceptable; the bad news was that they were once again giving way to the idea of a coup. What enraged Allende, however, was further news that Altamirano had delivered a speech boasting of his meetings with naval ratings and announcing his intention of holding more. The president felt it "paves the way for a *coup d'état*. We can expect the worst."[253] Millas noted, "[Allende's] conclusion was that the forces that were opting for a violent solution from different angles were too great; that some on the left were deceiving themselves; the leadership of the christian democrats were also miscalculating; and those, on the other hand, who were playing a masterly hand would seem to be the Pentagon."[254]

The president had arranged to see the commanders-in-chief at 1.00pm on Sunday to tell them of his decision to hold a plebiscite and that he would announce it over the airwaves at noon on Tuesday 11 September. When the communist leaders protested that this might prompt the conspirators to launch the coup beforehand, Allende replied that this was possible only if the commanders-in-chief were "criminal monsters" [*monstruos de felonía*].[255] Isabel and Tencha returned late to find "an atmosphere reeking of tension".[256] Although Pinochet appears to have been still uncertain, the Pentagon had made ready. The Argentinian periodical *Panorama* later reported that, according to reliable sources, as a precaution on 7 September thirty-two US aircraft – including

---

[251] Corvalán, *De lo vivido*, p. 153.

[252] Corvalán, "Había que hacer algo", *Época*, 11 September 1994.

[253] Millas, "Las dramáticas gestiones".

[254] Ibid.

[255] Ibid.

[256] Isabel Allende, "Recuerdos del 11 septiembre de 1973", *El País*, 11 September 1993.

reconnaisance planes – landed at El Plumerillo in Mendoza, near the frontier with Chile.[257] It has also subsequently been reported – though not independently confirmed from archives still firmly closed – that in offices a few streets back from the Hotel Carrera, CIA deputy director Vernon Walters had set up shop along with general Westmoreland's son-in-law Hernández Westmoreland to observe the coup at close quarters. In a recently declassified telephone conversation that took place after the coup, Kissinger reminded Nixon that "we helped them. [deleted] created the conditions ..."[258] The fact that the coup was set up by the US government via the Pentagon has also been confirmed by a former senior US official in a position to know.[259] For Walters's role, though, we thus far have Hernández Westmoreland's testimony and the carefully crafted obituary in the *Times*: "he was alleged to have had a hand in the downfall of Salvador Allende in 1973".[260] The hotel overlooked the Plaza de Constitución and at one level provided a view directly into the president's office.[261]

According to Hernández Westmoreland, Walters was operating through captain Ariel González Cornejo, head of naval intelligence. It was González who arrived in Valparaíso early on the morning of Sunday 9 September to give admirals Merino, Huidobro and Pablo Weber the precise timing of the coup.[262] That day, unknown to Allende, Merino sent a handwritten message to both Pinochet and Leigh:

Gustavo and Augusto,

You have my word of honour that D-Day will be the 11 at 06.00 hours. If you cannot accomplish this phase with the total of the forces at your command in Santiago, explain overleaf. Admiral Huidobro is authorised to deliver this and discuss any matter with you. Greetings in the hope of your complete understanding.

J. T. Merino.

[257] *Panorama*, 20 September 1973.
[258] Telcon, 16 September 1973: *NARA*. Reproduced on the *GWU, National Security Archive* website.
[259] Source (A).
[260] *The Times*, 15 February 2003.
[261] Chierici, "Unidici Settembre", p. 40. The information was provided by Hernández Westmoreland, who retold the tale many times in exactly the same way.
[262] Ibid., p. 49.

On the back of the message he added:

> Gustavo: This is the last opportunity. J. T.
>
> Augusto: If all the forces in Santiago are not committed from the first moment, we will not live to see the future. Pepe.[263]

On the morning on Monday 10 September the PCCh leadership convened prior to a cabinet meeting at La Moneda. The minister of the economy, José Cademártori, was called in to take a letter to Allende from Corvalán. It pressed the president to announce the plebiscite earlier.[264] But it had no effect. That evening chief of the national defence staff Carvajal calmly told his family that he would be up at 4.00am "because we are going to seize the government".[265] Meanwhile Allende's daughter Isabel arrived at Tomás Moro for dinner, proudly carrying with her the presents from Mexico. They included two summer jackets for her father. Allende broke off his discussions with his advisers to try one on in the bathroom. "I hope I will in the end be able to make use of them", he said. "Is the situation that bad?" Isabel blurted out tearfully, prompting him to attempt to calm her down. The dinner carried on into the early hours and included Letelier, Briones, Olivares and Garcés. "We tried to make the dinner normal, but from time to time we were interrupted by various calls with alarming details about troop movements and other rumours."[266]

At 6.00am on Tuesday 11 September the defence staff met. The first action was taken by the marines, who were under the command of Huidobro. At 6.30am, according to plan, a marine corps unit in Santiago blew up the radio transmitter at the state technical university. This gave an excuse for forces stationed in its vicinity to move out of the area. The naval squadron moved back into Valparaíso, which it had left to join the Unitas XIV exercises with the United States, and by 6.45 the navy had effectively seized the port. The prefect of the carabineros phoned Allende to report this crucial news, but it was easily assumed in Santiago that this

---

[263] Merino, *Bitácora*, p. 229.
[264] Millas, "Las dramáticas gestiones".
[265] Carvajal, *Téngase presente*, p. 81.
[266] Isabel Allende, "Recuerdos".

was merely another raid for arms caches. Allende needed reassurance. He therefore tried to contact army chief Pinochet, but he obtained only Pinochet's second-in-command, general Brady. Not entirely satisfied with the reassurances he was given, Allende left for La Moneda within the hour.[267] Nixon later said to Kissinger "our hand doesn't show on this one".[268] The "hidden hand" had, indeed, finally moved.

[267] Information from Chilean Naval Intelligence: "Events Leading Up To The 11 September Military Coup in Chile …", *NARA. Chile Declassification Project. DOD.* US Department of Defense Intelligence Information Report, 29 October 1973.
[268] Telcon, 16 September 1973: *NARA.* Reproduced on the *GWU, National Security Archive* website.

CONCLUSIONS: ALLENDE'S SUICIDE AND THE DEATH OF EXCEPTIONALISM

One has to consider, then, that Chile has conditions different from other countries.

Salvador Allende to Fidel Castro, 1971

"Allende is not going to surrender, you military shit [*milicos de mierde*]", the president shouted in the hearing of David Garrido, one of seventeen detectives involved in the defence of the palace. When bombardment made evident that further defence was futile, Allende ordered everyone to evacuate. "I went with them", recalls Patricio Guijón Klein, one of Allende's doctors, "but I remember [sic] that I have left my gas mask and I wanted to take it, so I came back." He saw the president sprawled in an armchair, the right of his skull smashed, the brain spilling out, his helmet on the floor, a machine gun still resting precariously on his knees.[1]

Frei and Aylwin, in particular, showed themselves visibly pleased in private meetings with foreign ambassadors, believing that the military would now hand Chile over to them. Aylwin spoke out publicly in support of the coup the day after in the name of but without authorisation from the PDC *consejo nacional* (and to the Catholic News Agency on 24 September), only to be repudiated two days later by sixteen other leading christian democrats.[2] Others reserved their thoughts for the like-minded. "It was … with a certain sense of relief that the Vatican heard of the overthrow of the Allende Government", archbishop Benelli, deputy to

[1] Interview: BBC *Panorama* programme 10 December 1973. For the visit of the documentary team: *FCO 7/2416*. Also, more embellished testimony: "Relato desde La Moneda", *El País*, 11 September 2003. Allende's daughter Isabel now accepts this: *http://psrdc.org/archivo/informaciones 44.html*

[2] Tomic, "Respuesto a Julio Silva Solar…", in Gil et al., *Chile 1970–1973*, p. 334.

the cardinal secretary of state, told the British.[3] The British ambassador and the British-Chilean Chamber of Commerce in private expressed themselves equally satisfied. But as news of dead bodies floating in the rivers began to reach the world's press the form of justification necessarily became increasingly elaborate. Foreign secretary and tory veteran Sir Alec Douglas-Home, for instance, went so far as to claim that "Chile had been on the verge of civil war."[4] If, indeed, that were so, it was not least due to the best efforts of Britain's key ally.

History took an unexpected turn when Pinochet ruthlessly snatched power for himself alone. Both Merino and Leigh, who preferred a constitutionalist outcome, were increasingly sidelined and rendered ineffective. 11 September thus proved a personal tragedy not only for Allende but for many families across the entire country and meant an end to democracy for the foreseeable future, not its rapid re-installation on the basis of constitutional renewal. Its restoration was to happen many years later and only after persistent pressure from a very different government in the United States, the godfather of the whole process. As the UP popular song put it in the very different circumstances of victory three years before: "it is not just a question of changing a president but making a completely different Chile". That was certainly also the philosophy of the conspirators.

A notable feature of the coup that always suggested special outside management was the extraordinary degree of efficiency and ruthlessness in its implementation; this included detailed lists of those to be arrested and interrogated or eliminated, categorised according to their level of importance. That planning appears to have been critical to its success. Former foreign minister Almeyda has remarked that "U.S. influence in inducing the Chilean military to set up a *coup d'état* was significant because the technical and professional assistance which was provided helped to retain unity while subversion was being planned."[5] Many died as a result; many not in hiding were also brutally tortured on the third floor of the national stadium and at the Chile stadium in Santiago, or behind the silent walls of the barracks in distant places. In a city known for radicalism,

---

[3] Crawley (Vatican) to London, 14 November 1973: *FCO 7/2416*.
[4] Meeting with the Anglo-Chilean group of the Labour Party, 1 November 1973: *FCO 7/2416*.
[5] Almeyda, "The Foreign Policy of the Unidad Popular Government": in Gil et al., *Chile 1970–73*, p. 128. CIA officers "compiled lists of persons who would have to be arrested": Corn, *Blond Ghost*, p. 251.

Concepción, for example, an ageing head teacher and socialist activist was brutalised for nearly a week to within an inch of his life. Lives were elsewhere otherwise ruined, promising careers bluntly cut short.

It was subsequently officially estimated that 3,500 people were killed, some of whose bodies have yet to be uncovered. This is almost exactly the same estimate given by Merino at a British embassy dinner in early December 1973: 2,800 civilians and 700 members of the armed forces; though this obviously excludes all those who died thereafter.[6] The numbers who fled or were forced into exile were astonishingly large. By late October more than 1,598 people had obtained safe conduct out of the country, of whom only 243 were foreigners. Many embassies actively sought and obtained the extraction of the vulnerable, and not merely their own citizens. But there is no record of the US embassy having done so.[7] The only citizen sought out was a scholar from Wisconsin University because of intense pressure from his senator, William Proxmire.[8] Indeed, two US citizens (Charles Horman and Frank Teruggi) notoriously disappeared and perished in the face of callous embassy indifference – and, it is claimed, with the active complicity of US officials.[9]

Several myths also perished, not least that of Chilean exceptionalism. A product of the unusually favourable conditions in the formative years of the Chilean state, it had become for the president a pillar of faith to cling to in a crumbling world. These special conditions, Allende was assured, meant that "the Chilean [revolutionary] process is irreversible".[10] It was therefore not without a trace of bitterness that Allende's rival and one-time heir apparent, Altamirano, many years later referred to "the myth of a 'unique country' without analogies or precedents".[11] After all, torture had long been practised on occasion by the authorities – as those imprisoned in 1948, such as Corvalán, had reason to remember; and there are several reported instances of it being inflicted on the right under Unidad Popular.[12]

---

[6] Spedding (Santiago) to London, 4 December 1973: *FCO 7/2416*.

[7] These details are to be found in Dos Santos Roca (Santiago) to Secretary of State (Brasilia), 29 October 1973: *MRE. Ofícios Recibidos*, vol. 9, 1973.

[8] *FCO 7/2416*.

[9] T. Hauser, *Missing* (London 1982).

[10] Olivares, *El diálogo de américa*, p. 10.

[11] Altamirano, *Dialéctica*, p. 216.

[12] Secretary of the PyL youth wing, Patricio Jarpa, was a victim: Câmara Canto (Santiago) to Brasilia, 9 October 1972: *MRE. Ofícios Recibidos*. Chile 1972. vol. 12. Also Jarpa's testimony in Fuentes, *Memorias Secretas*, pp. 149–50.

It was the scale of the events that shook the notion of difference and superiority which, only with the temporary, luxury incarceration of Pinochet in London, some thirty years later, came to the consciousness of previously deaf ears of the coup's beneficiaries, including the closest members of his family.

Some, such as Bernardo Leighton and – less directly by virtue of youth – Joan Garcés recalled the Spanish Civil War; its combustible ingredients were not so different from those in Chile by 1973. There too one could see an explosive mixture of a minority elected government pushing radical social change, pressed from the extreme left for complete revolution in the face of mounting opposition from the far right, and with the centre ground disappearing within a vise tightened at both extremes; the Spanish situation too was capped by a foreign intervention – in that case increasingly overt and long-drawn-out – which finally erased the revolution.

In Chile, the use of force had seemed unnecessary to those who believed that UP was heading for eventual defeat of its own accord by September 1976, if not earlier. The decision by Allende to hold a plebiscite actually provided for more immediate peaceful means by which a halt could be called to the socialist experiment. The coup was, however, brought forward to forestall the announcement of the plebiscite. At the White House tolerance for Allende had long been tested and found wanting. It was unfinished business and with the Watergate scandal threatening the very life of the Nixon administration, a new sense of urgency had taken hold, a determined reluctance no longer to wait upon events and the sense that any display of weakness abroad would be interpreted as impotence. The top-secret operation may have kept the truth from the public eye, but the White House must have been certain that their main adversaries would sooner or later discover more of the truth and draw the logical conclusions.

Not that preceding administrations, republican or democrat, had shown greater patience in matters Latin American. Here continuity had long been more real, though not always apparent, than change. And Kennedy, in this as elsewhere, set a pattern blindly followed by Johnson. So why should Nixon have behaved differently? The rationale was genuine. What Guevara had failed to achieve through the Bolivian gambit, Allende promised through more peaceful means: Cuban penetration of the Cono Sur. These concerns were not confined to Washington. They were shared in London and Bonn, themselves significant creditors to and investors in Chile. Their preferred solution did not coincide with that of the United States. But the US government held the whip hand. And Allende's Cuban orientation compromised him considerably in Western eyes. The fact, which took time to emerge indisputably, that this was prompted as much by the power of emotion as the power of principle or the dictates of reason proved all the more alarming because all the less subject to control. A great deal inevitably hinged upon the person of Allende, which caused a degree of bitterness for some of those involved. "Allende had what the Communists in France and Italy want," Teitelboim bluntly confessed to Adam Watson, "and he threw it all away."[13]

The argument that it was necessary to overthrow the régime because of the dangers of the virus spreading formed the consensus between the United States and its allies. But another view existed. "Economically weak, a population of no great number, located in a position beyond the normal circuit of Latin American political life, Chile counts for little", wrote Brazilian ambassador da Câmara Canto in July 1971, coolly noting the outlook of some "observers" who may well have been on his own staff.

> Its border could be neutralised by the deployment [*se dispuser*] of the Argentine army; and to the north the means of access bring one to areas of lesser importance for any major collision [*açõs de "impacto"*]. Furthermore, following Cuba's example, in so far as the Government decides to reduce drastically the standard of living of its people, the economy does not have the wherewithal to finance idealistic and quixotic projects as attempted by Che Guevara for the subversion of the continent.[14]

The degree of violence used in the overthrow of Allende caused even CIA veterans to look on with dismay and in retrospect furthered scepticism about the need for a coup. Keith Wheelock wrote:

> Elected with scarcely a third of the popular vote [Allende] was constantly obliged to reshuffle cabinets and to restrain the extremists, even within his own Socialist party. The ensuing administrative chaos and economic

---

[13] *Listener*, 24 September 1973.
[14] Da Câmara Canto (Santiago) to Brasilia, 28 July 1971: *MRE. Oficios Recibidos*. Chile. vol. 3.

bankruptcy was a predictable result. This, in my view, is a tragedy of Chilean politics, but it is no basis to conclude that Allende was leading his country lockstep towards revolution.[15]

To justify the use of overwhelming force, the incoming junta came up with the argument that a coup had been imminent from within UP – the *autogolpe*. The christian democrat Aylwin argued that "Chile was on the verge of a 'Prague coup'."[16] Yet the idea was rapidly discounted after 11 September by the navy, who were the best-informed and those who had been pressing the hardest in Chile for an insurrection; Leigh admitted he heard of the existence of "Plan Z" only after the coup.[17] Aylwin himself has since said that "no one believed it";[18] and the idea sounded remarkably similar to the alibi given by the Brazilian military (who had also been aided behind the scenes by Vernon Walters) nine years earlier. Robert Moss, equally well informed as the CIA, "said that the evidence about Allende's complicity in such plans was far from conclusive, and he himself doubted the existence of the documents claimed to have been found in [the communist under-secretary of the interior] Daniel Vergara's safe", though he readily acceded that such views were entirely consonant with those of Altamirano, Garretón and the MIR.[19]

The PCCh had, indeed, once held out momentary hopes for an *autogolpe* with a compliant military; Castro advocated as much earlier in 1973. But Allende firmly dismissed such daydreams while offering no practicable alternative. The MIR, the left socialists and MAPU had then belatedly indulged in what Havana contemptuously dismissed as "revolutionary game-playing" and had been debating an *autogolpe*; but, as elsewhere, the talk always far exceeded practice. It never became a reality, not least because the serious operators, the Cubans, backed Allende and counselled extreme caution. "What I find worthy of condemnation in my own UP", recalls Alberto Jerez Horta, who was senator for Concepción in 1973, "is that there were people who, without needing to, systematically and repeatedly raised the question of armed confrontation. I regard this as a suicidal policy.

---

[15] Letter dated 22 September 1973: *New York Times*, 5 October 1973.
[16] A reference to the seizure of power by the Czech communists in February 1948: *El Mercurio*, 18 September 1973.
[17] Spedding (Santiago) to London, 6 December 1973: *FCO 7/2416*.
[18] Aylwin, *El reencuentro de los Demócratas*, p. 30.
[19] Lunch with Rosemary Allott (IRD, FCO), 29 October 1973: *FCO 7/2415*.

And we ended up as we did. Moreover we had no arms. That is the most serious fact of all: Where were the arms? Nowhere."[20] The probability of decisive action by Washington had already been flagged in Moscow. Allende instead aimed at a plebiscite which it seemed likely he would lose, and the MIR and the left in general simply did not have the wherewithal to realise their dream of a truly revolutionary dictatorship.

A Soviet ambassador to Chile, Latin Americanist Yuri Pavlov, recalls: "it was well understood in Moscow that although the CIA had a lot to do with the coup d'état, it was not the main reason".[21] In both instances – Spain in 1936 and Chile in 1973 – domestic turmoil could simply not be insulated from the storms of the outer world. But that turmoil was a direct consequence of UP policy.

In exile the astute former christian democrat Julio Silva Solar produced the most penetrating critique of Unidad Popular errors in the political sphere. He considered most fundamental a failure in political leadership: a dual line existed within UP that was never resolved. Here he meant the contending conceptions of reaching socialism epitomised in the gradualism preferred by the PCCh and the more rapid transition favoured by the PS. "It was impossible to manage the most difficult situation that the government had to confront without a clear, coherent and unitary line." Resolving the duality, however, would have fractured the government.

> But in not doing so, the two lines ran together, mutually negating and offsetting one another. This translated into an absence of leadership and initiative, along either of the two lines. The president was always trying for reconciliation but the differences showed themselves to be irreducible.

Second, the road to socialism was institutional and democratic. Yet "the theoretical framework [presumably he meant Marxist-Leninism] corresponded to a socialism that does not proceed from democracy. Our experience in this sense made clear a gap and an imbalance in theory with important consequences." Third, given that the advance was not to be by force of arms, the broadest possible front was required – not a mere 51 percent of all votes. "Unidad Popular had no idea of the need for a broad

---

[20] "Alberto Jerez. Recuerdos Políticos: Cita con la historia", Patricia Arancibia – *www.finisterrae.cl/cidoc/citahistoria/emol/emol_2*

[21] *GWU. NSA. Cold War Oral History Project.* Interview 10841.

front that went much much beyond itself, and even less of how to create one." Thus it had no clear policy towards christian democracy.

> Any dealings with or dialogue with christian democracy was cause for suspicion on the part of the socialist leadership, which saw in it a deal or compromise of a reformist kind. More than the behaviour of christian democracy determined in the end whether it was the right who were to be isolated or, vice versa, Unidad Popular. There was scarcely any clarity about this.

Not only was there no policy directed at dividing the PDC. "Quite simply there was no policy towards the PDC."[22]

What had also made the régime so vulnerable as to render predictions of its demise so plausible were the obvious contradictions in economic policy and the attempt to press a revolutionary agenda on a population that had in the main not voted for it; in the process sacrifices were demanded of them that no class was willing to make; the refusal to sacrifice consumption to investment and private property to state ownership undermined the economy regardless of world copper prices. These elements are no secret and, except for diehards, never have been. Other factors, however, have been systematically understated or ignored.

Throughout events the misplaced sense of exceptionalism played its part. Ironically the exceptionalist illusion initially played to Allende's advantage. US officials were struck by the conviction still firmly held in Chile after the inauguration "that the 'Chilean character' will somehow miraculously preclude a Marxist take-over of the country".[23] Yet the right was ultimately quicker to discard comforting notions of exceptionalism than the government itself. Perhaps the most significant illusion was that the military were as apolitical as legend had it. This meant that the margin for error for UP was never as great as those who believed in this illusion imagined. The focus on Prats and on securing his loyalty threw the majority of the senior officer corps completely out of focus. Furthermore, the economic programme was from the outset bound for

---

[22] "Errores de la Unidad Popular y crítica de la Democracia Cristiana", Gil et al., *Chile 1970–1973*, pp. 318–20.
[23] Charles Meyer for the State Department speaking to a meeting of the 40 Committee: *NARA. Chile Declassification Project. NSC*. Minutes of the 40 Committee, 17 November 1970.

disaster, particularly since those who were supposed to benefit most found their hopes dashed. The belief that international capital would simply ignore the attack on private enterprise and investment; that the United States as the directing hand in world financial institutions would merely stand by and allow the Chilean market to be closed; that the laws of the market were not critical to the health of the economy until the entire system had been taken into state hands; that the Eastern Bloc and China would bail Chile out of its difficulties on blank-cheque terms similar to those given Havana by Moscow; all these were a collective delusion marked by Chile's psychological as well as geographical isolation. The Russians effectively wiped their hands of the whole affair, not least because of manifest Chilean incompetence. Why was Allende not better informed from his foreign ministry of Eastern Bloc attitudes? The economic chaos was also due in large part to the fact that Allende was no administrator and certainly no economist. Given his top-down vision and practice of socialism, which meant state rather than workers' or peasants' control, this inadequacy had fatal consequences. Another factor in the régime's vulnerability was the far left, which the president indulged beyond the degree to which judicious caution dictated, and which played a critical role as catalyst. The MIR, though too small to make a revolution, was just large enough and sufficiently well placed, socially as well as politically, to provoke counter-revolution. The left within the PS, MAPU and IC talked revolution, of "advancing without compromise", of "a final confrontation", yet failed to find the means to effect it and to forestall the inevitable backlash from those threatened in lives and property by any such victory. As Francis Bacon wrote, "it is the solecism of power, to think to command the end, and yet not to endure the mean". Christian democracy too played its part: "we have to recognise", said Tomic, "that the blame was not solely that of the Government".[24] Last, the US government was the architect of the coup, whatever Dr Kissinger claims. Yet it could scarcely have succeeded but for the failings of the UP régime. The blunt fact remains that only a superpower can sustain an exceptionalist tradition, as the United States every day confirms.

---

[24] Italy: *Archivio Centrale dello Stato, Carte Aldo Moro.* Busta 43, F.2, SF4. Ministero degli Affari Esteri, "Posizione della Democrazia Cristiana Cilena nei confronti del colpo di stato dell'11 settembre 1973" (Riassunto dell'interventi di Radomiro Tomic nella riunione del Partito democristiano cileno – 7 novembre 1973).

APPENDIX
ACCOUNTING FOR INFLATION

Accounting accurately for the rate of inflation in an economy is by no means a precise science. The normal indicator is a government's retail/ consumer price index. This assumes that all government is doing is measuring the increase in retail prices for a particular basket of goods taken as typical for average consumption. Problems can emerge when an original basket of goods no longer reflects consumer need or choice. This usually happens during periods of high inflation which alter consumer choice. Updating the basket then causes controversy and in so doing highlights the unavoidably subjective element of judgement in calculating the contents of the basket. Failure to update the basket will, however, seriously distort the index. Once the overt signs of inflation – listed prices – are curbed through artificial means by government in the market, reliance on the retail price index becomes even more problematic. The major effect of government price-capping is the emergence of the black market in goods now sold at prices substantially above the listed price. Thus the price consumers pay for the goods is not the price recorded in the index by government.

In respect of Chile from 1970 to 1973 all the above applies. As a result we face competing indices: that of the National Statistics Institute (INE), the Inter-American Committee for the Alliance for Progress, the World Bank, the International Monetary Fund, and the University of Chile Department of Economics. In respect of the first index, Sergio

Ramos, secretary of the economic committee of ministers in the Allende government, has since told us that

> ... the estimation of the prices of each commodity or service that formed part of the index was compromised as the inflationary process accelerated, as speculation and the black market grew, and as the problems of partial supply became more generalized. Since the price of each product was determined by direct observations of a restricted sample, it was very probable that under the conditions described generalizations grew increasingly less valid. The great distortions provoked by speculation and by those who were cornering markets could not but restrict the validity of sample values for the totality of effective prices in each zone or region; moreover, this restriction differed for each type of product.[1]

For our purposes we have used the World Bank index, which instead of using the official index, recalculates the rate of inflation on the basis of the growth of the money supply and assumptions about the rate of circulation of money. It rejects the alternative from the University of Chile because of its distorting effect. The rationale is given in its report on Chile:

> ... the official CPI understates by a substantial margin the full extent of inflation over this period. In addition to the distortion of the price trend in time, the official index never fully caught up with actual price behavior. During 1973, a consumer price index based largely on household surveys was independently constructed by the Institute of Economics at the University of Chile. The composition of the market basket and the weights applied were similar to the INE index. When prices were freed in October, the official price statistics began to record the accumulated tariff adjustments, the effect of the escudo devaluation, the October wage adjustment, etc. However, instead of recording these increases *via* INE's standard surveys and in relation to the December 1969 base, the official CPI simply incorporated the monthly price increases for October–December reported by the University of Chile index. But these increases, in percentage terms, were calculated from a base which had already taken black market prices into account. Thus, the rate of price increase shown by the UC index during the

---

[1] Ramos, "Inflation in Chile and the Political Economy of the Unidad Popular Government", Gil et al., *Chile 1970–73*, p. 330.

last quarter of 1973 is less than would have been calculated relative to the artificially depressed official CPI. In splicing the two indices together, what in effect took place was a discontinuous shift in the official index's base from December 1969 to September 1973, producing a gross underestimation of the total inflation which had occurred during 1970-73. On the basis of price data collected by INE during the last quarter of 1973, it is estimated that the understatement amounts to around 40 percent. In other words, the consumer price level in Chile is currently about 40 percent higher *relative to December 1969* than is indicated by the official CPI.[2]

---

[2] Levy et al., *Chile: An Economy in Transition*, p. 282.

SELECT BIBLIOGRAPHY

This list contains only works directly used in the writing of this book. To list the entire range of works on Allende's Chile, most of a polemical nature, would have served no useful purpose.

ARCHIVES

CHILE

Ministerio de Asuntos Exteriores (Santiago). *Memorias de Embajada 1970–1973.* Cuba. URSS.

BRAZIL

Ministério das Relacões Exteriores (Brasilia). *Arquivo Histórico. Ofícios Recibidos.* Chile. 1970–1973.

FRANCE

Ministère des Affaires Etrangères (Paris). *Archives. Amérique 1964–1970.* Chili.

GERMAN DEMOCRATIC REPUBLIC

(1) *Bundesarchiv* (Berlin). *Institut für Geschichte der Arbeiterbewegung.* Zentrales Parteiarchiv. Sozialistische Einheitspartei Deutschland. Zentralkomitee. Internationale Verbindungen.

(2) *Bundesarchiv* (Berlin). *Auswärtiges Amt.* Abteilung Internationale Verbindung.

GERMAN FEDERAL REPUBLIC
Politisches Archiv der Auswärtiges Amt (Berlin).

ITALY
Fondazione Gramsci (Rome). *Archivio Partito Comunista Italiano. Esteri. Cile. 1970–1973.*

Archivio Centrale dello Stato (Rome). *Aldo Moro Papers.*

UNITED KINGDOM
Public Record Office/National Archives (London). *Foreign Office Correspondence (1925–1966); Foreign and Commonwealth Office Correspondence (1967–1973).*

UNITED STATES
US National Archives (College Park, Maryland, and the Worldwide Web). *Department of Defense/Central Intelligence Agency/Department of State/National Security Council.*

Most of the Chile-related material of value is available online at *http://foia.state.gov/Search Colls* from the Department of State FOIA Electronic Reading Room:

Chile Declassification Project Collections
NARA Chile I, II, and *III,* for the US Department of State;
CIA Chile I, II, and *III,* for the CIA;
DOD Chile I, II, and *III,* for the US Department of Defense; and
NSC I, II, and *III,* for the US National Security Council.

George Meany Memorial Archive (AFL-CIO) (College Park, Maryland)

PUBLISHED PRIMARY SOURCES

V. Farias, ed., *La izquierda chilena (1969–1973): documentos para el estudio de su línea estratégica* (Santiago 2000).

M. González Pino and A. Fontaine Talavera, ed., *Los mil días de Allende* (Santiago 1997) vols 1 and 2.

S. Allende Gossens, *Obras escogidas (1970–1973)*, ed. P. Quiroga (Barcelona 1989).

D. Aron et al., ed. *Los gremios patronales* (Santiago 1973).

Lo hermida: la cara más fea del reformismo (Santiago 1972).

Libro blanco: del cambio de gobierno en Chile 11 Septiembre de 1973 (Santiago 1973).

Communist Threat to the United States Through the Caribbean (Testimony of Orlando Castro Hidalgo). Hearings Before the Subcommittee to Investigate the Administration of the Internal Security Act and Other Security Laws of the Committee on the Judiciary, United States Senate, Part 20, 16 October 1969 (Washington DC 1969).

Covert Action in Chile 1963–1973. Staff Report of the Select Committee to Study Governmental Operations with Respect to Intelligence Activities. United States Senate (Washington DC 1975).

United States and Chile During the Allende Years, 1970–1973: Hearings before the Subcommittee on Inter-American Affairs of the Committee on Foreign Affairs, House of Representatives (Washington DC 1975).

US Intelligence Agencies and Activities: The Performance of the Intelligence Community. Hearings before the Select Committee on Intelligence. United States House of Representatives. 94th Congress. 1st Session (Washington DC 1975).

Soviet Activities in Cuba – Hearing before the Subcommittee on Inter-American Affairs of the Committee of Foreign Affairs, House of Representatives, 92nd Congress, 2nd Session, Part 3 (Washington DC 1972).

"Chile en los Archivos de la URSS (1959–1973). Comité Central del PCUS y del Ministerio de Relaciones Exteriores de la URSS", *Estudios Públicos*, 72, spring 1998, pp. 394–476.

I. Zorina et al., ed., *Uroki Chili* (Moscow 1977).

PERIODICALS

APSI (Santiago)

Atlantic (Boston)

Bohemia (Havana)

Bolsa Review (London)

Cambio 16 (Madrid)

Chile Hoy (Santiago)

Clarín (Buenos Aires)

Clarín (Santiago)

Corriere della Sera (Milan)

Daily Telegraph (London)

Discusión (Rosario, Argentina)

Economist (London)

Encounter (London)

La Época (Buenos Aires)

Estudios Públicos (Santiago)

Foreign Policy (Washington DC)

Granma (Havana)

Guardian (London)

Istoé (São Paulo)

Listener (London)

Los Angeles Times (Los Angeles)

Il Manifesto (Rome)

El Mercurio (Santiago)

Le Monde (Paris)

Mundo Diners International

NACLA's Latin American & Empire Report

New York Times (New York)

Las Noticias de Ultima Hora (Santiago)

La Nación (Santiago)

Nouvel Observateur (Paris)

Observer (London)

El País (Madrid)

Panorama (Buenos Aires)

Panorama Económico (Santiago)

El Periodista

Punto Final (Santiago)

Qué Pasa (Madrid)

Ramparts (San Francisco)

El Rebelde (Santiago)

La Segunda (Santiago)

El Siglo (Santiago)

Studies in Intelligence (Washington DC)

Sunday Times (London)

La Tercera de la Hora (Santiago)

Time (New York)

The Times (London)

Washington Post (Washington DC)

MEMOIRS, DIARIES AND PUBLISHED INTERVIEWS

P. Agee, *Inside the Company: CIA Diary* (London 1975).

"Reportaje a Isabel Allende, hija de Salvador, a 30 años del golpe", *www.pagina12. com.ar* (7 September 2003).

C. Almeyda Medina, *Reencuentro con mi vida* (Santiago 1987/88).

C. Altamirano Orrega, *Dialéctica de una derrota* (Mexico 1979).

P. Aylwin Azócar, *El Reencuentro de los Demócratas* (Santiago 1999).

R. Cline, "Policy without Intelligence", *Foreign Policy*, no. 17, winter 1974–75, pp. 121–35.

Jacques Chonchol, *Chili: de l'échec à l'espoir*, ed. T. Nallet (Paris 1977).

P. Arancibia Clavel, ed., "Jacques Chonchol. Ex ministro de Salvador Allende: la revolución en libertad y la socialista" (*www.finisterrae.cl/cidoc/citahistoria/emol/ emol/_1*).

W. Colby, *Honourable Men: My Life in the CIA* (London 1978).

"Contribuciones para una historia del MIR", *Estudios Públicos*, 85, spring 2002.

Luis Corvalán, *De lo vivido y lo peleado: memorias* (Santiago 1997).

N. Davis, *The Last Two Years of Salvador Allende* (Ithaca 1985).

Régis Debray, "Il est mort dans sa loi", *Nouvel Observateur*, no. 462, 17–23 September 1973.

Jorge Edwards, *Persona Non Grata: An Envoy in Castro's Cuba* (London 1976).

Entrevistas de Sergio Marras: confesiones (Santiago 1988).

D. Frost, "An Interview with Richard Helms", *Studies in Intelligence*, fall 2000.

Manuel Fuentes W., *Memorias secretas de Patria y Libertad y algunos confesiones sobre la guerra fría en Chile* (Santiago 1999).

G. García Marquez, "La última cueca feliz de Salvador Allende", *Salvador Allende*, ed. A. Witker (Guadalajara 1988).

F. Gil et al., *Chile 1970–1973: lecciónes de una experiencia* (Madrid 1977).

F. Gaudichaud, ed., *Poder popular y cordones industriales: testimonios sobre el movimiento popular urbano 1970–1973* (Santiago 2004).

Sergio Huidobro Justiniano, *Decisión naval* (4th edition, Santiago 1999).

P. Arancibia Clavel et al., ed., *Jarpa: Confesiones politicas* (Santiago 2002).

P. Arancibia Clavel, "Alberto Jerez. Recuerdos políticos" (*www.finisterrae.cl/cidoc/citahistoria/emol/emol_2*).

U. Alexis Johnson, *The Right Hand of Power* (New Jersey 1984).

E. Korry, "Los Estados Unidos en Chile y Chile en los Estados Unidos. Una retrospectiva política y económica (1963–1975)", *Estudios Públicos*, no. 72, spring 1998, pp. 19–74.

"Entrevista – El Embajador Edward M. Korry en el CEP", *Estudios Públicos*, no. 72, spring 1998, pp. 76–112.

Nikolai Leonov, *Likolet'e* (Moscow 1995).

Gonzalo Martner, *El gobierno del Presidente Salvador Allende 1970–1973: una evaluación* (Chile 1988).

José Toribio Merino Castro, *Bitácora de un Almirante: memorias* (4th edition, Santiago 1999).

O. Millas Correa, *Memorias* (Santiago 1993).

P. Neruda, *Confieso que he vivido: Memorias* (2nd edition, Buenos Aires 1974).

Augusto Olivares, "El pensamiento del comandante en jefe del ejército: General René Schneider", *El Caso Schneider*, ed., P. García F. (Santiago 1972).

Augusto Olivares, *El diálogo de américa: F. Castro/S. Allende* (Santiago 1972).

A. Pascal Allende, "El Mir, 35 años". Worldwide Web. *Kolectivo La Haine.*

D. Phillips, *The Night Watch* (New York 1977; London 1978).

Augusto Pinochet Ugarte, *The Crucial Day: September 11, 1973* (Santiago 1982).

Patricio Carvajal Prado, *Téngase presente* (Santiago 1994).

Carlos Prats González, *Memorias: testimonio de un soldado* (4th edition, Santiago 1996).

O. Puccio, *Un cuarto de siglo con Allende: recuerdos de su secretario privado* (Santiago 1985).

R. Rossanda, "Successi, limiti e scogli di un anno di governo di Unità Popolare", *Il Manifesto*, November 1971; reprinted in *Il Cile: saggi, documenti, interviste* (Milan 1973).

S. Sideri, ed., *Chile 1970–73: Economic Development and Its International Setting. Self-Criticism of the Unidad Popular Government's Policies* (The Hague 1979).

Jaime Suárez Bastidas, *Allende: Visión de un Militante* (Santiago 1992).

Raúl Cardinal Silva Henríquez, *Memorias*, vol. 2 (Santiago 1991).

C. Sulzberger, *The World and Richard Nixon* (New York 1987).

F. R. Tomic, "Aclaraciones sobre ciertos hechos historicos", *Chile 1970–1973: lecciones de una experiencia*, ed. F. Gil et al. (Madrid 1977).

Florencia Varas, *Conversaciones con Viaux* (Santiago 1972).

Vernon Walters interview: *Istoé* (Brazil), no. 1644, 20 December 2000.

Paul Wimert interviews: *National Security Archive, George Washington University, Cold War Oral History Project*. Interviews 10837, 10838.

A. Witker, "El Hombre de las Grandes Alamedas", in A. Witker, ed., *Salvador Allende: una vida por la democracia y el socialismo* (Guadalajara 1988).

José Yglesias, "1909–1973. Salvador Allende: A Personal Remembrance", *Ramparts*, vol. 12, no. 4, November 1973.

"Cristián Zegers a Todo Dar", *Mundo Diners International*, vol. IX, no. 107, October 1991.

SECONDARY SOURCES

Don Américo: un chileno comunista. Homenaje postumo (Santiago 1992).

D. Avendaño and M. Palma, *El rebelde de la burguesía. La historia de Miguel Enríquez* (Santiago 2001).

O. Boye, *Hermano Bernardo: 50 años de vida política de Bernardo Leighton* (Santiago 1999).

Cambridge History of Latin America, vol. VIII, ed. L. Bethell (Cambridge 1991).

M. Chierici, "Undici Settembre", *Allende: L'altro 11 settembre/30 anni fa* (Rome 2003).

E. Condal, *Il Cile di Allende e il ruolo del MIR* (Milan 1973).

D. Corn, *The Blond Ghost: Ted Shackley and the CIA's Crusades* (New York 1994).

R. Cruz-Coke, "Síntesis biográfica del doctor Salvador Allende G.", *Revista medica de Chile*, vol. 131, no. 7, July 2003, pp. 809–14.

P. Drake, *Socialism and Populism in Chile, 1932–52* (Urbana 1978).

R. Hansen, *Military Culture and Organisational Decline: A Study of the Chilean Army*, PhD thesis, UCLA 1967.

T. Hauser, *Missing: The Execution of Charles Horman* (London 1982).

Julio Cesar Jobet, *El Partido Socialista de Chile*, vol. 2 (Santiago 1971).

A. Joxe, *Las fuerzas armadas en el sistema politico chileno* (Santiago 1970).

E. Kaufman, ed., *Crisis in Allende's Chile: New Perpectives* (New York 1988).

R. Kaufman, *The Politics of Land Reform in Chile, 1950–1970: Public Policy, Political Institutions, and Social Change* (Cambridge, Mass. 1972).

J. Koehler, *STASI: The Untold Story of the East German Secret Police* (Boulder 1999).

P. Kornbluh, *The Pinochet File: A Declassified Dossier on Atrocity and Accountability* (New York 2003).

F. Levy et al., ed. *Chile: An Economy in Transition* (World Bank 1980).

G. Marin, *Una historia fantástica y calculada: la CIA en el país de los Chilenos* (Mexico 1974).

Rafael Otano, "De Talca a Silicon Valley. Fernando Floes: la historia de un outsider", *APSI*, no. 432, 7 September 1992.

T. Powers, "Inside the Department of Dirty Tricks", *Atlantic*, vol. 244, no. 2, August 1979.

V. Riva, *Oro da Mosca: i finanziamenti sovietici al PCI dalla rivoluzione d'ottobre al criollo dell'URSS con 240 documenti inediti dagli archivi moscoviti* (Milan 1999).

Pedro Naranjo Sandoval, *Biografía de Miguel Enríquez* (Havana 1999).

P. Sigmund, *The Overthrow of Allende and the Politics of Chile, 1964–1976* (Pittsburgh 1977).

R. Sobel, *I.T.T. The Management of Opportunity* (London 1982).

Oscar Soto, *El último día de Salvador Allende* (Santiago 1999).

K. Tarasov and V. Zubenko, *The CIA in Latin America* (Moscow 1984).

A. Witker, ed., *Salvador Allende: Una vida por la democracia y el socialismo* (Guadalajara 1988).

Juan Baptista Yofre, *Misión Argentina en Chile (1970–1973): los registros secretos de un difícil gestión diplomática* (Santiago 2000).

INDEX